WHO IS MICHAEL OVITZ?

WHO IS

MICHAEL OVITZ?

WH
ALLEN

1 3 5 7 9 10 8 6 4 2

WH Allen, an imprint of Ebury Publishing,
20 Vauxhall Bridge Road,
London SW1V 2SA

WH Allen is part of the Penguin Random House group of companies whose
addresses can be found at global.penguinrandomhouse.com

Penguin
Random House
UK

First published in the United Kingdom by WH Allen in 2018
First published in the United States by Portfolio/Penguin in 2018

www.penguin.co.uk

A CIP catalogue record for this book is available from the British Library

Hardback ISBN 9780753553367
Trade Paperback ISBN 9780753553374

Printed and bound in Great Britain by Clays Ltd, Elcograf S.p.A.

Penguin Random House is committed to a sustainable future for our business, our readers
and our planet. This book is made from Forest Stewardship Council® certified paper.

MIX
Paper from
responsible sources
FSC® C018179

Judy, for the journey,

Chris, Kim, Eric, Minty, Ara, Jordan, Kendall,
and Marco, for my purpose,

My grandson, Pax, for my light,

Tamara, for the laughs and new adventures

CONTENTS

CONTENTS

WHO IS MICHAEL OVITZ?

PROLOGUE

I COULDN'T SLEEP LAST NIGHT, SO I SLIPPED DOWNSTAIRS and started watching *Terminator 2* on television. It was so late it seemed like no one else was awake anywhere. From my living room, high in Beverly Hills, the glitter of Los Angeles below felt like key lights burning on an empty soundstage.

As I watched Arnold Schwarzenegger bulldoze his enemies, I had a sudden realization. *That was me. I was a Terminator.* When we built Creative Artists Agency, Hollywood's premiere talent agency, I'd get banged around, hurled through a wall, plaster dust exploding everywhere . . . and then I'd climb out from the rubble, red eyes glaring, and hurl my opponents through the wall even harder than they'd hurled me. I completed my mission. The fear my opponents felt derived from sheer hopelessness: How could they beat someone so tireless, so relentless? So inhuman?

That was the image I took great care to project, anyway. It was an image I grew to hate. Who wants to scare the living shit out of people? But it was so effective. Our sell was simple: if you were with us, as an agent or a client, CAA would protect you 24-7, take care of your every need. At a time when other agencies were full of solo acts, we had teams of four or five agents on each client. By working longer and harder and smarter than the others, we became a mighty fortress. You were either with us or you were against us, and if you were against us, our phalanx of agents would stream forth from our stone walls, eager for combat.

We could demand $5 million for our best directors, double what they'd gotten at other agencies. We could package the stars and the writers and the directors of huge films like *Ghostbusters* and *Forrest Gump* and *Jurassic Park* and insist that studios make the film we gave them. We could collect almost $350 million a year in commissions from our 1,350 clients, who included everyone from Isabelle Adjani to Billy Zane, from Pedro Almodóvar to Robert Zemeckis, from Andre Agassi to ZZ Top. And it was all because our agents carried a heavy club: the implied threat of terrible consequences if the buyer didn't do what we wanted—a boycott by our talent; all the best films going elsewhere; total humiliation. I taught our agents to reach for the club every day, but to never—or almost never—pick it up. Power is only power until you exert it. It's all perception.

I was that club. The most persuasive point our agents could make to a stubborn exec was "I don't have the authority to close the deal at that number, so you'll have to talk to Michael." That was the last thing the exec wanted, because he or she knew I'd ask for even more. Better to close at an unpalatable number now than to be upsold into stratospheric realms once I got on the phone.

Most of our 175 agents uttered some version of that threat five times a day. My name became a kind of hex, a conjuring. In just twenty years I went from a complete unknown, to a comer, to being hailed as the most powerful man in Hollywood—a man the press invariably described as a gap-toothed, tightly scripted, secrecy-obsessed superagent. After a few years of that, I became the most feared man in town. And once I left CAA, when it became safe for everyone to vent, I became the most hated.

"Mike Ovitz" was such a potent bogeyman because he wasn't a person, he was a specter. I avoided red carpets; I'd enter and leave parties through the back door; I kept the rights to almost all photos of me;

I didn't do any press for the first ten years, and very little after that. When conducting business, I was so soft-spoken I made people inch their chairs closer. I rarely lost my temper (which was an enormous strain because I'm a perfectionist, and everything—*everything*—bothered me if it wasn't just so). I drank barely at all, I didn't use drugs, I didn't even dance. I never understood why you'd want to shower and change for a dance just so you could go get all sweaty. This set of traits made me seem freakishly composed and controlled. And you know what? I was.

My clients played characters on-screen; I played them offscreen. Ninety-nine out of a hundred people, their act is who they are. But anomalies like me manufacture their characters from bits and pieces of those they're with. I was a chameleon, becoming whomever I needed to be to make everyone comfortable and close the deal. My basic character was buttoned-up, omniscient, wise, loyal, indomitable. But I could be a sports car aficionado with Paul Newman just as easily as I could discuss fiscal policy with Felix Rohatyn, the banker, or dive into the specifications of the Walkman with Akio Morita, the head of Sony. So to those I worked with I was a control freak. A shape-shifting machine. A Terminator.

Yet the private me, the one only my closest friends saw, was ultra-sensitive to every slight and constantly concerned about threats from every direction. This me, the man with back pain and uneasy memories, wandered into my living room to look at Jasper Johns's *White Flag*, his 1955 masterpiece. I bought it from a bankrupt Japanese construction company years ago, and a condition of the sale was that I couldn't show it in public for a year because the company wanted to hide the state of its imploding finances. So for that year I kept the painting in an empty room in my house behind a locked door, the way Bluebeard guarded the secret room where he was truly himself. I'd go look at *White Flag* every day, and sink into a reverie, admiring Johns's talent, his fluidly expressive brushstrokes, his extraordinary will and imagination. Great art brings out the boy in me, the insatiably curious kid who has to know everything about everything.

I'm a frustrated artist. I couldn't paint or sculpt, I wasn't musical, and I sure couldn't act: when Albert Brooks asked me to make a cameo appearance in his movie *Real Life* I froze up completely. So I did the next-best thing with my life. I spent it around artists: appreciating them, admiring them, helping them become their best, fullest selves. I was the whetstone that sharpened them so they could slice through anything. Our pitch at CAA was "better material, better information, better deals—and we'll make your dream project happen." James Clavell's *Shōgun* moldered on the shelf for four years before my partner Bill Haber and I came along and turned it into a huge miniseries; *Tootsie* was just another dead-end script for six years before I began representing Dustin Hoffman and put him together with the director he loved to hate, Sydney Pollack.

Yet agents make dreams happen at a terrible price. When a painter paints, other painters may be jealous of his success, but they don't believe he's personally screwing them over with every brushstroke. It's not a zero-sum game: there's room for everyone to do his best. When an agent agents, though, the list of the personally embittered lengthens with the size of the deal. If we poached a new client, his old agency hated us. If one of our movies went to Universal, six other studios hated us. CAA's goal was to have all the clients, and therefore all the conflicts; we used to say "No conflict, no interest." It was a heroic goal, but it cost us. And it cost me.

RAIN MAN, FOR INSTANCE, CAME TO CAA IN 1986 AS A SCRIPT by Barry Morrow about a mentally disabled man named Raymond Babbitt and his brother, Charlie, a hard-boiled con artist. I instantly thought of Dustin Hoffman for Charlie, packaged with Bill Murray as Raymond. Dustin had made only one film since *Tootsie,* in 1982—the legendary flop *Ishtar,* a movie so ill-starred I had tried to squeeze him out of it by refusing to do his paperwork or take a commission. He needed a great role to get back in the public eye, and we needed him to start earning his $6.5 million fees again. Dustin wanted to play Raymond, unexpectedly, but fine, whatever. He was what I called a motor, a force potent enough to singlehandedly get a project green-lit.

Unfortunately, Warner Bros., which had a first-look deal with the film's production company, Guber-Peters, passed. I told Peter Guber I wanted to run with *Rain Man*, and he said great. It was dead, so why not let me try? The script had no sex, no car chases, and no third act, but I was convinced that if we could keep the budget to $25 million, we could earn back $50 million from date-nighters and grown-ups. So I started talking up the project. Nothing in Hollywood is anything until it's something, and the only way to make it something is with a profound display of belief. If you keep insisting that a shifting set of inchoate possibilities is a movie, it eventually becomes one. Sometimes.

I needed a second star and a great director. I introduced Dustin to my close friend Barry Levinson, who'd directed *Diner*, and they became fast friends. Then, in one of our packaging meetings—where we worked to assemble all the talent for a film, to make it completely ours—our agents Paula Wagner and Jack Rapke suggested putting Tom Cruise into the mix. After his success in *The Color of Money* opposite Paul Newman, we believed he'd be terrific as Charlie, and the combination of stars would make the film special. Everyone in Hollywood scoffed: given the age difference (Dustin was fifty, Tom twenty-five), how could the actors possibly play brothers? The conventional wisdom was that the project was CAA packaging run amok; the movie would collapse under its own weight and all three clients would fire us.

Barry Levinson dropped out to do *Good Morning, Vietnam*, and we brought in Marty Brest, who'd done *Beverly Hills Cop*. Screenwriter Ron Bass, another CAA client, rewrote the script. Ron's firmer structure helped us get United Artists to commit to the film. Then Dustin decided that Raymond should be autistic. Autistic people can't be cured, so now the film couldn't deliver any real redemption—but Dustin lived for difficulties. Without anguish he got bored. Marty Brest left to do *Midnight Run*, and Steven Spielberg came aboard. He developed it for a while, then left to shoot an *Indiana Jones* movie. We kept Tom Cruise busy by getting him cast as a babe-magnet bartender in *Cocktail*. Tom shot the whole movie while *Rain Man* inched along. Sydney Pollack came in and brought in four new writers. Then he dropped out.

When the original director leaves a project, it usually dies, having lost its primary profound believer. We'd lost four directors. But I refused to give up because Dustin was determined to play that role, and because I felt so warmly about him and his family (not that I ever wanted to show anyone, even Dustin, the strength of my feelings, because I worried that emotions were a fatal weakness). I called Barry Levinson and told him, "You were the right guy from the start." He read the latest script and decided that it needed to be a road movie: "It's not a three-act movie," he said, "it's a one-act movie. The movie goes on the road, and it meanders, and then it ends, but it's not an *ending*. Raymond's not going to change, and he can't live with his brother. It's too bad, but that's the way it goes." *Rain Man* would wind up with so little overt action that Dustin and Tom privately titled it *Two Schmucks in a Car*. But the developments that matter in a Barry Levinson film take place beneath the surface.

United Artists was in for $25 million but not a penny more, so CAA guaranteed the deficit. If *Rain Man* went over budget, the agency could lose its commissions, and then some. As we had money, relationships, and friendships on the line, I haunted the set and got a daily briefing from Mark Johnson, the film's producer. I couldn't rely on Barry to keep me informed, as he tended to ignore life outside his viewfinder. (During *Good Morning, Vietnam* I sent roses to Barry's wife in his name—"I miss you!"—so she wouldn't feel neglected.)

Dustin went into every role, he once said, "full of fear and pain and self-loathing." During the first week on location, Barry shot a scene by the duck pond outside the institution where Raymond Babbitt has been living. As Raymond and Charlie sit together on a bench, Charlie feels out his long-lost brother. Raymond stares into nowhere and mutters "I don't know" over and over. I watched ten takes and at least five seemed flawless. Tom had his character nailed. But I should have noticed that Dustin seemed mopey.

After flying back to L.A., I called him: "How's it going, Dusty?"

"Not good."

"What's the problem?"

"I can't find my character." His voice was shaking. "I thought I had it, but I just can't find it."

For three days Dustin phoned me every few hours in a growing panic. He went so far as to nominate Richard Dreyfuss to replace him. "This is the worst work I've ever done," he moaned. I asked if he wanted us to shut down the movie so he could gather himself. Even at $100,000 a day, it would be less costly than reshooting later.

"No," he said, "I want to keep working at it." People called Dustin a prima donna, but all he cared about was the end product.

I called Barry: "Dusty can't find his character."

"I know," Barry said, "but I can't get him to tell me if he likes anything he's done. I'll just keep going till he figures it out."

Ugh.

Finally, Barry asked Dustin to look for just five seconds in the dailies that felt right. Once he found them, they had their foundation. By the time they shot the underwear scene ("I get my boxer shorts at Kmart"), Dustin had dialed in.

A good package matched directors and actors who elicited the best from one another, even if they didn't always get along. Barry's equanimity was perfect on *Rain Man*. When Dustin stayed in character off camera and refused to make eye contact, Barry took it in stride. When Dustin shouted, Barry filtered out the noise, took the point, and moved on. He gave his actors room to find funny or poignant moments that weren't on the page. The scene where Raymond enters the darkened hotel room and mimics the sounds of Charlie and his girlfriend having sex was all Dustin, and all hilarious.

Rain Man came out in 1988 to very low expectations, and shocked everyone by grossing more than $400 million around the globe. Our clients with a share of the profits, or what's called back-end participation—Dustin, Tom, Barry, and Mark Johnson—made many multiples of their salaries. And then the film was nominated for eight Academy Awards.

During the Oscars ceremony, in March of 1989, my wife, Judy, and I sat one row behind Dustin. Barry Morrow and Ron Bass won for Best Original Screenplay early in the night, a good omen. Then Dustin's name was called out for Best Actor, and I felt a thrilling jolt of pride. My friend had joined an elite club of multiple Oscar winners: Spencer Tracy, Fredric March, Gary Cooper, and Marlon Brando. Dustin was nearly ten years older than me, but I felt like a father to him, and to all my clients—I was the dad holding on to the back of their bikes and running them down the street shouting, "Pedal, pedal!"

Dustin had brought *Tootsie* to CAA, but I had steered this film to him, a vital difference. Even so, I was startled when he began his acceptance speech by saying, "I thank my agent Mike Ovitz for making this project stick with glue when it was falling apart." I'd been mentioned at the Oscars as a name on a list, but never like that. Barry Levinson then won for Best Director, and said, "I have to thank Michael Ovitz, who worked to keep this movie alive a lot of times when it may never have happened." And when we won Best Picture, Mark Johnson thanked me for "standing by this for weeks and years." The editor of *Variety*'s column about the awards would be headlined MIKE OVITZ—AN OSCAR HERO. I was on cloud nine.

At the Governors Ball afterward, I walked in and was surrounded by well-wishers, a cluster that included Dustin and Tom Cruise. Tom Hanks, another Best Actor nominee, sauntered over to throw his arm around me (not long afterward, he, too, would become a CAA client). But off to the side I saw Gene Hackman and Alan Parker, the star and director of *Mississippi Burning*, both clients, and both losers that night. They were visibly seething. I had signed them, and though other agents represented them day to day, I felt a sense of responsibility for their successes and failures, just as I did for all our clients. I felt particularly sorry for Gene, Dustin's old roommate, who had been superb in a tricky role as a conflicted FBI agent. I also felt like a father caught favoring one child over another.

I was adept at palliating conflict—or at least I thought I was—so I walked over and congratulated them. They turned away, snubbing me dead. They were convinced that I'd somehow fixed it so *Rain Man* won. I had privately voted the straight *Rain Man* ticket, following my heart, but there was no way for me to influence the balloting, even if I'd wanted to. That was the problem with CAA: we only *almost* ran everything. *Rain Man* won—but *Mississippi Burning* lost. What should have been the greatest night of my life had just become one of the worst.

Ron Meyer, my partner and closest friend, was standing ten feet away. Ron was the soul of CAA, to hear everyone tell it, and I was the ass-soul. He wore sweaters and jeans and Cole Haan loafers; I was buttoned up in a blue suit. He was perpetually tan and relaxed and charming; I was perpetually pale and tense and vigilant. He was the velvet glove; I was the iron fist. But we were like Siamese twins, with one brain and one heart. I went over and told Ronnie what had just happened, and he grinned wryly, which made me feel better, as always. "It goes with the territory," he said. The year before, Michael Douglas and Cher, two of his best clients—people he thought of as great friends, and worked incredibly hard for—had won Best Actor and Best Actress. It was a very rare double for an agent, yet neither Michael nor Cher thanked Ron in their remarks. He was devastated.

Cher did thank her hairdresser, though.

———

AS AGENTS, WE DIDN'T CREATE ANYTHING. WE WERE SELL-ers; we sold our clients our time and expertise, and then we sold the buyers our clients. Our tenuous capital was the hours in the day, less the few we slept, and we spent that capital at a frenzied pace. I'd drop everything to get you the right cardiac surgeon, the right car, a place for your kid at the John Thomas Dye or Harvard-Westlake schools—whatever you needed. I was everyone's chief psychiatrist, legal adviser, financial adviser, fixer, cultural translator, and shoulder to cry on. With so many clients' very lives seemingly our responsibility, I obsessed about what might go wrong for them—and for the agency. At one point in the '80s we found an operative rooting through our trash, and after that I was always checking to make sure that memos got locked up or destroyed and that our lines weren't bugged. The phrase of mine that my assistants conspiratorially intoned to one another, with an eye roll, was "Is the line cleared?" I felt you could never be too paranoid, because our competitors were out to get us and our clients were weak and easily wooed.

Though my ruling desire was for complete control, I often felt at their mercy. I had little knowledge of what went on in their homes, production offices, and dressing rooms, but I hated the rumors I occasionally heard. Hollywood has always been a ruthless business, a machine designed to exploit talent and beauty, and the word was that a few of my male stars were treating younger women as sexual objects. When I learned about abuse in our office, I could and did address it. When one agent's assistant told me he was chasing her around her desk, I called him in, ripped him a new one, and suspended him for a week. Then I transferred her to my office, where she worked very productively for ten years. He returned noticeably chastened, and as far as I know didn't repeat his mistake. But with clients the dynamic was different; it was they who could fire me. Because of that imbalance—I was the parent, but the children had all the power—and because my focus was frankly on our business rather than on social justice, I let the matter go. I deeply regret that. Now, in the post–Harvey Weinstein era, a reckoning has finally come led by women braver than I was. It is absolutely necessary and long overdue.

Part of the reason I let the rumors slide is that I had a powerful need to take care of my clients; I thought of them as a very large, very fractious family. But when clients tried to reciprocate, I got embarrassed. I forbade toasting at the two birthday parties I allowed my friends to throw me; I liked giving gifts, not receiving them. I always wanted credit for everything I accomplished, the small and large miracles I achieved, and I was upset when I didn't get it—but I was mortified on the rare occasions when I did. So, for the most part, I gave, and people took. Every day I felt like each of my clients had installed a spigot in my gut and turned it on full blast. With 1,350 spigots in my gut, I often felt drained by noon. It's a thankless business, but you can't say that. You're getting paid, and that's your thank-you.

I always told our agents, "Make your clients think they're your friends—but remember that they're not." Yet it would be my clients who'd stay loyal, for the most part, and my friends who'd betray me.

Jay Moloney, the agent I thought of as a son and as my eventual successor, a man who modeled himself on me, down to the Armani suits he wore and the Lichtenstein painting he bought, would join the agency's posse of Young Turks who disowned me after I left CAA.

Michael Eisner, my great friend who ran Disney, would hire me as his number two, then publicly humiliate me and fire me after fourteen months.

And Ron Meyer, the blood brother I started CAA with, would leave to take a big job at Universal after I'd negotiated for us both to go there—and then disparage me all over town for twenty years.

I'd made it my life's work to understand people, to grasp what made them tick. I'd been certain that I was too wary to misplace my trust and too smart to be duped. So I'd like to think that these betrayals were random, and flagrantly unwarranted, and that I was the victim of some perverse instinct that destroys all human intimacy. I'd like to think that the problem was just that the tools and stratagems I'd used to get to the top inevitably created resentment, even among those who shared my success. That everyone hates a winner. That just because I sought money and power and intimidated everyone to get them didn't change me.

But I did change, of course. Because I could get movies that no studio would touch released and celebrated (*Stand by Me*), make stars out of nobodies (Steven Seagal, who'd been my martial arts instructor), even broker the sale of studios (Columbia and MGM once each, and Universal twice). With CAA's power behind me, I could, for a time, make almost anything in Hollywood happen through leverage, acumen, and sheer self-belief.

Those whom the gods wish to destroy they first give a gift.

CHAPTER ONE

IS THE GODFATHER HERE?

I MET DAVID LETTERMAN IN 1973, WHEN I WAS IN NEW YORK pitching TV shows for the William Morris Agency. Dave was a born comedian who for years had labored behind the scenes writing for crap like *The Starland Vocal Band Show*, but to me he'd always stood out. His humor was goofy but razor sharp. I tracked him as Johnny Carson's recurrent guest on *The Tonight Show*, and then on *Late Night with David Letterman*, which debuted in 1982 in the time slot after Johnny's on NBC. Dave excelled at the toughest job in show business: making people laugh, five nights a week.

No one could replace Johnny, the coolest, most charming host ever, but it was an open secret that Johnny wanted Dave to succeed him. Yet NBC made Jay Leno Johnny's permanent guest host, and seemed to be leaning Leno's way. In February 1991, during Johnny's twenty-ninth year at the helm, I was stunned to read a headline in the *New York Post*: NBC LOOKING TO DUMP CARSON FOR JAY LENO. Clearly, Helen Kushnick, Leno's hyperaggressive manager, was behind this ridiculous claim. She thought NBC owed Jay *The Tonight Show*—now.

The *Post* story made me take a closer look at late night. At CAA we kept a "dashboard" of every project under way in film, TV, music, and books. A copy was placed in each agent's black binder, together with the latest box-office data, TV ratings, bestseller lists, and other pertinent data that might give us an edge at our 8:30 a.m. staff meetings (which were themselves scheduled to give us an edge—we started sixty to ninety minutes ahead of our competitors). Our rule at staff meetings was "No idea is too stupid." I consulted the dashboard several times a day, looking for opportunities for clients, potential film packages, or new business, the crazier-sounding the better.

The late-night math seemed simple. There were two candidates to replace Carson, and Helen Kushnick had one. Letterman was the other. Dave had a top attorney in Jake Bloom, an able manager in Jack Rollins, and a nightclub booker who had nothing to do. Unlike Jay, who relentlessly played club dates on weekends, Dave never did stand-up. He shunned personal appearances. He didn't go out much, period. And he didn't have an agent. Dave was a star at 12:30, but I thought he could be a much bigger one.

Because it's human nature to resist being sold, I avoided cold-calling prospective clients. Better for them to come to me; better to be wooed than to pitch. I dispatched Jay Moloney on a recon mission to Peter Lassally, *Late Night*'s executive producer. Jay listened carefully to Peter's woes, then offered his opinion: "Dave is naked against all the forces lined up behind Jay. He needs help."

Afterward, Jay told me: "Dave is floundering." Dave's problem was that he was a regular guy from Indianapolis who didn't lobby or whine or throw his weight around. He thought that he'd inherit the biggest seat in late night on merit: he was clearly a more original talent than Jay, and therefore a more natural heir to Johnny. But that's not how the business works. Behind that biting sense of humor Dave was an innocent.

Warren Littlefield, the president of NBC Entertainment, favored Leno. But the man on the spot was Bob Wright, the canny finance executive who'd become NBC's CEO after General Electric bought the network in 1986. We sold NBC ten pilots a year and I held Bob in high regard. Optimistically, Bob hoped to retain both Leno and

Letterman, one on *Tonight* and the other in the bullpen. He thought Dave would do as he was told, because where else could he go? Ted Koppel was entrenched on ABC's *Nightline*, and CBS seemed whipped after a string of failed challenges to Carson. Its latest pretender, Pat Sajak, had been canceled after just fifteen months.

In May, three months after the *Post* story, Johnny announced that he'd retire in a year. At sixty-five, he wanted to go out on top. After waiting a respectful two weeks, NBC announced that Jay Leno would take Johnny's chair. Jay's mainstream appeal made him the safer bet for the $100 million franchise—corporate thinking, cautious but understandable. I was stunned, though, to hear that the network had kept Dave in the dark until two days before the announcement, particularly as Leno's latest contract had secretly locked him in as Carson's replacement. No one at NBC was looking out for Letterman, who brought the network $55 million a year. (Then, as now, the networks made most of their profits from late-night and daytime programming.) Indeed, the network's bean counters had been hassling Dave on expenses, going so far as to reject his invoice for a car phone. Even when Dave told Warren Littlefield to his face he'd have to quit if he didn't get *Tonight*, Littlefield made no real effort to assuage him.

NBC was driving Dave into our arms. After Peter Lassally called the agency that summer to suggest a meeting, we scrutinized Dave's contract. It was ugly. "It's like he's in prison," said Lee Gabler, our number two in television, a tall, judicious man our clients instinctively trusted. Dave was barred from negotiating with anyone else for a year and a half, until February 1993, two months before his contract was up. Even then, NBC retained the right to match any offer. If Dave turned them down, the network could keep him off the air for *another* year.

Agents used to be like firemen: they ran from one crisis to the next, reacting to offers and ultimatums, never knowing what tomorrow would bring. At CAA, we prided ourselves on making tomorrows. Could we create a more brilliant one for Dave? We put five people on the project under Lee, and I asked them to analyze Nielsen ratings and late-night time slots and every conceivable bidder for his services. All the data I needed was distilled into three pages of single-spaced type, and we spent hours and hours discussing the game theory of how to play the networks against each other. By late summer I was ready for our one shot at Dave.

OUR FOCUS ON FIRST IMPRESSIONS WON US MANY NEW clients before we'd uttered a word. When Dave and Peter Lassally pulled into CAA's underground garage that August, one of our five parking "concierges" welcomed them by name. Dave and Peter then walked to the elevator through a gallery of vibrant prints—Johns, Stella, Close, Rauschenberg. I'd chosen those pieces to compel attention and announce our values. When I gave visitors a tour, I'd stop by the prints and talk with actors about composition and mood, with directors about the power of the images, and with execs about being well rounded and having a life outside the business. The art works were secretly my favorite feature of the building because they always made me pause, made me feel something, made me remember the person I kept hoping to become—a man very different from the personage Dave and Peter had come to see.

After taking an elevator up one floor, they stepped into the atrium of our I. M. Pei–designed building, which was fifty-seven feet high and topped by a glass hemisphere. Other agencies looked like accounting firms, and as Dave and Peter crossed the travertine floor to the reception desk and took in the massive Lichtenstein on the wall, I hoped they'd be thinking, *Wow!* As they checked in they couldn't help but notice the traffic on the open bridges of our upper floors, a constant churn that suggested CAA's high metabolism.

En route to the next bank of elevators, Letterman yelled out, "Is the Godfather here?" Which was pretty funny, and also the first and last time anyone yelled in our lobby.

My third-floor office was modest in size and flooded with sun from the floor-to-ceiling windows. Gigantic offices are stupid and counterproductive. Personal meetings should be intimate; larger ones belong in conference rooms. On one end of my office sat a half-moon desk of French ash with two Giacometti chairs. A sitting area held a couch and two Josef Hoffmann chairs. The single canvas, *Circle in a Square* by Robert Mangold, echoed the core elements of the building's design.

As I shook Dave's hand, I did a rapid scan. I always scanned people head to toe. Was their hair dyed, did they wear a wig, did the elements of their outfits match? Were they clean-shaven? (This was before the scruffy look pervaded the business.) Someone with hair curling out of his ears or dirty fingernails wasn't someone I wanted to cultivate. If a guy walked in with a huge gold chain and gold watch, he'd better be a hip-hop artist. Otherwise, he was announcing his insecurity.

Anyone who scanned me would see a thoughtful dresser in a blue suit, with a white or blue shirt and black shoes—never brown— accessorized only by a leather-strapped watch. I wore no jewelry, not even a wedding band. I sat up straight, I was sympathetic, and I focused intensely on you, always turning the conversation away from myself. As I discovered by seeing my persona reflected in the eager eyes of my clients, that focus drew them in. And the contrast between the relaxed demeanor and the humming engine underneath, which people felt subconsciously, was comforting if you were on my side of the table, and curiously alarming if you were across from me. It suggested untapped power.

What I saw in Dave was a preppy midwestern man who wore white socks with penny loafers, was ill at ease, but was candidly seeking aid and comfort. I saw someone who felt alone, vulnerable, and lied to. When I smiled at him, he grinned back. Noting that we both had that distinctive gap between our front teeth, he said, "Are we related?" In a way—in our wariness, our skepticism of human motivations—we were. One reason I became so determined to help Dave was that he reminded me of myself. Of course, he was more trusting than I was, easier to read, and much, much funnier. Also, he truly believed he was going to get *The Tonight Show*, while I knew better.

When Peter Lassally launched into their tale, I cut him off. I understood their problem; I needed every minute to convince Dave I could solve it. "Peter," I said, "I know Dave's circumstances. And so I know why you're here. Dave is a star of such compelling stature that, frankly, it makes me personally angry he finds himself this abused. We pride ourselves here at CAA in developing a career plan for our clients that protects them as much as enriches them. David has had such an incredibly high professional standard, and yet he's going disturbingly unrewarded. That just doesn't make sense. It's bad business practice. Obviously," I continued, "we have an intense interest in establishing a business relationship with you, Dave. And with you, Peter. Frankly, we have worked out a career plan for David, and it includes securing everything for Dave that he wants. Everything." I let that sink in. "Of course, that means an 11:30 television show." However, I added, "The geometry of the deal will be far larger. The studios will be in, the syndicators, the full range of the entertainment industry. We'll frame a deal that will make you one of the giants. And if you give us the privilege of working with you, CAA will take care of everything your talents deserve."

My pitch to Dave later featured in a made-for-TV movie called *The Late Shift*. The scene was unusually accurate because the producer was my client Ivan Reitman, and I told Ivan exactly how I'd done it. Treat Williams, who played me, got the even tone I maintained in order to keep clients calm, as well as my compulsive hand washing. I'd wash my hands thirty times a day, and insist that my assistants not touch my food—which seems bizarre, I know, but I was in a people business, meeting dozens every day, and I was determined not to get sick. (And I never did, until one of my rare vacations, when I always collapsed.)

My pitch ran the risk of sounding fulsome: another salesman, full of blarney. But it's only blarney if you can't make it happen. If you can, then it's the truth—and the truth is the supreme sales tool. When I accurately foretold future events, my client: (a) felt good about getting the outcome I had predicted; (b) thought I was a genius for predicting it; and (c) spread the story, which helped us sign the next client. I knew from talking to CBS, ABC, and Fox that the other networks were interested in Letterman. The syndicators were bound to come knocking as well. Dave was too valuable to be ignored.

Dave talked about what he'd been through. Losing *Tonight* was his first soul-crushing disappointment, and he was still depressed. He was also forty-four, no longer a kid. One day soon he'd age out of the 12:30 demographic, and then what? I told him that all his options, including *The Tonight Show*, remained open, except for one. He could not stay on *Late Night*. Jay Leno was a likable personality with millions of fans, and Dave would be twisting in limbo, waiting for the guy to screw up. Could he wait five years? Ten?

"If we don't get involved," I said, "you'll end up at 12:30 on NBC by default, because you're the nicest guy in the world and you won't fight them. But you won't be happy." He nodded in agreement, and I moved to close. "We're ready to do this for you," I said. "Do you want us to do it or not?"

At that point, ninety-nine times out of a hundred the potential client would say, "It's been a great meeting. Let me sleep on it." Despite CAA's power—maybe because of CAA's power—he'd be reluctant to yield too easily.

"Let's do it," Dave said.

Walking him to his car, I said, "There will be times when you'll want to jump ship. Lots of people have a grudge against me and will do anything to work with you. They'll say we're destroying you—they'll try to put a wedge between us. If you think they could get to you, don't take this step." I always tried to instill the negative in advance, inoculating my clients against the worst things our competitors and buyers would say about us. It was like vaccinating them against the flu. With eleven companies eager to land Dave, the odds were high that at least some of them would try to stick a wedge between him and his advisers.

Dave said, "First of all, no one can reach me." Outside the studio he was a hermit. He laughed and added, "I'm not sure *you're* going to be able to reach me." We shook hands and something clicked. We were going to get along.

David Letterman was a huge test of CAA's strength. The situation could blow up in ten different ways, and under a national spotlight. The safe play was to let it be somebody else's headache. Two of our top execs and an astute corporate lawyer advised me to stay far away. If Dave wound up trapped at 12:30—or, worst of all, out of a job—how could the next client buy in? But something about Dave's helpless decency made me want to take his part. And I could never resist a challenge.

My first move was to call Bob Wright at NBC. "I'm glad you're involved," he said heartily, which was probably untrue. There's nothing sincere in entertainment: every call has at least one agenda, and usually two or three. Insincere flattery was actually more flattering than sincere flattery, because it was a tacit acknowledgment that I had power and had to be propitiated. But understanding that dynamic did make it hard to trust anyone.

"I'm not here to tell you what to do," I told Bob. "You've got two great choices. But the guy who loses—you're really expecting to hold on to him?"

"I've got a contract with both of them."

"I understand that, but let's get beyond the contract and look at the human being. Are you telling Dave he has to stay eighteen months to back up a guy who will take three years to build? You're going to lose Dave anyway. I don't get it."

"Well, that's a point," Bob said.

I was planting two seeds with that call. One, the choice of Jay Leno for *Tonight* was not irrevocable. Two, it was unconscionable as well as shortsighted to lock Dave in at NBC. Bob needed to give him the job he wanted or let him go. I had Jay Moloney send a memo to our 550 employees: "We are pleased to advise that we now exclusively represent David Letterman." News of the memo turned up the heat on NBC.

———

BEFORE THE DVR AND VIDEO ON DEMAND, THE TV BUSIness was all about counterprogramming. The networks eyed their programming boards, which displayed the competition's shows, and asked, "What'll play against this? And that?" *The Tonight Show* had always seemed unassailable because nobody could match Johnny.

While the 11:30 Carson/Leno audience was squarer than the 12:30 Letterman crowd, I knew Dave could adjust. Thanks to Brandon Tartikoff, who'd made NBC much younger in prime time, Dave could take *Tonight*'s audience "down," or younger, with him. There was a middle ground between Carson and the hip sarcasm of *Late Night*, and Dave was smart enough to find it. If Warren Littlefield thought Dave was too edgy for 11:30, other buyers burned to prove him wrong. We could spin Warren's brush-off as proof that our client was *different*, the alternative choice for discerning viewers. What's more, Dave's show was a plug-and-play commodity with no development costs. What better counter could you have to Jay Leno?

We wanted Dave to realize that he was in demand. But his contract prevented him from talking to his would-be suitors, and in our discussions with NBC the network was adamant about holding him to it. "We can't do any meetings," Lee Gabler kept telling me. It occurred to me that Dave wouldn't be in breach if we confined our talks to what might happen *after* he became a free agent. You couldn't kill a guy for planning his future.

I always tried to plot out, at the beginning of any complex negotiations, the desired end point. After we discussed the problem from every angle, it became clear that CBS was our desired end point. In June 1992, shortly after Leno took over at *Tonight*, I called one of my favorite executives, Howard Stringer, CBS's president. Howard was bright and calm and lethally witty—and I knew he was determined to plant his flag in late night. "Dave's not available now," I said, "but we're looking at possibilities after his contract expires. It might be a good idea if you started thinking about it."

"But how can I legally talk to him?" Howard asked.

"It falls under no harm, no foul. I'll set up some social meetings and you'll give it your best shot."

Next was ABC. I liked Ted Koppel's show so much that I often taped *The Tonight Show* to watch Ted live on *Nightline*. Yet I broached the unthinkable. "I know this is crazy," I told Bob Iger, the president of ABC Entertainment, "but would you ever consider moving Koppel to another time slot?" Iger didn't reject the idea out of hand.

As everyone in the business talked to everyone else, those two phone calls got the ball rolling.

———————

WE SET OUR BUYER MEETINGS ACROSS FOUR DAYS IN JULY and decked the black marble table in our meeting room with plates of fruit and homemade chocolate chip cookies. When the leading figures in television entered our lobby, we kept them waiting long enough to be spotted by anyone who happened to be in the building. We wanted our very private discussions to be very widely discussed.

Howard Stringer led with his top trump, an 11:30 slot on a true network. He made an impassioned presentation, telling Dave he was "much too decent a person to go with Fox!" As I said, lethally witty. Our concern was CBS's clearance rate, the percentage of affiliates with an 11:30 slot available to carry this potential new show. NBC's clearance for *Tonight* was well over 90 percent, but our research suggested that CBS's clearance would start at about 65 percent, then surge after Dave debuted. The low rate was a negative but not a deal breaker. Money was off the table for now. We couldn't address it without running afoul of Dave's contract, and Dave, with his midwestern ethos, was glad to skirt the subject, anyway.

Next came Fox. I considered Rupert Murdoch the top executive in modern media—cagey, prescient, with an unmatched appetite for risk. Rupert floated the idea of an 11:00 p.m. start to get the jump on Leno, and he could make it happen. But while Fox had the younger viewers we wanted, it was just emerging as the fourth network. To really compete with Jay, Dave needed a network that could clear more than two hundred stations.

Next came Columbia Television, King World Productions, and Paramount. I had warned Dave that I was skeptical of syndication.

What if ten southern stations pushed his show to a different time slot? What if the local baseball game ran late? Who knew what Dave's lead-in would be, or the lead-in to his lead-in? The variables scared me. Syndicators would offer ridiculous sums ("Oprah money," Dave called it), and that would make CAA's commission lavish. But Dave needed a solid core audience, night after night. Still, I told him to keep an open mind. It was a vital part of my self-presentation not to reflexively pronounce as most agents did, but to address questions or difficulties by taking a beat, then saying, "I'm not sure about that," or "Let me look into it." I wanted it clear that I didn't just make shit up.

Last, we heard from Bob Iger at ABC. Nothing was off the table, Bob said. He might shorten Koppel to half an hour and start Dave at midnight. He might even move *Nightline* to prime time, which Koppel probably would have welcomed. It was an exciting conversation, but I privately doubted that ABC would mess with success. (Iger's sales department soon informed him that neither of those ideas was feasible.)

We then flew to New York, where we met with Chris-Craft and Disney and Viacom. Viacom volunteered that it would pay Dave some $50 million a year. We told him to let it all marinate. Bound by his contract for another nine months, he couldn't commit even if he'd wanted to. Besides, his top choice, NBC, had yet to pitch.

For Dave the process must have seemed surreal. After a decade building *Late Night* as his stepping-stone to *The Tonight Show*, he'd found himself casually discarded. Now he had his hyperactive agents calling him five times a day and a who's who of television wooing him—and, of course, trying to undermine us.

But Dave shut out the gossip and whisper campaigns. There was no end of rumors about Dave's future and no shortage of reporters on the story, but our buyers kept their mouths shut. We had told them all that our discussions had to stay private, given Dave's contract with NBC— and that anyone found leaking would be out of the bidding.

In any case, the real story was being written inside our heads. Though we privately favored CBS, we had to give everyone a fair shot, or at least the appearance of one. And we had to get Dave a *Tonight Show* offer, not just because he wanted it, but because that way he could leave them, rather than slinking off as the rejected suitor.

Two scenarios troubled me. One was a bold or reckless bidder backing up the money truck. Say Rupert Murdoch said, "We'll give you a five-year commitment on the air and twenty-five million worth of stock options in Fox." And then he told Peter Lassally and Robert "Morty" Morton, the show's producer, "You'll each get five million in options. And instead of paying your guests scale"—about $400— "we'll budget five thousand dollars each to get the best people every night." That would blow Howard Stringer and everyone else out of the water.

My other fear was what might happen if Dave got offered *Tonight*— which we wanted only as an offer, but which he desperately wanted as a job. If he took *Tonight*, I could foresee him getting off to a slow start and Leno's camp conspiring to unseat him. What was to stop NBC from reinstalling Jay on the show? (Seventeen years later, the network would do just that with Jay and Conan O'Brien.)

We wanted to set a record for a host's salary on an initial deal, and we wanted to make Dave happy—and the best way to do that was to have downside protection. We wanted Dave at a network where no one was waiting for him to fail. More selfishly, my preference to marry Dave to CBS—after an amicable divorce from NBC—was also in CAA's interest. We needed to stay on good terms with Bob Wright and Warren Littlefield *and* Howard Stringer. In a zero-sum business, as I've noted, that's almost impossible.

HELEN KUSHNICK HAD BEEN A GREAT REPRESENTATIVE FOR Jay, but after she started executive producing *Tonight*, she got drunk with power. When Bob Wright asked her to have Jay say something warm about Johnny Carson on his first show, she flatly refused; and after that show taped, she muttered an audible, "Fuck you, Johnny

Carson." She banned stars who appeared on competing shows, such as Arsenio Hall's, and battled with Letterman's producers. Then, one night in August, she canceled the whole broadcast after the Republican National Convention ran into Leno's monologue time. NBC had to scramble to plug in a rerun, and we began to hear rumblings from the network: *Out of control. Knife to the throat.* (My source was Dick Ebersol, president of NBC Sports.) Jay Leno was supposed to be the low-maintenance host, but it wasn't working out that way. NBC fired Kushnick in September.

Throughout all this drama, Dave's camp in New York was pressuring Bob Wright to change his mind. But Warren Littlefield and John Agoglia, the executive vice president of NBC productions, were holding firm, particularly as Leno's ratings were strong. When I saw Bob at an industry function that fall, I appealed to him for a waiver to allow us to solicit hard offers. After all, NBC would retain its matching rights. After Dave tested the waters, I said, he'd be more open to whatever the network proposed.

Bob agreed, in exchange for a three-month extension of Dave's contract through June 1993. They'd sold *Late Night* that far in advance, and networks hate giving money back to advertisers. We shook on the quid pro quo, a no-lose proposition for our side. It took a new show six months to find a space, build a set, and assemble a staff. Assuming Dave went elsewhere, he couldn't start before late '93, anyway.

We asked our bidders to respond in writing on nine deal-point questions, including salary, budget, ownership, and time slot. Once we saw Dave's options on paper, the choice was obvious: CBS and Fox were the finalists, with CBS the front-runner. We kept hashing out the details with Howard Stringer, and by December we were satisfied.

We asked Dave to come in. "It is CAA's formal recommendation," I told him, "that you accept the CBS offer and so inform NBC." We laid out the deal points. CBS was offering Dave's company, Worldwide Pants, two hours a night, including whatever show Worldwide chose to produce at 12:30 a.m. Dave's three-year pay-or-play deal would be

$14 million a year, double his *Late Night* salary. The production budget was generous. The network's prime-time lead-ins were thriving. The 11:30 time slot was ironclad.

Dave agreed that CBS's offer was the best—though he clearly still hoped to use it as leverage with NBC. We gave Howard the news and made consolation calls to the rest, beginning with my friend Michael Eisner, the chairman of Disney. Michael's standard move was to low-ball (he'd offered Dave just $6.5 million a year) and then complain vociferously when he lost. "I can't believe you did this to me!" Michael said, launching into his customary guilt game: *Disney was the greatest company in history. Therefore this was a strategic mistake, an immoral decision, downright un-American.* He spent more time trying to make you feel bad so you'd give him the next deal than he did trying to win the deal in the first place. I said I was sorry and called the next also-ran.

After Dave approved the terms from CBS, Lee Gabler detailed the offer to John Agoglia, who had a month to put up or shut up. NBC had made noises about matching, but I doubted they would. The rich CBS package, which included guarantees for Paul Shaffer and his band, announcer Bill Wendell, and Dave's writers, was plausible for an 11:30 franchise. But in the 12:30 slot, with its lesser ad revenues, the math wouldn't work. At the shrewd suggestion of Bert Fields, the lawyer advising us on the contracts, we'd had CBS agree to pay a $50 million penalty in the event Dave failed to get the 11:30 slot it had promised. The point was to block NBC from matching and then stalling Dave on *Late Night* or keeping him off the air entirely. It was one of the subtle ways we loaded the dice to favor CBS.

Bob Wright offered to move Dave to 10 p.m. That was the wrong time—the audience that was accustomed to seeing the networks' dramas at 10 p.m. skewed both older and younger than the late-night sweet spot—and we turned him down. Two weeks later, Bob asked to see Dave alone. I was against it, but Lassally and Morton outvoted me, and they proved to be right. Dave used the meeting to satisfy Bob that he could adapt his style to 11:30.

The next day Jay Leno told the *New York Times* he would "leave

NBC immediately" if *Tonight* went to Dave. He mustered his friends at the affiliates, and their pro-Leno position made it into the *Los Angeles Times*. The pressure was building on Bob. When we met over New Year's in Aspen, he sought assurances that Dave could be a "team player" on *Tonight*. He seemed ill at ease—an encouraging sign, I thought. According to our sources, NBC's research showed Letterman beating Leno head-to-head. (We had similar findings from CAA's focus groups and supermarket exit polls.) The network buried the report and cherry-picked a new study to get data more favorable to Leno. But it was clear that, seven months into Jay's tenure, *Tonight* was still in play. I could tell that Bob wanted Dave. But he didn't want to jam through a move that could come back to haunt him.

———

ON JANUARY 8, 1993, JOHN AGOGLIA CALLED WITH NBC'S decision. Agoglia was unloved by agents, as he could be abrasive, even overwrought. But when I picked up, I heard ruefulness in his voice. Forced to make a one-eighty, he saw the humor in his situation.

"We want Dave for *The Tonight Show*," Agoglia said. But as he sketched the offer, it became clear that they didn't want Dave all that much. NBC had no intention of matching CBS. The salary was much lower, the production budget tighter. Most disturbing was NBC's proposed start date of May 1994, when Jay Leno's contract expired. That gave the network sixteen months, an con in television, to see how Jay's ratings held up. If they cratered, Dave was plan B. If Jay rallied, NBC could stick with the status quo. Either way, Bob Wright would keep his two biggest stars in the fold.

It was crafty work by NBC's lawyers but a terrible deal for Dave. At best, he'd be perceived as the second man in on *Tonight*. At worst, he'd be the guy not quite good enough to get a shot. To me, Agoglia's bid was a nonstarter. But what would Dave think? Years before, when asked about *The Tonight Show*, he'd said, "If I weren't asked someday to do it, I'd feel kind of sad. Yet doing it—that's my worst nightmare. . . . Maybe the prudent thing would be to let some other poor bastard walk into the fray for several months and then try doing the show." NBC was leading us to precisely that point, with Jay Leno playing the poor bastard.

We were encouraged by how weak NBC's offer was; we could recommend against it without reservation. But even novice agents know that the first offer is never the best or final one. We could have shown up en masse at Warren Littlefield's office and called Bob Wright with Agoglia in the room. Knowing how much Bob dreaded Dave's departure, we could have shaved the sixteen-month delay and boosted Dave's salary and production budget. I was a deal maker. I could have hammered home a deal to get Dave his dream job. But I didn't do it, or even tell Dave that I could, because it wasn't right for him. A late-night show wasn't a one-off, like a book or a movie; his career hung in the balance. Sometimes, representing a client's best interests means not getting him what he thinks he wants. The judgment part of the job requires knowing when to redirect a client's desires.

In a conference call with Dave and Peter, we told them what Dave was eager to hear: "We've got NBC if we want it." But as we compared the offers for them, CBS won on every count. It also won on the crucial perception question. Jay Leno was pulling a 4.9 rating at 11:30, while CBS was languishing at 2.7. A 3.8 on CBS would make Dave a hero; the same number on NBC would be disastrous. For someone with Dave's strong fear of failure, that was a weighty detail. Flipping the frame to emphasize the positive and to spark Dave's competitive nature, I said, "If you go to CBS, you'll have the chance to beat NBC's pants off." Peter backed us. But Dave was still agonizingly unsure.

From the start, two summers earlier, Dave had asked for my unfiltered opinion. I'd told him everything, even the ugly stuff—the negative gossip about him at NBC, the concerns about his style at 11:30—that agents usually edit out. On each call I'd think, *Is this the moment to push him over the cliff?* I decided, now, that it was finally time. I told Dave *The Tonight Show* was dead for him. It had died six months before, the instant Jay Leno took over. From that moment, Dave was no longer the crown prince; he could only be Jay's usurper.

Their needling aside, they admired each other. If Dave bigfooted Jay, he'd have a hard time living with the fallout—and with himself. His self-respect was even more important to him than his childhood dream.

Dave didn't want to hear this, but he needed to. I closed by repeating our recommendation: CBS. There was a long pause. Then Dave said, "You know, it's every race driver's dream to drive a Ferrari. I need more time." His heart was overwhelming his head.

Playing for the time Dave needed, I asked Agoglia to come in over the weekend and start papering the contract. On January 9, a Saturday, he and his seconds met with Lee Gabler, Jay Moloney, and Steve Lafferty, CAA's head of TV business affairs. I stayed away to preserve Dave's option to bail. We orchestrated it that way because in a pinch I might have to disavow any agreement they came to.

Lee called afterward and said, "John's not looking to make a deal." He'd offered a few small concessions but refused to put them in writing. A seasoned agent like Lee could read his body language. Agoglia was following Bob Wright's orders against his own inclinations, and he didn't want to close.

Agoglia followed up not by faxing the deal points to us, as arranged, but by reading them over the phone. NBC was temporizing like crazy, which meant one of two things:

1. They weren't sure they wanted Dave. A faxed deal memo, initialed by Dave and messengered back, was binding.

2. They weren't sure Dave wanted them. They feared we might turn them down, leak their offer to the press, and drive an embittered Jay Leno to quit.

At Peter Lassally's urging, Dave called the one person who'd truly understand his dilemma, the one person with no ax to grind. Johnny Carson told him he couldn't decide what was best for someone else. But if NBC treated him the way they'd treated Dave, Johnny said, he "would probably walk." The king gave Dave permission to relinquish his long role as the prince-in-waiting. When Dave and I spoke that evening, Dave said, "Let's proceed with CBS." He sounded at peace.

Before we could inform NBC, Agoglia pulled the network's proposal. We guessed that Carson had told someone he had spoken with Dave, and the grapevine did the rest. To cover its ass with Leno, NBC then held a press conference to deny any offer had been made. Uh-huh.

THE LATE SHOW WITH DAVID LETTERMAN DEBUTED ON CBS on August 30, 1993. I came to New York for it with my thirteen-year-old son, Chris, who wore a suit for the occasion. Standing in the glass-walled control room at the back of the Ed Sullivan Theater, we heard the audience erupt when Dave came onstage. As the applause washed over him, I felt real satisfaction at having gotten him his own show. You couldn't know what Dave was feeling deep down unless he told you, and he'd never tell you, but he looked assured in a double-breasted suit—a pointed departure from his old blazers—and he nailed his monologue. Bill Murray, a client and great friend of mine, was Dave's first guest, and Paul Newman, another client and great friend, did a cameo from the audience. The show went over like a dream.

Afterward, in his office backstage, Dave was characteristically self-lacerating—he told me the taping had been a disaster, and when Howard Stringer called to offer congratulations, Dave muttered that he'd call him back. Seeming embarrassed by all the attention, he focused on my son. Apropos of nothing, he reached into his humidor and offered Chris a cigar, which cracked him up. As we left, Dave caught my eye and nodded, just once.

Howard Stringer underpromised and overdelivered. Within three years, CBS reached an affiliate clearance rate of more than 90 percent. With two to three guest spots per night, *Late Show with David Letterman* gave the film business an additional venue for promoting new releases, which helped all of our film clients. Worldwide Pants became the producer of CBS's *The Late Late Show* and *Everybody Loves Raymond*, and Dave was set for life.

IN THE MIDDLE OF THIS LONG, TENSE PROCESS, ON CHRIST-mas Eve, 1992, my family was in Aspen playing board games. I was going upstairs for a deck of cards when the phone rang in my bed-room. I was annoyed, because Christmas week is a hall pass for agents. What now?

"Michael?"

"Yeah?"

"It's Dave. I'm sorry to call you on Christmas Eve."

"Dave, I'm Jewish." I often tried to make him laugh, but this was one of the few times I succeeded.

He cleared his throat. "I have something I wanted to tell you," he said. "Um . . . I was in a bad place, and you're helping me get to a good place. You're really saving my life." He went on in that sweet, generous vein for three or four minutes, a long time for such a reserved guy.

I was stunned. After saying good-bye, I sat alone for a while. In my twenty-five years as an agent, through thousands of transactions, I had never heard so much heartfelt sincerity and gratitude. This—*this*—was what I had always secretly hoped the business would be like.

It was the last time it ever was.

CHAPTER TWO

THE
FIRST VALLEY

MY LIFE IS A STORY OF THREE VALLEYS. I BEGAN IN THE SAN Fernando Valley, wound up in Silicon Valley, and spent the intervening decades in a Valley I'd dug for myself.

I was raised in Encino, a nondescript part of the San Fernando Valley, the most nondescript part of greater Los Angeles. I loved Encino until I knew better, and then I hated it. We were on the wrong side of the hill from all the action.

My father, David Ovitz, had grown up in the Depression, the son of Jewish immigrants from Romania. He never made it to college. He married my mother, Sylvia, another second-generation American, and worked as a Seagram's salesman, wholesaling to liquor stores in Chicago, where I was born in 1946. As the local liquor market flattened, the company encouraged its salesmen to transfer to Los Angeles, which was booming. When I was five years old and my brother, Mark, was a baby, my parents traded in our third-floor walk-up for a $3,000 tract house in Encino.

My father was a sweet, hardworking, conscientious man who was fabulous with people. He kept broken cases of Seagram's bourbon, gin, and vodka under a blanket in his garage, and he'd hand out bottles to the local cops, the plumber, the laundress—everyone got one. In return, he got great service and endless good will. But even though he worked weekends selling patio furniture in Santa Monica, in a good week he made just $400. He'd give my mom $50 out of that to feed a family of four, and she was always running short. Our one luxury was Sunday dinner out, usually at a Cantonese joint called the Samoa House. Dress-up occasions were at the Smoke House, where my dad made sure we got in for the early bird discount. It wasn't until I was in college that I went to a restaurant after six p.m.

My dad's dream was to open his own liquor store. "You need to be in charge of your destiny," he drummed into me. "It's no good working for somebody else." I remember him pointing to the display of Seagram's Seven in a store—at eye level, the best position. "Power is all about shelf space," he'd say. "And to get shelf space, you've got to be big." But even his modest dream was out of reach; a liquor license cost $25,000. He wanted the license nearly as much as he wanted one of the big Fleetwoods in the window at the Casa de Cadillac on Ventura Boulevard. My father was not a superficial man, but it killed him that my mother's uncle, Sam, always had a gaudy new Fleetwood. Sam ran the two small Westwood hotels he co-owned with his nine siblings, and somehow he seemed to live higher than the others. He made my dad feel small.

A big weekend for us was to drive five hours to Las Vegas, stay in a thirty-five-dollar room at the Sands, and take in the shows. The Rat Pack was on the marquee, and you might see Sinatra in his tux at the tables. "Look at this place," my dad would say. "Did we pay admission?" I'd shake my head. "See those girls coming around with free drinks? Seagram gets paid for that booze. Where do you think the casino makes its money?" He'd nod toward the crowds around the roulette wheels and craps tables: "From all those stupid people, Michael. Maybe one in a hundred leaves a winner." Once or twice, to prove his point, he had me watch him play blackjack. He'd lose a little, then quit. "Just remember," he'd say. "The house always wins."

I absorbed the lesson, at least as far as gambling went. In every other way, I bucked the house. Because while I loved my father, I hated his boxed-in life. Like many who'd grown up in hard times, he feared risk. My mother's mother, Sarah, was a blunt-spoken widow who lived with us for years. She played on my mother's resentments, telling her, "You deserve more." My mother took good care of us, but when the mood came on her, she was a fuzzy Xerox of Sarah, just as querulous and demanding but less forceful. Sarah would gather me on her lap to watch *Days of Our Lives* together, and she'd protect me from getting spanked. She paid attention to me and seemed to think I was special— she was my second mother—and I felt horribly conflicted when she'd tell me, "You can be better than your father."

On certain Sunday afternoons, my father and Sarah and I would go to one of Uncle Sam's Westwood hotels and listen in an auditorium, with the other relatives, as he gave an update on the family holdings. These were really just occasions for him to demonstrate his acumen and to receive adulation. He was a cold, distant figure, a dictator who'd entertain petitions and grant favors. We'd stand in the back—I think because my dad hated being there at all. Indicating Sam, Sarah would whisper to my father, "Why can't you be like that? Why don't you own a hotel?" She was agenting him, brutally. And, like Malcolm McDowell's character being forced to watch scenes of violence in Stanley Kubrick's *A Clockwork Orange*, I couldn't turn away.

Sarah kept dosing me with this poison until I was fourteen, when my father finally kicked her out of the house. By then her incantations— a dark version of the immigrant's creed that in America you can be anything you want—had cast their spell. Instead of trying to emulate my father, a kind and loving man, I would be what Sarah expected of me. I would succeed at all costs. She was depressed, of course, sunk in her own miseries, so I'd save her by taking extraordinary measures to reward her faith in me. Later in life, I'd go the extra mile for anyone who seemed sick or lost. But when Sarah left our house, she took the most feeling and hopeful part of me with her.

At nine, I got a paper route and raced my Schwinn through the neighborhood. Then I asked for a second route, cutting my free time to the bone. But I always felt free inside my head. As a kid, I'd drive my dad and my teachers crazy with questions: "How can gasoline explode if it's a liquid?" When I was in fourth grade, I saw a scoop of melting lemon custard on the sidewalk of Balboa Boulevard, near a Baskin-Robbins. The scoop was fast becoming its components, and I explained to Mark, who accompanied me everywhere, "It's ice cream—but it's *not* ice cream." I went home and looked up ice cream in our *World Book*, and then I went to a Cornet dime store and bought a four-dollar machine to make some. It tasted horrible. But that was the kind of mind I had: observe, analyze, then reverse engineer.

I was a head shorter than my classmates and annoyingly curious, so I was bullied in elementary school. My father had saved me from older bullies once, in the stairwell of our building back in Chicago, but he wasn't around at recess or in the deadly hours right after school let out, when it was open season on outliers. I absolutely hated that feeling of powerlessness, of cowering and being craven and hoping just to pass unnoticed. I couldn't bear it.

I always stood out academically, even if none of my teachers took particular notice or encouraged me. I read everything I could, but my favorites were biographies of successful men: Andrew Carnegie, Winston Churchill, Nathaniel Rothschild. I also did a lot of drawing and model making. I wasn't a gifted draftsman or builder, but I'd construct model boats and planes in my room and entertain dreams of commanding flotillas and squadrons. If I built a fighter plane, I'd promptly draw a futuristic version of it, projecting what the next model should look like. Alone in my room, I'd try to see around the corner to what the 1960s would bring. I was always fascinated by what was coming next.

AT NINE, I DISCOVERED MOTION PICTURES. FOUR BLOCKS from my house, behind a chain-link fence and a security shack, sat a place of mystery—the back lot for RKO Pictures, the studio owned by Howard Hughes. The first time I eluded the watchman and snuck through a hole in the fence, I came upon another world. Mounds of lighting equipment, cameras, microphones, and cables, and row upon row of false-fronted buildings, from old western towns to gritty urban streets. Hundreds of actors in makeup: cowboys, Indians, policemen, spacemen. And hundreds more people in street clothes who peered through lenses, strung lights, hammered and hauled and ran about until a director yelled, "Action," and the fantasy began to take shape. The first production I saw was the schlocky serial *Queen of the Jungle*, but I was hooked.

My parents desperately wanted me to become a doctor, but the movies became my obsession. I tried to catch every new release, and I became a student of the business, both the creative side and the bottom line. In high school I subscribed to the weekly *Variety*. I loved *Fort Apache*, an RKO western about the cavalry and a great leader (John Wayne) who overrules an incompetent one (Henry Fonda). I became obsessed with building forts, and with the Spartan idea of the phalanx, the battle formation in which you're only as strong as the guy on your left. I was also impressed by an Errol Flynn western where he drew a line in the dirt during a mutiny and said, "You're either with me or against me." That formulation—*you're totally in or totally out*—became my mantra. It helped me enormously later. And it hurt me in equal measure, because it didn't allow for shades of gray. Most of life turns out to be in shades of gray.

When I was thirteen I was bowled over by *Cash McCall*, an otherwise mediocre film about a businessman named Cash, played by James Garner, who lived in a hotel penthouse, flew around in his own plane, bought failing companies, and resold them at a profit. "I'm a thoroughly vulgar character," he explained. "I enjoy making money." As a negotiator, his stance was "You can either take my very generous offer or go home and cut your throat." The concept of private equity was far beyond me, but I was struck by how Cash conceived a plan to fit his companies together into a conglomerate, then put his plan into practice with a band of specialist associates. I was also struck by his thesis that life was more than just business. I could run the world like Cash and still be home at six p.m., just like my father, to enjoy my family. He was a romanticized version of Uncle Sam: all the good parts, and none of the bad.

————————

AS A NINTH-GRADER AT PORTOLA JUNIOR HIGH, I GOT clobbered in an election for class historian. Losing this extremely insignificant contest depressed me for months. I could have accepted my shortcomings as a politician and folded my tent. Instead, vowing never to feel so humiliated again, I analyzed the loss and realized that I had no constituency. I needed to expand my relationships beyond the nerds who haunted the library and the ne'er-do-wells who snuck into RKO.

The following year, at Birmingham High in Van Nuys, a school of 3,500 students, I put my analysis into action. I made friends with the chess team, the football players, the debaters, joined five or six clubs, and built a base of support across various cliques. It seems funny to me now, but I had no sense of humor about it then. I'm sure I came across as a brown-nosing kid in a hurry. But I was an effective brown-nosing kid in a hurry! I ran for tenth-grade president and won. The following year I ran for student-body vice president. Because we were such a big school, I had to give my campaign speech to three separate assemblies. I got up to speak and discovered that I was extraordinarily comfortable on my feet. I looked people in the eye and pointed to them, calling them out, saying "You can do it! And you! Together we can make this a better school!" I personalized the battle—and won easily. Each victory made winning more addictive.

After I won that election, my father told me, "If you want to be treated like a king, you have to act like one." I started wearing J. C. Penney suits to student council meetings. I set up a program to bring in guest speakers and I initiated a clean-campus campaign, in which we'd all get out fifteen minutes early for every day the campus was deemed clean. In my zeal, I totally missed the signals from our student-body president, Mike McConahay, that I was stepping on his toes. It surely didn't help that when I ran for president that year, aiming to succeed Mike, I ended my speech by saying "I would much rather be a president who has done something that can be criticized than one who has done nothing and can't be criticized." I won again.

By then I was working eight-hour shifts as a box boy at our neighborhood Piggly Wiggly, 4:00 p.m. until midnight, saving toward a car and college and thinking about my future. Being student-body president made me an ex officio member of the Encino Rotary Club, so I met once a month with the Rotarians—car dealers and insurance agents who'd made something of themselves. They were no smarter or more hardworking than my dad, but they had something he lacked: a college degree. That had given them options, and now they composed the local power structure. But I didn't want to be just part of a local power structure.

Eight miles from where I grew up, across Sepulveda Pass, stood the mansions of Beverly Hills. I'd stare at them as we drove to family dinners in Westwood, a trip that in those prefreeway days took ninety minutes. That was when I began to hate the Valley, which lacked museums, institutions, a cultural center—any real stimulus for my brain. In the Valley, people grew up carrying a football under their arms. I wished I'd grown up in New York, where people grew up carrying a newspaper. The west side of L.A. seemed like the best local version of New York. And—though I didn't make the connection at the time—it was where Uncle Sam had his hotels. I wanted to live there.

This grudge against my surroundings, this sense that I had been raised in the wrong nest, like a cuckoo's egg, fueled me when I began my working life. I always felt one step inferior to the people around me, and one step superior. I wasn't as creative or cultured as they were, but I was a lot smarter and more hardworking than most of them. Insecurity and ambition make a powerful cocktail.

A MONTH BEFORE I GRADUATED, IN 1965, I HEARD ABOUT A job I actually wanted. After a hiatus of thirty years, the Music Corporation of America, known as MCA, was reviving its studio tour at

Universal's back lot. They were hiring ten young guides, five men and five women.

North of Ventura Boulevard in Encino, people lived in houses like ours. South of it were vast homes that cost $50,000 or more. The local melting pot was the town's Little League, which my dad ran. Through baseball he knew a south side father named Herb Steinberg, MCA's head of publicity, who agreed to recommend me. I had a strong résumé, but Herb's referral really helped. That was my first lesson in the business: who you know matters. I was the only high school student MCA hired.

Our training began in May with four weeks of evening orientation. In June the studio set us loose on the thirty-odd departments on the lot: makeup, hairdressing, set design, props, costumes, electrical, and so on. A memo went out to the department heads about the young people in yellow-and-white seersucker jackets who'd be dropping by. The rest was up to us.

The other guides worked from nine to six, but I came in at seven each morning and stayed until nine at night. Universal owned the last full-fledged working lot, and I walked its four hundred acres end to end. I read and reread and underlined my studio guide as if I were cramming for a final, writing out lists of questions for execs and technicians and keeping a notebook full of the answers. At the end of each interview I arranged to come back to observe. I had carte blanche at the busiest film and television studio in the world—and I was getting paid for it!

I spent hours around people putting up sets or taking them down or lighting them for the next take. I'd ask the production manager any dumb thing that came into my head. *Why are you breaking for lunch now, at ten a.m.?* It turned out that lunch was a subtle calculation. It might pay to take a meal penalty—enforced by union regulation—and skip the break if you could squeeze in one more shot before quitting time. Because after quitting time came overtime (when union members were paid at time and a half). And after overtime—that is, if you worked more than sixteen hours beyond your call time—the crew went into a glorious, devoutly-to-be-wished-for state known as golden time, when they got paid a full day's wages for each extra hour.

What I learned at Universal, the way glorious films blossom out of an intricate mesh of mundane practicalities, enthralls me still. I went in even on Sundays, when I could wander the empty soundstages to my heart's content. I passed through *Dracula*'s castle, the courtroom for *Inherit the Wind*, the battlefield in *All Quiet on the Western Front*, the Bates Motel from *Psycho*. I once disturbed some props on a TV set marked as a "hot set"—meaning one in the midst of shooting—and the director chewed me out the next day. I said, "You're one hundred percent right—I'm new. I'm sorry, and it won't happen again!" I post-mortemed everything, and never made the same mistake twice.

The heart of the tour for visitors was a two-hour ride on a candy-striped Glam Tram. I sat up front, wired for sound, and gave my spiel. As we passed the white house from the popular sitcom *Leave It to Beaver*, people *ooh*ed and *aah*ed. I went into the characters' back stories and how the show was produced. I might halt the tram and open Beaver Cleaver's front door to reveal the emptiness within (an irony lost on most visitors). Or dispense tidbits about historic Universal movies, such as *The Phantom of the Opera*.

The back lot was overseen by Al Dorskind, an MCA vice president who tried to evoke the Golden Age by inscribing actors' names on their bungalows. If our guests were impressed by seeing "Lana Turner" on a door, they went wild when they saw an actual star. I chased after Cary Grant, Jimmy Stewart, and Lee J. Cobb, but they all raced off. I had better luck with the young Michael Caine, then shooting *The Ipcress File*. Michael liked to walk to the set or the commissary instead of riding the studio golf cart. Telling my driver to wait, I'd call out, "Michael, come say hello to your fans!" Then I'd go on about Michael's fabulous career until I shamed him into signing some autographs.

I was a great guide because I believed in the product. By eighteen, I'd absorbed a basic rule for success: love what you do. (Too many people fight their job, a battle they cannot win.) My supervisors picked me to run the once-weekly VIP tour on a deluxe single-car tram. It was reserved for the friends and favor recipients of Lew Wasserman, MCA's legendary CEO—and a man whose career would intersect with mine in ways I could never have imagined. He'd be the making of me and, in a sense, I'd be the unmaking of him.

Some of us Valley kids followed the studios like boys in New York tracked the Yankees. I wasn't interested in the stars, but in the *process* of making pictures and in the people who were truly responsible. I loved the book *Frank Capra: The Name Above the Title*, which explained how the famous director took his writers to Palm Springs for ten weeks and worked with them until they had a script they could shoot. The idea of sitting in Palm Springs with a close pal, drinking mint juleps and making art, entranced me. And I loved reading about Irving Thalberg, "The Boy Wonder" who became the head of production at MGM at twenty-six. It gave me the idea that film could be a young person's game.

All the foul-mouthed magnates who founded the modern film business were fascinating: Harry Cohn, Louis B. Mayer, Jack Warner, William Fox. But the one who interested me most, in part because I worked at his studio and in part because he had the most far-reaching ideas, was Lew Wasserman. As I learned when I scrolled through microfiche to find old newspaper stories about him, Lew was a top Democratic Party fund-raiser and wielded unmatched power in show business. (To hedge his bets he had a senior MCA executive help out the Republicans.) Some said he was tied to the mob, and Lew never denied the connection; if anything, he liked being feared. It was good for business.

He began as a talent agent. After moving to Los Angeles from Chicago in the late 1930s, Lew built the town's paramount talent agency. His rules were simple: tend to the client, dress appropriately, divulge no information about MCA, do your homework, never leave the office without returning every phone call. He insisted on dark suits, white shirts, and a dark blue or dark gray tie, and he'd sweep papers left on people's desks into the wastebasket at the end of the day. His credo was "Messy desk, messy mind." On the one occasion I saw Lew's office as a tour guide, his desktop held only a phone, a clock, and a handsome desk set. Not one scrap of paper that could yield a secret.

He invested being an agent with power and respect—for a time, anyway. In 1950, when MCA insisted on half the net profits for Jimmy Stewart in a western called *Winchester 73*, it rewrote the rulebook. There were back-end deals before that, but never for such a big hit. *Winchester 73* became a *moment*. Cornering the market on movie stars, Lew swung decisive leverage to the talent and their representatives and helped finish off the old studio system. Later, he bought the Paramount library of old films when no one thought it was worth a dime. MCA was everywhere, packaging a huge number of TV shows and taking up to 75 percent of their production costs. The company's reach was so vast it became known as The Octopus.

In 1962, after MCA bought Universal, the U.S. Department of Justice (run by Lew's friend Bobby Kennedy) moved against the company for antitrust violations. Lew could have sold his agency intact to the next generation, as we did later at CAA. Instead, he used Kennedy's threat as a pretext to break it up and scatter his top agents to a dozen boutique outfits. Sellers were Balkanized and their power neutered— brilliant!

Lew coming on the lot was a visit from royalty. One day he took my VIP tour with his friend Mort May, of the May Department Stores Company. Lew was tall and imposing in his big glasses and dark suit. He looked at me, unsmiling, and said, "How's it going with the tour; are you enjoying it?"

"I'm enjoying every second of it!" I said. That was our last conversation for twenty years, until we went at it hammer and tongs over Robert Zemeckis's directing deal. I never reminded Lew that he'd given me my start in show business, though maybe I should have, just to piss him off.

I worked weekends at Universal throughout my first year at UCLA. Because I was putting myself through college, where I was majoring in psychology, I had to work every spare hour. I returned full time the following June, when the tour really took off. The studio added rides and concessions and threw up a building for demonstrations of stunts and makeup. After getting off the tram, guests could pick and choose where they wanted to go—it was like a mini-Disneyland. I signed on for extra shifts.

My immediate boss was the assistant operations manager, Tom Center. Tom was older, around thirty, but we talked about movies all day. A few weeks into the second summer, he left to start a weekend tour at 20th Century Fox and asked me to come along. The new job was year-round and closer to UCLA, so I quit Universal to go with him. I'd be making almost $600 a week at Fox, at age nineteen—more than my father. As Fox's back lot was too small for trams, we improvised with walking tours around the soundstages. There weren't many movie fans from Dallas or Philadelphia—or from the Valley, for that matter—who'd seen the infrastructure behind the magic. They were as slack-jawed as I'd been at RKO.

A few weeks after our Fox rollout, Tom joined the art directors' union. "I'm leaving," he said, "and I'm recommending you for my job." To my surprise, I got it. I hired my college roommate as my number two and a dozen guides from my fraternity. We brought in twenty attractive sorority girls as hostesses.

Business boomed. By fall I was working sixty-hour weeks while going to school full time. If I had a midday class, I'd hop into my '65 Mustang for the ten-minute ride to campus and dash back an hour later. I parked in a corner of Fox's parking lot and changed out of my jeans and white J. C. Penney T-shirt, the college uniform of the day, and back into business attire. My bosses were never the wiser. At school I was a total liberal, counseling my classmates on how to evade the draft; at work I was the best organization man you could ask for.

In my first innovation, I took a shot at the packaged bus tours run by Gray Line at Universal. It was a sweetheart deal for MCA, which sold blocks of tour tickets to Gray Line. But after I slashed half off Universal's block price, Gray Line agreed to divert a few weekend buses to us. I gave discounts to larger groups and threw in an option for lunch at the Fox commissary. Within a month, the feedback was so positive that Gray Line switched all its weekend business to Fox.

Al Dorskind, my old boss at Universal, called. I had cut sharply into his weekend profits, and he was furious. "Michael," he said, "you stole Gray Line from us. It's inappropriate, and I'm not sure it's legal. You need to stop."

I should have been cowed. Al—bald, tanned, fit, and rough around the edges—was Lew Wasserman's hatchet man. Instead, I felt a strange rush. "The last time I checked, this is America, and competition's a good thing," I said. "But I want to thank you for calling, and I'll certainly refer this to our legal department."

I went to Fox's top lawyer and told him the story. He grinned and said, "You didn't do anything wrong. And you tweaking Al Dorskind is going to play really well up the ladder." It was true. My bosses were delighted that some college kid had shaken MCA's tree.

Standing up to Al Dorskind taught me two things about myself. One, for reasons I cannot explain, I was fearless in confrontations. Two, I liked the entertainment business.

I MET JUDY REICH THE FIRST DAY OF MY SOPHOMORE YEAR. After registering for classes, I went to get a coffee at the student center and spotted a gorgeous blonde reading a book. There were a dozen tables open around her, but I walked up and said, "Hi, is that seat taken?"

"No," she said, eyeing me like I was deranged. An hour later, without my ever having told her my last name—I was just "Michael" to her for some time—she agreed to our first date: pizza and a Hollywood jazz club called Shelly's Manne-Hole. Great plan, but they wouldn't let Judy in because she wasn't yet eighteen. For our second date I took her to a rooftop restaurant and spent thirty bucks, a ton of money at the time.

Judy was an engineer's daughter from Beverly Hills, but she'd grown up in the flats south of Wilshire, the poorer part of town. So she

was a reach for me, but not totally out of the question. She was bright—
a better student than I was—sweet-tempered, vivacious, and crazy
about the theater. She dreamed of singing and dancing on Broadway.
When I met her, she was pledging Kappa Alpha Theta, the big gentile
sorority, and dating a handsome but wooden fraternity man. I convinced her that an ambitious guy from Zeta Beta Tau, the Jewish frat
I would become president of, could be more fun. From day one, I was
content just to hang out with Judy, a first for me. She made me feel like
I was working for someone other than just myself. She loved my drive,
the way I got everything out of my days—what she called my "last
squeeze of the toothpaste" lifestyle. I loved that she loved it, that she
got me. We were in total sync. In the summer of 1969, my BA in hand
after just three years in school, I married her.

CHAPTER THREE

MAIL MAN

AFTER GRADUATION I APPLIED TO THREE COMPANIES: WIL-
liam Morris, the oldest talent agency in the business; Creative Management Associates, or CMA, an up-and-coming talent agency led by
MCA alumni Freddie Fields and David Begelman; and the ad agency
J. Walter Thompson. Only Morris called me in for an interview. I went
to their Beverly Hills office in my ninety-nine-dollar navy blue suit,
wing-tip shoes, rep tie, and white button-down Oxford shirt. I looked
like a rookie FBI agent.

Almost everyone at William Morris started in the company's mailroom. After a year or two, trainees were sent to secretarial school for
shorthand, or "speed writing." They came back as an agent's secretary.
If they did well at that, they became an assistant, then a junior agent,
and finally a senior agent. It could take three years to become a junior
agent and four more to start signing your own clients as a senior
agent—and more than 80 percent of the trainees washed out along the
way. The way you got ahead at WMA was nepotism: everybody was
somebody's nephew. It was an old, soft, corrupt place.

I didn't know anybody, so I needed another way to stand out. I told
the head of personnel, "I have a proposition for you. I think I can learn
all I need to know to become an agent in 120 days. If I can't, I'll give

back everything you paid me." I was agenting him, and he knew it. He broke out laughing. "That's the craziest thing I ever heard," he said. "But I'm going to hire you. You start Monday." My salary would be $55 a week.

I said, "I'd like to start tomorrow." I showed up at 7:00, two hours early, to learn my way around the building. At 9:30, we received our assignments for the day. A few senior trainees snagged the plum jobs as substitute secretaries, which gave them the chance to impress an agent. The rest of us piled into company Volkswagens to make the morning mail runs to studios, networks, lawyers, and clients. There were three routes: the Valley, Hollywood, and Beverly Hills. Before the days of fax or email, all business not handled by phone was conducted via hand-delivered memos and contracts. Our bags were full and heavy.

There were twenty mailroom trainees, which meant I had nineteen rivals for advancement. I set out to finish my route in half the allotted time. Mapping out routes with my spiral-bound *Thomas Guide* to the city's roads, I played a game I called Keep On Moving. The trick was to avoid red lights. I got back to the office before noon, way ahead of the rest, for any errands my bosses needed in-house. They dispatched me to accounting or legal, where I learned the ins and outs of the byzantine company. People came to rely on me. Soon they stopped sending me outside Beverly Hills, and raised my salary to $75 a week. I was embarrassed by the low pay, embarrassed that I could take Judy out only to Mexican restaurants, which were the cheapest. You could get a five-course meal at Casa Escobar, on Pico, for $3.95: two dinners, two beers, and a tip and we were out for $16—slightly more than I was making in a twelve-hour day at William Morris. But Judy gave me the line I'd use later when I recruited people to an entry-level job at CAA: *You're investing in your life.*

I despised the mailroom but fell in love with the world it served. Working for William Morris was a means to an end—to get close to our creative clients, people who did things I could not do myself. I had no interest in being a cigar-chomping schlepper, like many of the agents there, and I was repulsed when I learned the methods of one of our agents: he'd sign aspiring actresses just to screw them, then toss the contracts. Agents in those days were functionaries, fielders of offers—they weren't respected in the creative community, and they didn't respect their clients all that much, either. They didn't poach, because they weren't aggressive. They lived by quantity of work, not quality. Two phrases you often heard were "A happy client is a working client" and— if an offer for a crappy project came in—"Sell 'em, don't smell 'em."

I aspired to build my own company someday, but that was in the distant future. I figured I'd be at WMA for twenty years. The agency had a rigid caste system: the mailroom guys used VWs; young agents got reimbursed for their mileage; rising agents got Buicks; senior agents drove Cadillacs. Los Angeles had to report to the New York office, which still ran everything. And film was our prestige division. The big movie agents were on the ground floor, near the top executives; TV agents were exiled a floor above. Even as made-for-TV movies such as *Brian's Song* were smashing old boundaries, there was no mingling of the worlds at WMA. Morris ruled in television, music, literary (books that became films or shows), nightclubs, theater, and Las Vegas. In film, though, CMA was killing us. Because there was no culture of poaching, we had no plan to reverse CMA's dominance—but the fact that our flagship division was our weakest created significant internal tension.

One day I was buttonholed by Abe Lastfogel, chairman emeritus and the living link to William Morris himself. He handed me a screenplay to bring to Warren Beatty's apartment at the Beverly Wilshire Hotel. I needed help to find the secret stairway to Beatty's penthouse, the spot where he entertained Julie Christie and many others. The outer door was open, and I peered through the screen into a simply furnished one-bedroom suite. As Warren came to the door barefoot, in jeans and a T-shirt, I saw a woman in the background, identity unknown. He took the script and asked me about myself. He couldn't have been nicer.

That image of a carefree man in the penthouse—shades of Cash McCall—stuck with me. Some fifteen years later, incredibly, I'd be Warren's agent.

Another day I was asked to drive around Sam Spiegel, the renowned producer of *Lawrence of Arabia* and *The Bridge on the River Kwai*. He was nearly seventy but still virile—his nickname, in reference to his amorous technique in the back of taxicabs, was "the Velvet Octopus." I was doing my best to make an impression, talking a mile a minute, when Sam cut me off.

"Kid," he said, between puffs on his cigar, "you looking for advice?" I nodded excitedly.

"Okay, kid, here it is," he said. Puff, puff. "When you have the chance to fuck a girl, fuck her. Don't let her get away."

A lot of show business advice turned out to be about how to get laid.

WE HAD A FILE ROOM THE LENGTH OF A BASKETBALL court. It was lined with steel cabinets, the hard drives of the era, all packed with seventy years' worth of manila folders. I viewed those files as an encyclopedia of entertainment, albeit a helter-skelter one, so I helped the woman who ran the file room, Mary, with her mimeographing. And I brought her little gifts—a box of candy, a scarf. One day I said, "You know, I'd love to read some of the files." She told me to make myself at home. Within a week she was letting me stay on after she left. Then she gave me a key.

While other trainees waited to be told what to do and read and learn, I entered Mary's domain each morning at 7:00 and every evening after work. For ten weeks I made my way from *A* to *Z*, through the client files and the network and studio deals. I jotted questions for Sam Sacks, the head of television legal affairs, who was charmed by my interest and lent me a tape of a talk he'd given at USC on contract law in entertainment. I played it at home and came back with more questions. He gave me nine more tapes.

The legal office sat adjacent to the first-floor executives, and Sam Weisbord, the head of television worldwide and the top Morris executive in L.A., passed it on his way to dinner and again when he returned. He was a creature of habit. He stepped out to dine with Mr. Lastfogel—as everyone addressed him, including Sam—at 6:30 every evening. At 7:00 the senior people took off, all except Stan Kamen, the famed motion picture agent, who returned calls with a second-shift assistant until 8:00. And then the office was empty until Sam returned from dinner for another three hours to finish up.

I planted myself at a cubicle where he could not help but notice me, spreading out my files so he'd see them. A week later, around nine p.m., came the call I'd been waiting for. "Can you do me a favor?" Sam said. It was just a clerical task, but we were the only two people in the building, and he sure wasn't going to do it.

My play was totally calculated and manipulative. I'm sure Sam knew exactly what I was doing. He also knew that calculation and manipulation are prerequisites for the job. So three months after starting at William Morris, I became Sam Weisbord's guy. I worked as his after-hours assistant without being asked or paid. I never went by his office without ducking my head in to see what he might need. When his secretary took sick and went on leave, he asked me to fill in. I was a terrible secretary, but a spectacular assistant. Because I struggled with word-for-word dictation, Sam would say, "I want you to take care of so-and-so and tell him such and such," and then I'd flesh out the letter on my own.

Service organizations live or die by time management. I lined up the memos on Sam's desk by priority, subjects headlined in felt pen, and after Sam scrawled his replies in the upper-right-hand corner, I hand-returned them to their senders. I kept his refrigerator stocked with carrot and celery juice, the health drinks of the day. I called brokers for tips on stocks Sam should buy or sell. In short, I made myself indispensable. When his secretary returned, Sam asked me to retrain her according to my methods.

Though a compulsive skirt chaser, Sam never married. He was

devoted to his work and to Mr. Lastfogel, period. As the day wore on, his two devotions clashed. Agents returned calls between 5:30 and 7:00, after the clients came off the set and before they went out to eat. There was no way for Sam to finish all his calls before his dinner date. He had a bad eye that twitched when he was nervous, and by 6:10 the eye would begin to jerk and roll. He was the agent who taught me to think about creating work for the whole company—he was the only guy at William Morris who thought that way—but he just didn't have enough time to get it all done. At 6:20, Mr. Lastfogel, all five foot four of him, would stroll into Sam's office. He'd smile at Sam and continue into the bathroom and shut the door. Then he'd wash his hands, saunter out, and nod his head. Sam would drop whatever he was doing—he'd practically put the phone down in midsentence—and flash me a resigned look as he trailed the old man out.

After I started working for Sam, I conceived a new long-term goal: I wanted to run William Morris. To expose me to deal making, Sam had me assist a TV agent named Fred Apollo. I listened in on Fred's calls and soon was closing deals with the networks on his behalf. After seven months at William Morris, when I was twenty-two, I was promoted to junior agent—a title so demeaning we'd do away with it at CAA. My pay doubled to $150 a week. Though my promotion came in record time, I'd missed my own deadline by three months. I felt like I had to catch up before the world got away from me.

I was assigned to work in the music department, where my job was to place our musicians on programs such as *The Carol Burnett Show* and *The Glen Campbell Goodtime Hour* and to cover their live shows. One night I went to the Forum, in Inglewood, to work a Sly and the Family Stone concert. I'd been told to introduce myself to Sly and take care of the band, then count the gate and make sure the money was right. (In the days before Ticketmaster, music groups were routinely shortchanged.) My credential looped around my neck, I wandered through the maze of tunnels under the seats, asking if anyone had seen Sly. Around ten o'clock, with the band past due onstage, I came across a husky guy with a towering Afro and a guitar around his neck—Sly. His eyes were glazed and he was nearly staggering.

Realizing that if the show didn't go on I'd get the blame, I took a deep breath and said, "Mr. Stewart"—his real name was Sylvester Stewart—"I'm Michael Ovitz from the William Morris Agency."

"What's going on?"

"Mr. Stewart," I said, "you're a little late. I don't want to press you, but there's a curfew on the concert." It was a neighborhood ordinance, strictly enforced. "If you want to do a long set, you probably need to get going."

He gazed in my general direction and said, "Awww, I'll be there shortly. But could you check on my band? They're in the Lakers' locker room."

I wound my way through more tunnels to the locker room and opened the door. Jammed inside were about fifty men and women in various states of undress, shrouded in a fog of pot smoke.

The nearest woman looked at me and shouted "Narc!" and everyone scattered. I could hear toilets flushing.

I closed the door, retreated to the parking lot, and drove back to William Morris, where I typed a memo to my department head relating my encounter with the Family Stone and suggested that my services might be of better use elsewhere. The next day I was moved into TV packaging.

———

IN MY HOME NOBODY DRANK. WHEN MY FATHER TOOK US out to dinner, he ordered Shirley Temples for Mark and me and a Seagram's Seven and soda for himself. He nursed his cocktail before handing it to the busboy and asking for a second one he never finished. I was the same way. I'd gotten drunk once, at a frat party, and that was enough. I didn't like the feeling of losing control.

Tony Fantozzi was a first-floor agent with an enviable client list, from director Billy Friedkin to Carol Channing. Tall and skinny, with a big fuzzy mustache, he was extremely charming. A few weeks after I moved into TV, Tony asked me to join him for lunch with a producer named Hal Graham so he could pass off some legwork—that is, the actual work Graham needed done, such as making his deals and finding talent for his shows, all of which Tony was now above. I was thrilled.

We met at 12:30 at the Cock 'n Bull, an English pub on Sunset Boulevard with a famous buffet. I'd been at work since 7:00 a.m., a long time without food for someone with a high metabolism. I could smell the roast beef and chicken as I stepped inside—delicious. I was desperate to get on the buffet line but deferred to Tony, who lit a cigar and ordered martinis. Half an hour passed. My tablemates' glasses were empty; mine was four-fifths full. Tony called for another round.

The talk became more animated. Tony ordered a third round. As people returned to the neighboring tables with heaping plates, I was feeling light-headed. Tony ordered a fourth round. When the fifth round arrived at a quarter to three, my glasses were lined up like jets at LAX. Regretful about missing out on whatever pearls were to come, embarrassed, unsure of the etiquette, I stood and offered a useful all-purpose excuse: I had a ton of work back at the office.

After that, whenever Tony asked me out, I grabbed a sandwich and wolfed it down in my car en route. To stay vertical through the meal, I'd spill some of my drink on the carpet or pour the martini into my water and ask the waiter for a fresh water glass. My admiration for Tony grew. He might return to the office a little wobbly, but two coffees later he was full speed ahead.

One day Tony said, "I need you to help me with some daytime television guys." It was a strange request because William Morris had little to do with "day parts," as we called them, except for one or two ancient soap operas that ran themselves. But the brass had asked Tony to rehabilitate Jack Barry and Dan Enright, the producing team from the quiz-show-rigging scandal of the late 1950s. "They're having a horrific time getting back on the air," he said.

As I was just a kid when the scandal broke, I was dumb enough to see this as my big break. I had no idea how thoroughly Jack and Dan had been tainted. My Barry-Enright presentations kept getting turned down, not once or twice but eight or ten times. Perplexed, I nagged my superiors to contact the network execs who weren't taking my calls. They didn't want to get involved, but they couldn't blow off Sam Weisbord's protégé. It took us nearly two years to get a show called *Break the Bank* on CBS, with Jack not only producing it but serving as the host.

Agenting was a commodity business. If you didn't sign clients, no matter what you contributed elsewhere, you were dead wood. I started by going after people no one else cared about—soap opera and game show producers and, especially, serial writers. Daytime wasn't glamorous, but it was lucrative. I noticed that projects grew out of ideas and that ideas came from writers. I had a special respect for the people who created new worlds from thin air. One Saturday night, Judy and I were in bed watching *Lohman and Barkley*, a local TV variety show. It featured a skit with a roller-skating rabbi, a lanky guy who had fake *payess* (the Orthodox sidelocks) down to the floor. He had us roaring.

My first call Monday morning was to the show's office. I reached the guy who played the rabbi and said, "I'm Michael Ovitz with the William Morris Agency, and I think you're hysterical. I would love to meet with you." That's how a TV writer named Barry Levinson became my first client. It wasn't long before I got him hired on *The Tim Conway Show*—about as much as I could do, in those days.

Yet I was already meeting the up-and-comers who would later run the business. One day I ran into Michael Eisner on the set of one of our game show pilots. He headed up daytime at ABC. I asked him how he liked the show, and he noncommittally said, "Well, my wife liked it." So I sent roses to Jane Eisner, with a card. Michael called me and said, "Do not agent my wife!" He was kind of angry about it—but that sort of stunt got my name out there, and Eisner and I soon became friends. I've always had a weakness for smart people, and Michael was a smart, Eastern-educated guy who'd grown up on Park Avenue—exactly where I wished I had. He had staff to take care of all of his needs at home, and he was New York pale and he toggled between boyishly awkward and slick and smiling and he was even more manipulative than I was—and I fell for the whole package. After we started doing a lot of business together, Judy and Jane grew extremely close. In later years, our families would vacation as one big group in Aspen and Hawaii. Michael and I even had the same internist. When one of the Eisner boys disappeared one evening, as a teenager, Judy and I were at a Madonna concert with the Eisners, and Michael and I left and drove around town looking for him—finally locating him, naturally enough, at a party.

My next mentor at WMA was Howard West, a senior television packager. His job was to assemble the right mix of Morris clients (writers, directors, performers) and sell the loaded project to a network. Howard could mold the fuzziest concept into a viable TV show, such as *The Jim Nabors Show* or *Laugh-In*. The agency charged 10 percent of the cost of every show it assembled (half up front, and half deferred until the show went into profit), so if a show cost $1 million an episode, we'd make $100,000 every week. It was a much quicker way to cash in than simply representing individual clients.

Howard did the deals with the network, and I'd do the deals on behalf of the production company or the lead actor. Sometimes WMA represented both sides, as it did on *The Glen Campbell Goodtime Hour*, when we represented the producers and also Glen Campbell and Jerry Reed, whom the producers were paying. So I'd be negotiating against William Morris agents for my clients, and for my own fees. Those were the toughest deals of all to strike. But the experience would later give me the idea to represent all sides of the deal at CAA, working out any conflicts internally and raking in all the fees.

Howard taught me how to bring clients into a package and keep them happy, how to mediate problems, how to watch over budgets. He always made time for me. (Following his example, I had a series of trainees assigned to me at CAA. I'm afraid I was much less patient.) He was a model for follow-up and presentation and how to think on your feet. And he taught me to tell clients the truth. Agents always get busted when they tell the easy lie: "You look great in dailies" or "Your script is fantastic."

But Howard wasn't a client signer, so he hit his ceiling at William Morris. At dinner one night he told me he was leaving to set up a management company with his friend George Shapiro. (Later he and George became executive producers of the supreme TV package of all time, *Seinfeld*.) The news rocked me, and we downed two bottles of white wine. That was the second—and last—time I ever got drunk.

WMA EXCELLED AT CERTAIN KINDS OF PACKAGING, BUT WE had nowhere near the clout of Universal Television, which basically set NBC's lineup. The big New York sales week fell in late May, when agents peddled their clients' pilots for the fall season. With hordes of actors under contract and a soup-to-nuts production company, Universal churned out shows like a Ford assembly line. As the FCC barred networks from producing their own content—a rule that wasn't fully eliminated until 1995—NBC was dependent on Lew Wasserman's largesse.

Our WMA contingent stayed at the Sherry-Netherland, on Fifth Avenue, where all of Los Angeles gathered for the week. After flogging our pilots hard for days, on the night before the schedule was announced we'd see Lew Wasserman stride through the lobby to head to his suite. A few minutes later, NBC's vice president for programming would be ushered into the elevator and up to Lew's rooms. It was pretty obvious from the schedules announced the next day what happened up there:

NBC: "We need a detective drama for Wednesday night."

Lew: "We'll get you Peter Falk in a wheel with Dennis Weaver and Rock Hudson."

And that would become *The NBC Mystery Movie*, a rotation of *Columbo*, *McCloud*, and *McMillan & Wife*. Or Lew might say, "We'll give you a family show with Robert Young as a doctor who cares about his patients' lives"—and presto, *Marcus Welby, M.D.* Whether it was a Thursday-night comedy or a weekend western, Lew had what they wanted, or what he told them they wanted; he set the menu and they ate the food.

After NBC stuffed itself with Universal's programs, the rest of us fought over the remaining slots. As strong as WMA was, we were a pale shadow of the way MCA had dominated agenting in the fifties, or the way Universal ran television now.

You could not beat Lew Wasserman.

CHAPTER FOUR

GOOD COP/ BAD COP

NOT LONG AFTER I MADE AGENT, RON MEYER CAME TO William Morris from the Paul Kohner Agency and was assigned to TV talent. He was twenty-five, two years older than me, and the first thing that struck me was how *nice* he seemed, how skilled at putting people at ease. Gravel-voiced and sleepy-eyed, Ron was a high school dropout who'd served a hitch in the military—he had a Marine Corps tattoo on his arm—and who presented himself as a self-taught, well-read street fighter. He was terrific at his job but felt a little insecure at a place where a college education had become the norm. He reminded me a lot of my dad: a friendly street guy with savoir faire. But Ron was smarter than my dad, and shrewder.

We hit it off right away, two kids with no money who resented the guys with rich parents and fancy cars. (I drove a '65 Mustang, while Ron had an aging Porsche two-seater that barely ran.) Something about being around Ron made me completely comfortable; I felt happy with him, at home. I admired Ron because he had what I didn't—a relaxed charm, an ability to do things for people he hated with a warm, lazy smile.

Judy and I began to hang out with him and his wife, Dolly Colton, and their friends. Ron was a neat freak who liked the occasional home-cooked meal; Dolly was a gregarious redhead, born to wealth, who had no interest in the domestic arts. Friction was inevitable, and soon Ron wanted a divorce. He couldn't afford a lawyer, so I helped him choreograph an exit with Dolly and her formidable father. We agreed that he needed to be aggressive, like an agent. He'd open by asking *them* for alimony—after all, they had the money. Dolly and her father settled for a clean split of the couple's assets.

Single once more, Ron unleashed his ample charisma. One day, we saw Geneviève Bujold idling her Mercedes convertible in the office parking lot. Ron was obsessed with Geneviève, a Morris client and a very hot actress at the time. Now she was twenty feet away. Ron looked at me, then walked over to introduce himself as one of her agents. He told her how great she was and said he'd love to get to know her better. Then he asked if he could buy her an ice-cream cone someday. I saw Geneviève nod and smile—they had a date! Ron's invite was so innocuous it worked. It wasn't a drink or a nighttime proposition: it was an ice-cream cone. That was Ron Meyer.

———

PHIL WELTMAN CUT A WIDE SWATH AT WILLIAM MORRIS. He ran the training program and cycled younger agents through the departments—in effect, he decided our destinies. Square-jawed and no-nonsense, Phil was a born drill sergeant. One morning he summoned a guy named Jimmy Goldsmith. Jimmy had shoulder-length hair, as was increasingly common in the early 1970s, and Phil lectured him on the virtues of a good haircut. When Phil called him in again at 5:00 p.m. and saw that Jimmy hadn't made it to the barber, he fired him.

But we revered Phil, the one senior executive who valued both loyalty and initiative. While he vocally promoted the William Morris values, Phil called out the ugly stuff, too, such as the old guard's resistance to teamwork and promoting younger agents. We'd later make Phil's philosophy a central tenet of CAA, but it went against the grain at William Morris, where it was every man for himself.

Under Phil's tutelage, Ron and I decided to sign clients as a twosome—ideally clients who worked in prime time. We met a talented TV writer named Norman Lear, whose sitcom pilot about a working-class family in Queens had just been picked up by CBS. The new guy there, Fred Silverman, was ditching rural-themed shows like *Green Acres* for urban, contemporary programming. *All in the Family* debuted in 1971 and topped the Nielsen ratings five years running. The show's leads, Carroll O'Connor and Jean Stapleton, already had agents, but Sally Struthers and Rob Reiner were relative unknowns, and Norman introduced them to us.

When we visited the set, I wore my navy suit and Ron wore jeans and a pullover. We promised to find Sally, who wanted a more rounded career, TV movies and theater jobs whenever *All in the Family* went on hiatus. She liked the idea of two agents for the price of one, and by the second meeting she was ours. Rob had written for the Smothers Brothers but was straining to get his own material off the ground. We snagged him a job directing a TV movie called *Sonny Boy*, the beginning of Rob's distinguished run as a director and producer, and signed him and his wife, Penny Marshall, who later became the star of *Laverne & Shirley*.

Norman Lear had a genius for making hit shows. Over the next few years he put eleven more sitcoms on the air, including *Maude* and *The Jeffersons*. Ron and I dogged his cast members, signing John Amos from *Good Times* and Demond Wilson from *Sanford and Son*. We made a great team because we had a great rap. I was formal, reserved, analytical, and concise, and Ron was sociable, sympathetic, disarming, and loose. You needed a persona as an agent, something that made you unique. I'd heard that Sam Cohn, the famously rumpled New York agent, cut holes in his sweaters to make them look moth-eaten. Sam's persona was the absentminded genius. Ron's was the best friend and confidant, the "I'll fix all your problems" guy.

I had given a lot of thought to my persona. There were three options. Number one was standard agent: the schmoozer, the gladhander. But I didn't want to be standard in any way. Number two was

Leland Hayward, an absolute gent who had his own agency in the forties and handled such clients as Fred Astaire, Ginger Rogers, Jimmy Stewart, and Judy Garland. Leland was legendary for his consideration. If a client wanted to leave, Leland would let her go without a word of protest or a hint of rancor. Everyone loved him. That was incredibly appealing—but I sensed that Leland's persona wasn't the right fit for me.

Believe it or not, in those days I was affable and considerate, with never a bad word about anyone. But you need to pick a persona you can inhabit without strain, and I knew I'd do better as the opposite of Ron—as the all-business tough guy who'd protect you. I could see that that's what the biggest stars and directors wanted. So my persona became the "I'll make your dreams come true" guy, mixed with the "I'll fix your problems" guy. Ron was the good cop and I was the bad. Ronnie and Mike. (I actually always hated the lunch-pail nickname "Mike," and spent countless hours reminding everyone, "My friends call me Michael," but "Mike" stuck to me like a burr.) Underneath the roles, though, Ron and I were always more alike than even our colleagues realized. Ron's easygoing demeanor hid a personality as calculating and determined and tightly wound as mine was.

———

OUR BOSSES PERIODICALLY GATHERED US TO TRUMPET THE latest signings and whip up the troops. I usually sat in the back with Ron and the other young agents; we weren't supposed to speak at these rallies, just listen.

In the fall of 1974, CMA stole Steve McQueen from us. At the next meeting, Sam Weisbord proudly announced that he'd roped in an equally big name: Ann Miller. A mutinous murmur arose. Miller had been a star in MGM musicals—twenty years earlier. Ron spoke up, suddenly, to suggest that we go after some of CMA's biggest clients, some actual stars, to even the score. Sam Weisbord's eye started to twitch like crazy and he lost his mind, shouting, "You don't know what you're talking about! She's a star!"

I completely agreed with Ron, but I would have discussed it with Sam in private, where his ego wouldn't have been on the line. Ron was extremely direct, not tactical. I left the meeting deflated. Ann Miller was doing dinner theater and earning a decent income, which was all Sam cared about. But we cared about the company's image. When people asked about new clients, we wanted to brag about a Jane Fonda or a Jacqueline Bisset, not some fifty-one-year-old song-and-dance queen. Our feelings were ageist, sexist, lookist, and any number of other -ists—but then so is Hollywood.

The Ann Miller meeting was like the first time you realize your parents are old. I'd played by the rules at William Morris, and so far it had worked. But I began to ask, *What if?* What if guys like Ron and me had more of a say? And then: *What if we could run a company of our own?*

THE BEVERLY HILLS AND NEW YORK OFFICES OF WMA WERE bitter rivals. Movies were handled in Los Angeles, and theater in New York. Television was split, with sales on the East Coast and creative work and packaging in L.A.—and the two camps were insanely jealous of each other.

Late in 1974, we had a visit from Lou Weiss, one of the inner-circle executives around Morris president Nat Lefkowitz in New York. He asked to meet with the agents in charge of TV packaging: Rowland Perkins, who covered CBS; Mike Rosenfeld, who covered ABC; and Bill Haber, who handled NBC. I was present for my daytime work signing and packaging game show producers and directors. As a group we'd killed it. Rowland, Mike, and Bill accounted for twenty-one programs for prime time, and I had packaged seven more in daytime—more pilots altogether than any other outfit in town, including major studios such as Universal.

Lou breezed into Rowland's office in a stunning suit and Gucci loafers. We were huddled in our not-so-dapper suits, waiting for our attaboy. "We had a strong sales season on both coasts," Lou began. "*But*—we could do better."

Rowland Perkins, who'd counted on becoming the next West Coast head of television, bent forward as if he'd been gut-punched. (Nat Lefkowitz would slide a New Yorker into the job instead.) Happy-go-lucky Mike Rosenfeld looked like his dog had died. Bill Haber's left foot was tapping furiously. As Lou droned on, Bill's foot tapped faster and faster. After Lou left, everyone exploded. "That was unbelievable!" Mike said. "It's horrible!" cried Bill, dangerously flushed.

In 1973, when I had brought in close to $2 million in commissions on a weekly salary of $400, William Morris had given me a $7,500 bonus. In 1974, the agency's leaders recognized my seven pilots by upping my bonus to $15,000, which they thought handsome, given that all of us "could do better." Meanwhile, every day we walked past the office of Joe Rifkin, a Lastfogel crony who read the newspaper for hours with his feet up. There were three or four guys like that around, big wheels from way back when who were just diluting our bonus checks. The only way they'd leave was feet first. It drove Ron nuts.

PHIL WELTMAN'S DOWNFALL BEGAN WHEN THEY MADE him an administrator and he gave all but a few of his clients to younger agents. Though Phil and Sam Weisbord had been best friends, dating to their bachelor roommate days, they fell out after Sam got tight with Mr. Lastfogel. When Phil irked the bosses once too often, he had no rabbis left to protect him. It happened a few weeks before Christmas of 1974. Phil called Ron and me and a few of his other confidants into his office. Sam Weisbord had asked him to leave the company, he said: "They put my name in the computer and it came up wanting." The man who made confident agents quake, who taught me the meaning of strength—that tough, tough man broke down in front of us.

That lit the fuse. At dinner one night, Ron said, "Why don't we go into business for ourselves? We'll make more money, and they'll never be able to do to us what they did to Phil."

Ron was persuasive, but I felt conflicted. Sam Weisbord, my rabbi, was next in line for the presidency, and Walt Zifkin, the agency's controller, had told me I'd run the place someday. Judy and I were the fair-haired couple at the company. I had more to gain by staying than Ron, and more to lose by leaving.

Seeing me hesitate, Ron said, "You have no gamble in you. Sometimes you have to step up and roll the dice." That got me thinking. I was twenty-seven. If we busted in three years, I could land a new job and start over. But I wasn't about to gamble on a two-man boutique. If we left William Morris, I wanted to build a giant agency and beat them at their own game.

A few days later, Mike Rosenfeld confided to Ron that he and Rowland and Bill were leaving. They wanted Ron to join them and handle the talent while they packaged network and studio deals. Ron urged them to add me as well, and they agreed. I was surprised by Ron's willingness to throw in with Bill, who was famous for torturing his staff with work-related trivia quizzes. He drove Ron crazy every day. Nonetheless, I went to the rebels' first meeting, after work at a bar called the Golden Bull.

We were an unlikely group, united more by opposition to WMA than by any plan for an alternative. Rowland Perkins was the eldest, nearly forty, handsome, silverhaired—an agent out of central casting. But he was a salaryman at heart, comfortable with a guaranteed paycheck. Mike Rosenfeld was a fantastic agent, beloved by everyone, but he was obsessed with the idea that because his father had died young, he would, too—so he was out every night, burning the candle before it was snuffed out. Bill Haber was brilliant, creative, and prickly. Later on, it became important to him to drive around in a Volkswagen Bug, to be the "I'm not really an agent" agent. When CAA was running smoothly, he was always threatening to quit and go work with blind children.

Ron led off with his idea for a Meyer-Ovitz (or Ovitz-Meyer) Agency. The others quickly talked us out of it. Together the five of us had the three major networks covered. We'd earned our stripes in talent and in packaging, the two main facets of TV agenting. I gave us a beachhead in day parts, which generated cash flow every week, much faster than the returns from prime time—a key consideration as none of us had much money to plow into the venture. (I was making $45,000 a year, but I still owed William Morris $15,000 for the down payment on my house in Sherman Oaks, in the Valley.) Two clients were sure to follow us. Ron was very close to the character actor Jack Weston, and I thought of Kelly Lange, an L.A. news anchor, as the sister I'd never had. We rated a dozen others, including Sally Struthers and Rob Reiner, as probables. With a bunch of iffies, we had a list of about seventy-five names.

I weighed in on three points. It seemed to me that we should take advantage of the fact that we were young and aggressive—Ron, Bill, and I were all under thirty—to try out new ideas that could reshape the ways the town did business. First, I said, the equity had to be split evenly. Second, we had to try to get as big as we could. Third, we'd share our clients and serve them as a group—no turf wars, no silos. At William Morris we had many an agent who excelled at signing artists but stumbled in finding work for them. Wouldn't it be better, I said, if clients could rotate freely within our firm? We'd be five musketeers, one for all and all for one. Everyone would handle everyone, and everyone would tell our clients the truth. It was standard procedure in the agency business, when a client called with unpleasant news or a dangerous rumor—"I hear I'm getting fired off the film"—to say "Don't worry, I know all about it and it's fine," even if this was the first you'd heard of it. We would pioneer the calm, no-bullshit approach, saying instead, "Let me look into it and I'll get right back to you." We'd be better agents because we wouldn't agent you.

The other thing that would differentiate us—and it was a big one—was that we would create work for our clients, not just field offers. Everyone agreed.

Suddenly, the revolt felt real.

ON THE FIRST FRIDAY OF 1975, I KNOCKED OFF EARLY TO GO skiing with Judy at Mammoth Mountain, five hours away. There were no cell phones or pagers in those days, and no one knew where we were.

I needed to get away to think my future through before talking one more time with Ron.

When we got back to our tract house Sunday evening, a note was taped to the front door. It was from Mike Rosenfeld: "Call me before you talk to anybody." When I called, he said, "I hope you could afford that ski trip, because you're now unemployed with the rest of us." Before leaving town, I had applied for a credit line for our new agency at City National Bank. I listed the five partners' names on the forms. Unfortunately, the guy who ran City National was a friend of William Morris's CFO. The day I left town, Sam Weisbord had taken Rowland for a walk and said, "Is it true? Are you leaving?"

Anyone else would deny it in a heartbeat. Anyone but Rowland, the straightest arrow in Southern California. After he threw us all under the bus, Weisbord called in the coconspirators one by one. We were officially fired that day, but Sam wanted to see me on Monday—for closure, I guess.

You couldn't call Sam Weisbord personable, but he'd given me my first break and treated me with respect. Had he told me that he was hurt and that he wanted me to stay, there's a very good chance I'd have backed down and asked Ron to do the same. I felt no obligation to Bill and Mike and Rowland. If Sam had played it smart, he might have broken up the whole thing before it started.

Instead, he fixed me with an arrogant stare and said, "You've really screwed yourself this time." His bad eye was twitching up a storm. I said, "Look, it is what it is." I went to my office, packed up my Rolodex, and left the building for the last time.

WE'D COUNTED ON THREE MORE MONTHS TO GET ORGA-nized, but our future was now. We held an emergency meeting at Rowland's house in Upper Bel Air. As a former WMA vice president, he was the logical choice to run the show. But that night he hardly said a word. Having just lost an annual paycheck of at least $250,000, he was clearly in shock.

I had made a checklist of everything we needed to do: find an office, get stationery, get a license, come up with a logo, and so on. I was the most junior of the group, an afterthought. But as I moved down my to-do list, nobody else was chiming in. Ron was superb at managing in the moment but indifferent to administration; Bill Haber had a counterpuncher's style; Mike Rosenfeld had no desire for added responsibility. So I kept talking, and I never stopped. Through our first few weeks in business, jobs kept falling into my lap. We all liked the name "Artists Agency" because it denoted a client-centered culture—but another agency had previously used it. So I proposed adding "Creative" to suggest both our clients' creativity and our own. Mike and I sketched the CAA logo, and I ordered stationery.

David Wolper, the William Morris client who produced *Chico and the Man*, gave us temporary office space, a room on La Cienega with two phones. (WMA pressured him to throw us out, a hint of things to come.) Two weeks later we scraped together $100,000 by putting up our homes as collateral. Ron and I paid a deposit on a bargain-bin lease in a lower-end building on Doheny and Wilshire, at the very edge of Beverly Hills. The former tenant, the landlord said, had been a wigmaker.

CAA was a prototypical start-up. We brought in folding chairs and card tables for desks, and our wives each came in one day a week to answer the phones. We had one paid assistant—a bookkeeper—and two cars among the five of us. The Screen Actors Guild sent someone out to make sure we were for real. The guy came back a second time after the wigmaker turned out to have been an escort service.

To launch with a statement, we had slashed our packaging commission from 10 percent to 6. It was a go-for-the-throat move to undercut William Morris and the rest (and it sounded like more of a bargain than it was—we'd still take 10 percent on the back end, in syndication, where the real money was). But we quickly realized that no one was knocking the door down to take advantage of our cut-rate commission—or for any other reason.

OUR FIRST BIG PROBLEM WAS THAT JACK WESTON AND
Kelly Lange wound up staying at WMA. The agency's Norman Bro-
kaw convinced Kelly that he was going to make her a giant personality.
We'd have done the same thing in his place—we did do it many times
later. But it was a devastating blow; the other clients we had wouldn't
bring in enough to support us. For years, we used the story of Jack
Weston and Kelly Lange not following us, after they'd sworn up and
down that they would, to teach our young agents. "Don't ever think
that what is, is—because it isn't. Never count on anybody or anything."

Our second big problem arrived by messenger a few weeks in: an
envelope addressed to me from Leon Kaplan of Kaplan, Livingston,
Goodwin, Berkowitz & Selvin, the mammoth law firm that represented Warner Bros. and 20th Century Fox and almost everyone who
was anyone in the entertainment business. Their letterhead listed
seventy-two attorneys and made it feel like a whole country was declar-
ing war on you. Kaplan informed me that his client, Freddie Fields,
controlled the rights to both "Artists Agency" and "Creative Management Associates," Freddie's previous firms. We were therefore infring-
ing by using "Creative Artists Agency" and must immediately cease
and desist.

I reread the letter. I was puzzled about why he'd singled me out,
rather than writing to the partnership, but I figured I'd have to devise
our response. I knew Sam Weisbord and Leon Kaplan were close, and
that Kaplan's firm had represented the Morris agency forever. I also
knew that Kaplan did *not* represent CMA. And I knew that Freddie
Fields had recently cashed out of CMA to become a movie producer
and a client of Kaplan's. I connected the dots. Alarmed by our package-
fee discount, William Morris had deputized Fields to harass us into
relinquishing our name and starting over, a mortal blow to an infant
company.

This was serious trouble. If we slugged it out in court, the fees
would suck us under fast. Ron and I had just run into a young WMA

agent at a party. "You know what the betting is back at the office?" he said. "That you'll be out of business in six months and working as casting agents."

My one play, a long shot, was to intimidate my old boss. From working for Sam, I knew the Department of Justice was probing William Morris for monopolistic practices in their TV work—the conflicts of interest that we lived with daily. The rumor was that Lew Wasserman had tipped off the department because he was annoyed at having to pay WMA's package commissions. Nothing was likely to come of it, but the agency's leaders remained apprehensive.

I told my partners my plan, and, very anxiously, they finally agreed. They thought it was a lousy idea—but no one had a better one. I drained a glass of water and cleared my throat. I needed to believe in what I was about to say, and my voice absolutely could not crack. I rang Leon Kaplan. He sounded arrogant, and why not? He pegged CAA as weak, broke, and defenseless.

"Mr. Kaplan," I said, "we haven't met, but I know who you represent. I think you're trying to put us out of business. I think it's inappropriate and unfair, and it could be really interesting if this went to the Justice Department in the middle of their antitrust investigation." My tone was firm but matter-of-fact. I went on, "You can rip up this letter and we can all be friends and forget about it. Or you can pursue it and I will call a pal of mine who happens to work at Justice, and I'll ask him to throw this into the hopper, and we'll see how it all sorts out."

Dead silence. Then Kaplan said, "What are you suggesting?"

"I'm suggesting you send me a handwritten letter within the next two hours withdrawing the first letter. Or tomorrow morning I'll call my friend." Then I thanked him and hung up. I gave no thought to the repercussions—or to the fact that I was bluffing, because we'd be out of business before the feds could get around to dealing with the call I'd never make anyway to a friend I didn't have. I played my hand as calmly as I could and waited for the outcome. Only after I'd hung up did I realize my hands were shaking.

Time crawled by. Fifteen minutes before the deadline a messenger arrived with a new letter from Kaplan. In the space of an afternoon he'd moved from cease and desist to cease-fire.

That day forged our siege mentality. To defend our tiny position, we unleashed hell on anyone who crossed us. For starters, we refused to take on any client who used Kaplan, Livingston, and within five years the firm was defunct. I'm not saying we did them in, but we did help nudge them toward the edge. Our counterassault on William Morris took longer to deploy but proved nearly as effective. And a few years later, when Jack Weston told a friend of Ron's that he wanted to come to CAA, Ron replied, "Tell him he can go fuck himself. Not if he was the last client on earth." One of the strongest bonds Ron and I shared was a belief that any betrayal must be avenged.

For the rest of my time at CAA, I was a great friend and ally but an implacable foe. When you're twenty-eight years old and you've quit your job and there's no going back, and then the industry leader tries to smother your baby in its cradle, you steel up pretty fast. Kaplan's letter taught us to play hardball, and hardball we would play for the next twenty years.

CHAPTER FIVE

FROM ZERO TO ONE MILLION

NEEDING CLIENTS FAST TO PAY OUR RENT, WE FOCUSED ON TV writers and actors, two reliable sources of income. In TV, the talent got paid every Thursday, so the agents did, too. For six months we met with prospects by the hour, from 8:00 in the morning till 10:00 at night, when we'd collapse with a delivery pizza. It was close to midnight on a grueling Friday when we got a call from the actor Jack Cassidy, one of our first new clients. He was a heavy drinker who had once startled his neighbors by watering his lawn naked. Clearly blitzed, Jack started in like it was a normal business hour. We rolled with it, having lost all normal frame of reference—every waking hour was a working hour.

Our top client was Chad Everett, who played Dr. Joe Gannon in CBS's long-running *Medical Center.* When a TV movie script came in with a $100,000 offer for Chad, it was a godsend. The $10,000 commission would float us for another month. But after we all read the script and assembled to call Chad (we did everything together then, to showcase our esprit de corps), there were five long faces around the conference table: the movie was crap. Chad was Bill Haber's contact and Bill led off on speakerphone to warn against the project, but we all chimed in, unanimously recommending a pass.

It would have been easy to tell Chad to take his $90,000 and run. No one would have slammed us for putting him in a bad TV movie. But we killed the offer without a second thought—and that moment established our business bona fides. We were not going to be flesh peddlers. We would put our clients' long-term interests first.

We were able to stick to our ethical guns in part because I had sold a pair of game shows, *Give-N-Take* and *Rhyme and Reason*. (Judy worked as a model on *Give-N-Take* and another game show, and she booked jobs at Bullock's Department store and worked in the lounge at Pacific Southwest Airlines—for a while, she was paying all our bills.) That fall, NBC took *The Rich Little Show*, our first prime-time package. I still have the telex they sent to let us know. Buyers liked new agencies: the more sellers undercutting one another, the more leverage for them. In those days buyers ran roughshod. If one agent balked at a studio's terms, there was always another, more desperate agency that represented a client who'd serve equally well. Our goal—which seemed amazingly distant—was to flip the power equation by amassing so much talent the buyers couldn't go around us.

After nine months, we had 135 clients, and most of them had their best years in front of them (Anne Archer, Larry Hagman) or behind them (Hope Lange, Totie Fields). We didn't have expense accounts; we paid for everything ourselves and deducted it from our individual taxes. Early on, Rowland arranged a dinner for a couple of hot writers, Joe Bologna and Renée Taylor, at a fancy restaurant in Century City. We really wanted them, and we really wanted to show how all for one we were, so we brought our wives. Knowing that dinner for twelve was going to cost a fortune, we nervously reminded each other, "They picked the place, so let's hope they pick up the check. *Don't* reach for it!" As Joe was a regular there, we hoped the waiter would bring it to him. He did, but Joe just ignored it, puffing a big cigar. The check sat there, glowing ominously. Finally Rowland's wife, Diane, took it and gave it to Rowland. We were all horrified—I think that was the beginning of the end of their marriage. Rowland slipped the check to Mike under the table, but he didn't have a credit card, either. I was the only one who did, so I picked it up: $2,000 that we didn't have. Joe and Renée did sign with us, without ever having any idea how close they came to putting us out of business.

Broke as we were, we had to fake it till we could make it. At La Scala, a Beverly Hills bistro that was *the* place to be seen, I showed Tony, the maître d', a hundred-dollar bill. Then I ripped it in two and gave him half. "My wife and I will be in for dinner tonight," I said, "and I want you to give us the first booth on the right and treat us really, really well. If you do that, you'll get the other half of this bill—and many more to come." A hundred bucks bought some remarkable service in 1975, and CAA went on to do many big business dinners at La Scala. We tipped lavishly and were hailed like the second coming of Darryl Zanuck. Then I took out a car loan and bought five Jaguars for $15,000 a pop (but only $1,500 each down). We ordered CAA license plates, followed by a hyphen and the partner's initials. The cars were a rank extravagance for a company that would file zeroes on its tax returns its first three years. But in a city of fantasy, a big show was essential.

Though we had started to make a small mark in television, we had trouble persuading film stars to take us seriously. Sue Mengers, the biggest movie agent in town, mocked us as "the TV boys." She was being mean, but she was right—that was all we had. I'm still stung by the memory of a lunch Mike and I had at The Smoke House with Thom Mount, the "baby mogul" who became president of Universal Pictures at twenty-eight. He was the Irving Thalberg of our time, albeit briefly. We needed the anointment of his recognition, and we talked a great game. Then Thom asked to see our client list. I didn't want to show it to him because it began and ended with Ernest Borgnine in film and Chad Everett in television. He insisted. As he looked at it with amused disappointment, I nodded at Mike and we left without eating. I hated being pigeonholed as inferior.

We all took a meeting with Jacqueline Bisset at her house, and my partners gave the Agenting 101 pitch: *You're a great actress; you should be doing more; you should have bigger roles, Oscar-winning roles.* New agencies sell their youth and energy—"I'll kill for you!"—because that's all they have. Seeing her skeptical expression, I jumped in and said, "Take off your actress hat for a moment and pretend that you're a small corporation. You're now JB, Inc., and your revenue is X million a year. What can you do to increase your bottom line, and control the direction of your future growth? You need to take control of your projects, get involved in developing them." I believed that nobody wants to be treated as just what they are. Everyone wants to feel encouraged to become even more than they are—to become the best version of themselves.

Afterward, in the car heading down the hill, we quarreled. Mike said, "You can't look at her like she's a corporation—she's an *actress*." I said, "I don't agree. We have to differentiate ourselves from the other agencies, and this is a great way to do it." Bisset's lawyer called and said she wanted another meeting—only just with me. I met with her again, but she decided to go with another agency. That was okay. As we got bigger, she got smaller.

Mike was very close to Rick Ray of Adams, Ray & Rosenberg, a prestigious television literary agency that represented four hundred writers. A year or so after CAA opened, Rick proposed that we join forces. The two firms met in our cramped conference room to seal the deal. Together, Lee Rosenberg declared, we'd be "the best television agency in the business. Even if we never represent movie stars like Robert Redford."

Ron and I traded glances. "I plan on representing movie stars," Ron said.

Lee said, "You'll never get them, they're locked up by the big boys."

"We're going to represent *all* of them," I said. I suddenly knew we were going to try to get as near to the whole market as it was possible to get, to crush all comers. Our plan had been to wait five years before branching out to movies, but I was never good at waiting.

Ron looked at me and nodded. I stood up, and then Ron stood up, and then Bill stood up, and the meeting and the merger were over. Mike was crushed—he was really close to Rick and had dreamed of working with him. That was the moment we realized Mike might not be with us for the long haul. I looked at Ron and Bill and said, "We've got our whole lives ahead of us. We'll get the stars." I was twenty-nine; Ron, thirty-one; Bill, thirty-three.

THE JACQUELINE BISSET MEETING CONVINCED ME THAT the way forward was to sell our clients on our reach. We'd give them more info than anybody; they'd see every script and even get hot books in manuscript—preferential treatment befitting the CEO of his or her own corporation. We'd break into film by taking books and scripts and treatments to prospective clients—we'd bring the mountain to Muhammad. When *New York* magazine touted Mort Janklow as the hottest literary agent, I rang him up. It took me ten days to get him on the phone to ask if I could come see him. I flew to New York at a cost that made my stomach twitch.

Mort's Midtown Manhattan office was done in Charles Gwathmey modernism, all angles and curves and rich oak paneling. Trying not to seem overawed, I laid out our book-first strategy. I asked to call him every Thursday at 10:00 a.m. in case he had something for us.

Mort could have set his watch by my calls. I kept at it for a year, every week, no matter where I was, before he gave us a novel called *Chiefs*, a police drama set in the South. The story was solid, but Mort neglected to tell us that the networks had already turned it down. Bill Haber worked round the clock to get *Chiefs* produced and prove we were for real. His friend and client Martin Manulis, the producer of *Gunsmoke*, somehow wrangled Charlton Heston, a big-enough star to get *Chiefs* adapted into a successful miniseries on CBS. Ecstatic, Mort started sending us manuscripts by his most commercial writers: Jackie Collins, Judith Krantz, Danielle Steele. We went on to package pulp sensations like *Mistral's Daughter* and *Hollywood Wives*, each of which brought the agency $50,000 to $100,000 up front and millions in syndication when they were resold to the nation's more than six hundred independent stations.

Scores of independent lit agencies needed a liaison to Hollywood buyers, and once Janklow began to vouch for us, CAA rapidly became that liaison. We threw parties at Elaine's—the watering hole on New York's East Side frequented by Truman Capote, Woody Allen, Norman Mailer, and scores of agents—and won a lot of business. We offered a unique and attractive proposition: on any production that derived from the lit agents' source material, they'd keep their full commissions on the writers' fees. CAA would get paid by attaching actors and directors to the package.

Soon we had eighty agents sending us novels in manuscript, to be optioned by our producers and then lateraled to our screenwriters for adaptation. After copying the scripts in bulk, we slapped on bright-red covers with the white CAA logo and planted hundreds of them, with scrawled notes and scuffmarks for a "used" look, in beauty parlors, restaurants, and doctors' offices. Most had no chance of selling—and we didn't leave any really important screenplays lying around—but they generated free publicity. They helped establish our brand in our race against larger but less agile firms like William Morris and International Creative Management, or ICM.

We were making headway in our second year, but still barely breaking even. All I could think about was money, but Ron Meyer was the grasshopper to my ant. He suddenly flew off to see Richard Chamberlain on a TV-movie set in South Africa—an astronomical expense, especially when we needed Ron in L.A. We talked about it, not exactly in our indoor voices: I was the thrifty dad and he was the spendthrift son.

The subject recurred as we walked to our cars one Saturday. "Money is the scorecard of success," I said. "I don't get how it seems so unimportant to you."

Ron said, "But money doesn't bring you happiness. My father was broke all his life and he was the happiest guy you ever met." He took a quarter from his pocket and held it up. "See that?"

"Yeah," I said.

Ron flipped the quarter over a mesh-link fence onto the roof of a kiosk on the other side. I made a big show of scrambling to climb the fence to retrieve the quarter, and Ron laughed. We were both joking—but not really. That moment was us in a nutshell. Ron cared too little about money and I cared too much. I never wanted "Fuck-you money"—I wasn't greedy in that way—but I was hell-bent on making enough so I'd never have to go back to the Valley.

In 1977, after two and a half years in which we'd netted nothing at all, each partner was able to take $80,000 out of our profits. For Rowland, it was still less than a third of his William Morris salary, but at least the trend was in the right direction. Judy and I moved from Sherman Oaks to Brentwood, trading in our $75,000 house for one that cost $650,000. I'd wake up and think, "My God, I live in Brentwood."

IN LATE 1976, OPPORTUNITY HAD COME KNOCKING IN THE unlikely form of a fifty-two-year-old bon vivant named Marty Baum, an agent with his own shop and a beguiling line of blarney. He had a strong if graying list led by Peter Sellers, Rod Steiger, Carroll O'Connor, Sidney Poitier, Julie Andrews, Blake Edwards, and Joanne Woodward. Marty felt lonely and wanted to join us. We debated for months. Would Marty's aging clients help or hurt our image? Could he share his list and adapt to our collective culture?

We decided to make him a full one-sixth partner and never regretted it. He gave us a big foot in the door in films; his clients, whom he generously shared or outright handed over to the rest of us, made CAA a contender. And he made us all acquainted with haute cuisine. He didn't regret it, either; in five years, he went from $100,000 a year to $500,000.

Marty set me up with James Clavell, the bestselling author of *King Rat* and *Tai-Pan*. Clavell's latest opus was *Shōgun*, a sprawling historical novel about an English naval pilot shipwrecked in seventeenth-century Japan. The creator of these exotic tales led a simple life on Mulholland Drive. He rose each morning at 5:30, had coffee, took a walk, and was at his typewriter by 7:00. He worked till noon, when he went to lunch at Yamamoto's in Century City. We first met at Yamamoto's sushi bar, my initiation into eating raw fish. I liked the menu and the company so much that we met there several times a month for close to twenty years.

James was a proper British gentleman, all double-breasted blue blazers and bone-dry humor. He was tall and imposing despite a limp that required him to use a cane, a memento of his time as a Japanese prisoner of war. After a few pieces of tuna sashimi, he asked me to read *Shōgun*, which had bounced around town for years. The studios were always alarmed by its length: twelve hundred pages.

I packed the paperback on a weekend ski trip. At first I struggled to keep the dozens of characters straight and to pierce the thicket of Japanese names, but by page eighty I was hooked. When Judy got annoyed that I was responding to her only with grunts, I ripped out the first chapter and passed it over. We spent a few hours on the slopes and the rest on the couch, literally tearing through *Shōgun*.

Marty and I talked the book up to the director Richard "Dickie" Attenborough, another Baum client, and then Dickie gave it to Robert Bolt, the screenwriter who wrote *Lawrence of Arabia*. We pitched the package of Attenborough and Bolt and Sean Connery and the book to Barry Diller and Michael Eisner at Paramount, who agreed to develop it. Dickie's theory was that *Shōgun* could be squeezed into a two-and-a-half-hour film by leaving some big chunks aside for sequels. But the book was just too big to generate a tidy script. Our package fell apart.

Like most of America during the last week of January 1977, I had spent my evenings glued to *Roots*, the landmark miniseries about black America. ABC aired it for twelve hours over eight consecutive nights and garnered record ratings. A hundred million viewers watched the finale, the largest television audience in history. It hit me—why couldn't we do the same with *Shōgun*?

James Clavell was horrified. He was a cinephile who'd written the screenplay for *The Great Escape* and directed six movies. "Television will ruin my book!" he declared.

Only a miniseries, I insisted, could do justice to *Shōgun*'s scope and sweep. With the author's extremely doubtful approval, Bill Haber and I went to Paramount to meet with Michael Eisner and Gary Nardino, who ran the studio's television division. Gary was eager to bring the project to the networks. We began at ABC, our best buyer, but they turned us down. CBS said the same thing: "We don't think Americans care much about Asia."

But Deanne Barkley, the head of TV movies at NBC, fell for James's novel and ordered twelve hours. Her faith was tested when the new writers adopted the perspective of John Blackthorne, the British sailor trapped in the East. To make Blackthorne's bewilderment hit home, they had the Japanese characters speak in Japanese without subtitles. It was avant-garde for prime time, but we backed the writers and Deanne backed us.

NBC budgeted *Shōgun* at a lavish $22 million, which allowed it to be filmed in Japan and to therefore look and feel like an event. Paramount stepped up and agreed to "deficit" the project, by funding any overage in the production costs (they expected to make their money back by selling syndication rights worldwide, after NBC's first two runs of the series). We were on our way.

Deanne and our agency disagreed just once, over who should play Blackthorne. The network wanted Richard Chamberlain, best known as a teen heartthrob in the sixties' medical show *Dr. Kildare*. I thought he was light for the role, but I was proved wrong. Richard's vulnerability made the character work. A virile, swashbuckling Blackthorne like Sean Connery wouldn't have been as sympathetic.

Shōgun's first night, a three-hour installment in September 1980, told us we had a hit. Viewers loved the romance, the loyalties, and the betrayals—the Asian soap opera of it all—and they made it one of the highest-rated programs in NBC's history. (It remains the second-most-watched miniseries, after *Roots*.) *Shōgun* triggered a run of bestseller adaptations and helped set off the American craze for sushi. Never again would a network claim its viewers were indifferent to Asia.

James was gratified by the show's fidelity to his novel. He liked it even better when more than three million *Shōgun* paperbacks sold within a week of the last installment. He especially got a kick out of the "bumper" credits we'd negotiated. At each commercial break, the screen read "James Clavell's *Shōgun*." When the show returned, viewers saw a second card: "James Clavell's *Shōgun* continues." It was one of our earliest efforts to brand our clients.

A week after *Shōgun* concluded, James called and asked to see me the next day. "The usual place?" I said.

"No, I want to meet at the McDonald's on Ventura Boulevard, off Van Nuys."

"What?"

He started laughing. "Be there at 8:30 tomorrow morning."

I walked into the McDonald's in one of my better blue suits and found myself underdressed. There was James at a booth in his blazer, ascot, and creased gray slacks, his cane at his side. Before him were two trays. Each held a cup of coffee and an Egg McMuffin.

I sat down and he handed over an envelope. I sliced it open and found a check with a dizzying number of zeroes made out to Creative Artists Agency. James had persuaded Paramount to allow him to deliver our $1 million package commission. It was by far the biggest payday we'd ever had—nearly $3 million in today's money.

Shōgun had languished at William Morris for three years. CAA got it made. Never mind that the deal almost fell apart twenty times; deals always almost fall apart twenty times. That was the first time we took a client's far-fetched dream and made it come true.

––––––––––

IN 1978, ANDREA EASTMAN, AN ICM AGENT I RESPECTED, told me, "You guys should be in the movie business. The way you work would be a breath of fresh air." Ron and I had been discussing that possibility, and Andrea's remark made us revisit the matter. But first, we wondered, why had she said that? Agents always had an agenda; there were no genuine compliments or candid suggestions. Was she trying to get us to stop focusing on TV, where we were starting to kill it? Was ICM planning a raid on our television talent? What was her nefarious plan? It turned out, astonishingly, that Andrea was just being honest and generous.

Ron told me, "We should split this up. You do movies, and I'll straddle movies, doing film actors and TV." We were going after ICM, which had all the stars except those represented by Stan Kamen at WMA. In those days, the focus of representation was the social life: ICM's Sue Mengers would sign you, then invite you to the cocaine parties at her house in Beverly Hills. She'd also gossip about you—she called her stars "sparklies"—to her other clients. We built our business as her opposite: we'd take tables in the back of restaurants, where we couldn't be overheard, lean in, and present ourselves as very square. "You won't have a big social life with us," I'd say. "We're here to make you independent in every direction, to strategize for you. So what are your dreams?" We didn't bad-mouth Sue, or anyone else, but the unspoken message of our presentation was "Can any other agency deliver ten people who've already had a premeeting about how to move your career ahead?" Later on, before every meeting we took with our clients, I'd send a memo out to everyone in the company even faintly or potentially involved in his or her work, trawling for ideas, and we always had a minimum of five people in the room.

Hollywood was an archipelago of talent, thousands of separate islands—but directors and stars were the keystone islands. We needed to build bridges and connect the islands to make packages, which would turn us into a kind of studio. To get actors, we needed directors, because directors had the stars in their pockets: Sydney Pollack had Redford and Martin Scorsese had De Niro. I wrote a list of the directors I wanted and thought I could conceivably get, many of them in comedy, which wasn't taken seriously in the agency world. (Though

Jack Lemmon and Walter Matthau had made a fortune for WMA, agents there never treated them accordingly.) My directors list included Steve Gordon, Albert Brooks, Ivan Reitman, Sydney Pollack, and—here I was dreaming, though the dream would eventually come to pass—Martin Scorsese and Stanley Kubrick.

I was beginning to believe that I could converse with those guys, because when we launched CAA, I had started a private project (one that took me ten years) of watching every film that had won one of the five big-category Oscars. I discovered why *Gone with the Wind* had passed the test of time and *How Green Was My Valley* hadn't; I learned the relationship between vision and craft. At the same time, I was boning up on the deal structure of movies and on which actors and directors had currency. Film had its own language, and I needed to be bilingual.

But to get to the directors, there was a further step: we needed writers and their material. Directors wanted great material a lot more than they wanted to chat with me about the opening crane shot in *Touch of Evil*. The easiest way to make some headway through this obstacle course was to turn our television writers into movie writers and directors. I encouraged Barry Levinson to write a screenplay based on his youth in Baltimore, and he came up with *Diner*, his debut as a film director.

The second easiest way was to turn other agencies' television writers into movie writers and directors. We wooed Steve Gordon, a TV writer with a screenplay about a millionaire alcoholic with a romantic dilemma. Steve's agents at ICM couldn't or wouldn't sell it. I sent the script to United Artists, which ordered the movie with Steve attached to direct. After *Arthur* became a surprise hit, Steve signed with us. We'd poach by assumption: behave as if we were the client's agent already, make their dream happen, and then they'd sign. Tragically, the following year, weeks after we had attached Steve to a comedy with Robert Redford, he had a fatal heart attack at forty-four. I was close to Steve, and his death stunned me. But I'm now astonished when I realize how quickly I put it behind me and got back to work building

CAA. It took half a day. Don't look back; someone was definitely going to be gaining on us.

To get to writers, you often had to get to the executives they trusted. Marty Baum introduced me to Ted Ashley, the dashing ex-agent who'd become the chairman and CEO of Warner Bros. Ted was *the* guy in our business; early in my career I'd visited his penthouse at the Sherry-Netherland and marveled at a Rothko on the wall. Then he took me to La Côte Basque, where I watched in awe as he slid the maître d' a hundred-dollar bill.

Now, a few years later, Ted had heard that I was one of the rising new breed, along with Barry Diller, David Geffen, Michael Eisner, and Terry Semel, so he put me together with John Calley, Warner's cultured, soft-spoken production head. John had an artist's eye and ear. Directors loved him, and he was especially tight with Sydney Pollack and Mike Nichols and Clint Eastwood. When I learned that John was a speed-reader, I began shipping him three or four Mort Janklow specials per week. Most had no future on the screen, but John finished every one. I sent him piles of scripts, whatever I could lay my hands on. John appreciated the attention and guided his friend Bob Towne, the community's most prestigious screenwriter, to CAA. It was one of the great favors of my life. Towne, who wrote such legendary scripts as *Shampoo* and *Chinatown*, was friends with other A-listers like Warren Beatty and Jack Nicholson. Having him as a client gave me instant credibility: now I could make bold plans about whom to go after next.

No good deed in Hollywood goes unpunished. A few years later I met with Calley on Towne's deal for *Greystoke: The Legend of Tarzan*, a hot property. While his associates were based in Warner's administration building, John worked out of a bungalow nearby. He met me at his door in a cardigan and Hush Puppies and welcomed me inside. Logs crackled in the fireplace, and Mozart wafted from the stereo.

"John," I said, "I'm trying to make a deal for Bob, but Frank Wells"—the studio's president—"is killing me, and I can't get it done. I don't know what to do." We had asked for gross-profit participation, but Wells was offering only net. Gross was our holy grail, because the box-office receipts established how much the studio owed your client; net was nearly worthless, as studios took so many deductions in their accounting that they somehow never showed any profits. As one of David Mamet's characters says in his play *Speed-the-Plow*, "Two things I've learned, twenty-five years in the entertainment industry. . . . The first one is: there is no net." (A beat later, he adds, "And I forget the second one.")

"That goddamned Wells!" John exclaimed. "What an asshole! He's too tough on the artists we love and need. You walk over there. I'm going to call him right now."

I said, "John, I can't thank you enough. This is unbelievable."

"No, no, not at all!"

As I walked out, I passed John's open window. He was on the phone with his back to me. "Frank," I heard him say, "Ovitz is on his way over. *Kill him.*"

AND THEN, IN 1979, AHEAD OF SCHEDULE, WE GOT A STAR.

Having grown to fifteen agents, we needed more space. When a failed hedge fund decamped from a suite of furnished offices in Century City, I wangled a below-market sublease. In our new lobby one morning, I glanced at the tenant list and spotted an eye-catching name on the eighteenth floor. Gary Hendler was a tax lawyer who'd started a high-end firm with Art Armstrong, a top business attorney. Along with Barry Hirsch, Jake Bloom, and Tom Pollock, Gary was one of the premier entertainment lawyers, the people who structured and vetted artists' contracts. Gary's client list included Robert Redford, Sean Connery, Sydney Pollack, and Barbra Streisand, among others.

After I pestered his receptionist, Gary agreed to meet me for dinner at Scandia, the top restaurant of its day. I'd befriended the maître d', a gregarious little guy named Giuseppe Bellisario, and ate there four times a week. (CAA later financed Giuseppe when he opened Giuseppe's in West Hollywood.) By the time I intercepted the check,

Gary and I had established a rapport. He understood my ambitions, and I knew all about his passions. The next day I sent him a barrel of Hershey's chocolate Kisses; the day after that, a good bottle of wine; the day after that, a first-edition volume on the law. We met several times for lunch, until one morning he called and said, "I'd like you to meet with Sean Connery." It wasn't so much that I'd bowled over Gary with my qualities as that there was little downside for him to making the introduction: Sean's career was in a deep, dark hole.

Sean was in London, and a lot rode on our first phone call. I wouldn't get a mulligan. Like most men my age, I had grown up idolizing Sean Connery and the relaxed violence of his take on James Bond. But it would be a mistake to gush. I had to diplomatically tell him he was screwing up. A dock worker before he got into acting, Sean couldn't stand being idle and worked nonstop. Usually I liked that quality in a client, but Sean said yes to everything, and the script or the director or the costars were routinely beneath him—often all three. It had happened with *The Next Man*, his most recent flop, and it was about to happen again with *Meteor* and *Cuba*.

When Sean came on the line, I told him, "If you're going to build your brand, you can't take roles at random. You need to choose better projects." I told him he needed to have exposure to a range of possible scripts and to have them developed into packages with him as the star. I also said he needed to work with better directors and that we'd get him those introductions and those jobs. This became the pattern for how I'd sign a star: start by politely criticizing his choices; tell him he needed to see and choose better material and better directors; promise him both. I made no promises that he'd work with specific talent, because the easiest way to lose a client is to make a promise you can't fulfill; the client always remembers. Sean didn't ask which of our directors and actors I thought he should be paired with, which was fortunate, because we didn't represent anyone of his stature. If he had asked, I'd have said what I often said in those days: "The creative talent that's right for *you*."

Sean was quiet at first, but he gradually warmed to my candor about his decision-making process. The following week we bought a full-page ad in the trades, all in bright red: "Creative Artists Agency, Inc. is proud to announce the exclusive worldwide representation of Sean Connery." I tore it out and mailed it to Lee Rosenberg, the agent who'd scoffed at the idea we'd ever sign a movie star. (Lee later became my neighbor, and we got along well, but for years I sent him an ad each time we signed a star. The one I sent for Robert Redford was particularly satisfying.) I flew to England a few weeks later to visit Sean on the set of *The Great Train Robbery* and to cement our partnership face-to-face. But I never asked him to sign a letter of engagement. I thought written agreements were not just overrated—because clients could void them if they went ninety days without work—but downright counterproductive. With no papers to renew, our clients had no anniversary to jog them into thinking about leaving us.

We began by finding Sean a pair of prudently budgeted, low-risk science-fiction films. Then came something trickier, a remake of *Thunderball*, the vintage Bond film. Sean hadn't played Bond since *Diamonds Are Forever*, more than ten years earlier, when he'd sworn off the franchise to avoid getting typecast. I felt he simply *was* James Bond, and that if audiences and producers were reminded of that, other opportunities would follow. One night, I worked the conversation around to Roger Moore and his shortcomings as Bond. Sean remained the definitive 007, I said—and he could not dispute me. I made sure Micheline Roquebrune, a French-born artist who was Sean's wife, supported the move, and I had Gary Hendler support the idea, too (I cleared everything client-related with Gary, behaving almost as if I were his assistant). I wore down Sean's defenses until he agreed to sip the shaken-not-stirred martini one last time. The movie's title, *Never Say Never Again*, came from Micheline, who recalled him telling the press that he'd "never again" play James Bond.

Unfortunately, the shoot in the Bahamas was strained. Sean disliked the producer, and he wasn't wild about the script or the director, Irvin Kershner. Also, it had taken so long to put the film together, four years, that Sean was now fifty-two, and visibly creaky in some of his action scenes. John Calley scanned the dailies in vain for the debonair Connery he'd thought he was buying. Fortunately, Sean's fans were so hungry for the real Bond that *Never Say Never Again* was bulletproof— and even if it stunk, I'd put together enough subsequent movies for Sean, based on his growing momentum, that he was safe. The film picked up good reviews and performed decently well at the box office. I even think Sean was glad he'd done it. He was back from the brink.

Our next deal was strictly mercenary. Sean loved to make money. I told him we could take films for the payday, if it was big enough—but only if we had quality projects slotted in between. Golan-Globus, the Israeli-producer cousins who had a brief but colorful run of B-movie action pictures, wanted Sean to play the Green Knight in a period piece called *Sword of the Valiant*. For six days of work that would amount to twelve minutes on-screen, I set Sean's price at $1 million, plus a penalty of $250,000 per day if he was kept past the first week. No actor had earned so much for so little. (Better yet, because the shoot was in France, Sean wouldn't pay any taxes.) The producers balked, then, hours later, caved. They needed the Connery brand to sell the film.

Going into *Sword of the Valiant*, I told Sean, "Just show up and take the money. Don't try to be the producer and the cinematographer and the makeup guy. Have some fun for a change." Two days into the shoot, I visited him in Avignon. We went to dinner and I said, "So how does it feel to be doing nothing?" Sean spared no detail on what needed to be fixed. As my jet lag caught up to me, I began nodding off. "You young guys have no stamina," Sean said, reprovingly. He himself was tireless. He'd disembark in Los Angeles after a nine-hour time change and scoot off to play a couple of sets of tennis.

He remained extremely attractive; at restaurants, even with his hairpiece at home, women of all ages still gave him the "take me now" look. In 1989, when Sean was fifty-nine, *People* magazine would declare him the sexiest man alive. But he had entered the phase where leading men needed to downshift to more mature roles. I knew he'd fight me on that. My lever was *The Untouchables*, a Brian De Palma film starring Kevin Costner as Eliot Ness. It had an exceptional part for Sean: an Irish cop who was Ness's stern but avuncular mentor. Sean could steal every scene.

"You're the *eminence grise* in this movie," I said.

"But I'm not the lead," Sean said. "And I die midway through"— his character got gunned down by Al Capone's mob.

"That's the key scene. You give Costner the strength to go on against Capone."

"But I'm still dead!" He just did not want to play the older mentor.

After weeks of this, I appealed to Micheline. At first she took Sean's side. But when I explained why the job would position Sean for the next decade, she gently brought her husband around. I called Sean again and said, "Sean, you have to play this role. And with no hairpiece. It's time." You have to risk alienating your clients. When you tell someone the truth, all they can do is get upset—they can't call you an idiot. Sean finally gave in.

We were good until the first day of shooting, when the predictable complaints began. His character, Jim Malone, was made up to be in his sixties, and Sean loathed his shapeless period suit and tweed cap. But he liked Costner and De Palma, and he gradually, grudgingly came to embrace the role. And he did steal every scene.

The Untouchables earned Sean his only Oscar and it set up a distinguished late-career run: *Indiana Jones and the Last Crusade*, *The Hunt for Red October*, *The Russia House*, *The Rock*. He didn't want to play an even-older Russian in *The Hunt for Red October*, but I firmly said, "Sean, you're going to look great in a blue uniform." He wasn't the type to gush, but never was a client more faithful and appreciative. He became my friend and adviser, an honorary member of the Ovitz clan. He vented when something went terribly wrong—like the time I packaged him with Sidney Lumet and Dustin Hoffman in *Family Business*, one of the best-sounding, worst-executed movie ideas ever. But it was like fighting with family; Sean never threatened to leave us.

On his sixtieth birthday, in 1990, Micheline and I threw him a surprise party at Wolfgang Puck's brewery restaurant in West Los

Angeles. The two hundred guests were all people he had worked with or was close to or greatly respected, including Clint Eastwood, Michael Caine, Michelle Pfeiffer, Harrison Ford, and Steven Spielberg. As we walked Sean in, I could see that he was moved, and that moved me. When he stood on a riser to speak, he cried and couldn't say a word.

CHAPTER SIX

CAR PHONES

IF A LAWYER DID A FAVOR FOR US, WE'D TRY TO DO A BIG-ger one for them. In a business of favors, the chits added up.

Not long after Gary Hendler introduced me to Sean Connery, I found a way to repay him. I knew that Gary was badly overworked and that Barry Hirsch was restless at his firm. They embodied two of the city's top three entertainment-law firms. So why not package Hendler and Hirsch? I took Gary to dinner and sang Barry's praises. On my way home, I called Barry from my car and asked him to breakfast the next morning in Santa Monica. I pitched him on Gary, and the two of them met the following day. Less than a week later, Barry and Gary formed Armstrong, Hendler & Hirsch, a hub of motion picture talent. CAA would represent fifty of their clients within a year.

Then Sylvester Stallone told Ron Meyer he planned to fire his law-yer, Jake Bloom—who had brought Sly to us in the first place. Ron had a tough conversation with his star, and Sly agreed to sit tight. That meant something around town. It showed the lawyers that we valued them, and that they were better off on our side.

Bert Fields was my channel to Dustin Hoffman. Bert was a litiga-tor nonpareil—whenever there was a big Hollywood lawsuit, both sides would race to engage him. I met Bert when we were starting

CAA, and after our first lunch, I sent him a check for five dollars to retain his services, a mostly jocular way to give him a conflict to think about if anyone asked him to sue us. Dustin, having broken out in *The Graduate* in 1967, had lost his way, as well as his first marriage, to the intoxications of celebrity. Then an old family friend, a businesswoman named Lisa Gotsegen, came into his life. Lisa kept Dustin on the straight and narrow and made sure he read the scripts he got sent. They were engaged to be married in 1979 when Judy and I met them for dinner at Chasen's, the West Hollywood institution where Frank Sinatra and Gregory Peck kept red-leather booths on reserve.

Dustin had just shot *Kramer vs. Kramer*, which would win him his first Oscar, but prior to that he'd had a string of bombs, and his career was in a precarious place. He was extremely picky about roles, the opposite of Sean Connery, but my pitch was much the same. "We'll make sure you see *everything*," I said. I tried to turn a weakness (my inexperience and dearth of film clients) into a strength (he'd have my complete attention). I could tell I was scoring points with Lisa—she'd grown up near me in the Valley, and I felt instantly comfortable with her—but Dustin was harder to read. On impulse, I said, "Try us out and I won't charge you anything until you think I've earned it." It was the only time I ever offered to take less than 10 percent, much less work for free. If word of the arrangement got out, the haggling with other clients would never end. But we desperately needed a top-ten film star like Dustin Hoffman. I deluged him with material, and signed him six months later.

WHILE SEAN AND DUSTIN WERE COUPS FOR CAA, WE STILL needed directors. I'd long loitered near one of the best: Sydney Pollack. During my time at William Morris, Sydney was making standout pictures like *They Shoot Horses, Don't They?* and *Jeremiah Johnson*. I'd stumbled across him on the streets of New York in 1972, while he was filming *The Way We Were*, and watched behind the rope with the other passers-by. Sydney handled Robert Redford and Barbra

Streisand so lightly that they didn't even notice the bridle. The famously skittish Streisand seemed to trust him completely. As I watched
them, a vision of the future came over me: *I'm going to have all of these
people someday, in an agency that will represent the whole food chain
and flip the power from the studios to the artists.* Even then I had the
odd feeling that Sydney would be my master key.

Realizing that vision took years. When I heard about *The Yakuza*,
a film about the Japanese crime syndicate that Sydney would release in
1975, I cold-called him and offered to connect him to Ed Parker, a local
martial artist who could choreograph the movie. Ed didn't get the job,
but I kept in touch and stopped by Sydney's office every so often. I
stayed after him when we started CAA, escalating my soft pressure a
notch in 1977, after Sydney invited me to the premiere for *Bobby Deer-
field*. Al Pacino was outstanding as the hard-hearted race-car driver,
but the movie never really jelled. Because Sydney had yet to make a
blockbuster, he was ripe to be lured.

Sydney's longtime agent was Evarts Ziegler, a cultured, white-
haired Princeton man—a literary agent out of central casting. Zig went
his own way, living in far-off Pasadena even as his firm, Ziegler, Dis-
kant & Roth, represented A-list writers like William Goldman (*Butch
Cassidy and the Sundance Kid*) and Willard and Gloria Huyck (*Star
Wars*). He also had top-tier directors like Dick Donner (*Superman*)
and Jim Bridges (*Urban Cowboy*). I wanted them all, but how to lure
them away?

The unexpected answer came through my car telephone, a novelty
at the time. The radio-based phone, slightly larger than a shoebox, had
eleven channels: you kept pushing buttons until you found a dial tone.
Busy channels were like party lines—any subscriber could listen in.
On my way to the office one morning, I heard a voice that sounded like
Evarts Ziegler's. I pulled off the road to take notes, because Zig was
discussing his star-studded list with his assistant. I clocked in at the
same time the next morning, and there was Zig again, doing business
while commuting. He sounded old and forlorn. Zig was past sixty, and
at a time when we were swarming potential clients, he had just one

assistant and a junior partner named Steve Roth. I decided to try to buy him out. To make him more receptive—to soften him up—I escalated my campaign to sign Sydney Pollack.

"I'll *kill* for you," I told Sydney. All I had to sell was my passion and energy and the fact that I was thirty years younger than Evarts Ziegler. As Sydney wavered, we got screenplay after screenplay into his hands before Zig did. I pestered Mort Janklow for drafts of upcoming books and sent out summaries by the dozen. Each day I spent up to two hours on Sydney, far more than anyone would spend for his biggest *signed* client. Sydney was Hamlet reincarnated—he never made a fast decision. But in 1981, with our courtship in its second year, he signed with me at last.

Having dealt Zig a body blow, we offered him $750,000 for his agency, plus a lifetime royalty on his clients' work. He'd keep a piece of his business in perpetuity, even if he never came to the office. After we'd negotiated for six months, Zig passed. Either he doubted our staying power or he couldn't stomach surrendering to some whippersnappers. But during our discussions we'd discovered that Steve Roth serviced the cream of their younger clientele and that Steve was eager to leave. We promptly cut a deal for him to come to CAA. That got us most of what we wanted, including Dick Donner, Jim Bridges, and the Huycks, at the price of Steve's compensation—$250,000 a year and the potential to become a partner.

We had to build a critical mass of clients so we could reverse the power curve from the buyers (the studios) to the sellers (us), and anyone in our way was going to get rolled over. With his core business gone, Zig sold what remained to ICM in 1983, and he was done. The truth is that I didn't give a thought to Zig after he turned us down. You never heard that someone was unhappy afterward—they just lost. Ron sometimes had to remind me not to roll over *everyone*; Jack Nicholson was with a one-man outfit, Sandy Bresler, so we wouldn't go after Jack. "There are two hundred of these smaller agencies," Ron would say, "and you can't put 'em *all* out of business." That made sense to me, even then.

But flattening Evarts Ziegler was the beginning of my Sherman-esque March to the Sea.

———————

STEVE ROTH, OUR NEW HIRE, HAD GROWN UP IN BEVERLY Hills and knew how to handle himself around celebrities. He was glib and well dressed and unflappable. We offered him a full partnership after a make-good period. He started out guns blazing, but soon he was skipping the Saturday meetings. Then he started coming in late on weekdays. Steve was hanging out with producers like Frank Yablans and Robert Evans, people who blew off phone calls as a prerogative of power, and he started behaving like them.

Matters came to a head in a conference call with Dick Donner. Dick had used me as a sounding board since *Superman*. Now, as he was transitioning between Zig and CAA, he had asked us for comments on *Inside Moves*, an original screenplay by Barry Levinson and Valerie Curtin. As Dick and Steve and I talked through the script, I realized that something was off. Steve was parroting whatever Dick said. Forty-five minutes in, Dick asked, "What do you guys think about the scene where the nun gets raped on top of the bar? I'm worried it breaks the tone of the movie."

There was no such scene in *Inside Moves*—no nun at all, in fact. Before I could jump in, Steve said, "Dick, I agree with you a hundred percent." Dick Donner, a total sweetheart, hung up and then took his phone off the hook. We couldn't reach him for two days.

Steve Roth, it turned out, did not really like to read—or, for that matter, work. He began to remind Ron and me of the rich brats in the Morris mailroom. I went to Frank Price, Columbia's chairman and CEO, for a favor, as we had a couple of pictures in the pipeline with him, including *Tootsie* and *Stripes*. One week later Steve moved to the Columbia lot to begin work on his new production deal. We didn't usually fire people at CAA, but we did ease them out—and into positions where they could help us.

THE TIME I PUT IN WOOING SYDNEY POLLACK WAS THE BEST investment I ever made. He became my friend, my mentor, and my calling card. Two weeks after I signed him, we bought another red ad in *Variety* and the *Hollywood Reporter* for Robert Redford, as big a star as there was. The entertainment business was an infrared system. When you got hot, people gravitated toward your heat, which made you hotter. Along with Sean and Dustin, landing Sydney and Bob vaulted CAA into contender status with ICM and William Morris. In 1979, when I moved full time into film, television accounted for 90 percent of the agency's revenue. By 1982, 60 percent of our business was in film; we rapidly became players where it counted most.

Ron Meyer began calling me Rumpelstiltskin. "There goes Rumpelstiltskin," he'd say, "turning shit into gold." In the original fable, it was straw, but like any great agent, Ron improved things in the telling. In dealing with the studios, Ron and I developed an effective one-two punch. After I opened with a hard line, asking for an amount somewhere between more than we expected to get and ridiculous, execs would back-channel Ron and say, "My God, he asked for six million for Warren Beatty against ten of the gross"—meaning 10 percent. "Can you help us out?" Ron would smooth their feathers and say, "I'll talk to him," or "Try this." After they called me back, I'd tell Ron where things stood for the next round. On occasion I would offer a small concession. More often I'd hold firm and close the deal where I started, but the buyers always felt better because they'd been listened to. They never seemed to get that Ron was *my* agent.

Yet there wasn't a day when I didn't walk in the door and get hit by a rush of anxiety. What idea can I come up with today to pay the overhead? There'd be the adrenaline rush when we sent out the internal memo, "Robert Redford is now a client." Fifteen minutes later it was, What next? In 1979, when I was thirty-three, Ted Ashley at Warner Bros. took me aside and said, "I'm going to give you some great advice." He grinned ruefully. "And, knowing you, you're not going to take it.

But here it is: I could have worked ten percent less, and it wouldn't have made a difference in my professional success. But I would have been a lot happier."

Ted was absolutely right on both counts—it was great advice, and I didn't take it. I see now that I could have worked as much as 20 percent less, and it wouldn't have cost me. If I'd worked even 10 percent less, across thirty years, that's three whole extra years of life I'd have enjoyed. On the other hand, Ted himself stepped down from Warner Bros. at a relatively young age, in his late fifties, and when I saw him a few years later, I was stunned by how listless he seemed.

I had no interest in retiring young after midlevel success. The same year that Ted gave me the advice on slowing down, he put me in a room with Steve Ross, CEO of Warner Bros., in New York. Steve was a visionary. He was tough, forceful, generous, and impossibly charming—hard as nails yet widely liked. Starting with a few parking lots, he had bought and sold his way to the very top of the media and entertainment industries.

Ted wanted me to come to Warner, and I was flattered. But only five years into CAA I knew I wasn't ready for a studio position. "I'm really not that interested," I told Steve.

"Well, what job are you interested in?" he asked.

"Yours. I want to learn everything I can, and then someday I'd like to have your job."

He laughed. "That's the answer I was hoping for," he said. Instead of feeling threatened or offended, he found my ambition refreshing—the sign of a true leader. I took note of that quality, and tried to mirror Steve's best aspects at CAA.

It was hard to feel as relaxed as Steve seemed, though. Even when I'd visit an art gallery, and find myself blessedly unreachable, in those days before cell phones, I'd feel a stabbing anxiety in my gut because I knew twenty-five people were trying to reach me. Your clients burn through your energy, your expertise, your joy. For every Dusty Hoffman with a wife and five great kids, there are a hundred more who have only an all-consuming need for attention. If you're that kind of emotional gypsy, then the Sunday brunches at the Scientology building begin to look pretty good.

When Ron and I were in New York, one weekend in 1979, I suggested we take a walk in Central Park. I told him, softly but firmly, that the ownership structure of our company was way off. Rowland wasn't bringing in any income, and Mike, who'd always hoped that CAA would be a boutique agency, was clearly sidling toward the exit. I said that if I didn't get more than the 16.67 percent that each of the six partners owned, I'd have to consider other options. I knew Ron wouldn't want to jeopardize what we'd built. He often acted as my agent with the others, breaking tough news to them (or from them to me). He enjoyed being the Ovitz whisperer, so I was confident he'd deliver on my ask. And, indeed, when he spoke with the others, they took the obvious point that I had clearly become the firm's leader. I replaced Rowland as the firm's president, and got a larger allocation of shares. In 1982, Mike would retire and we'd buy out his shares for $750,000.

Professionally, mission accomplished. Emotionally, though, I had just hit the self-destruct button—only it would take sixteen years to go off. Bill Haber never forgave me; he would later say, "Agreeing to give to Michael some of my own shares is the only professional regret I have in my life."

Even worse, I never suggested to Ron that his stake also be increased—I wasn't emotionally aware enough to realize that he'd feel slighted if I moved up and he didn't. Ron wanted Bill's shares, and he wanted him gone.

The problem was that Bill was a magnificent head of television. Like Howard West, he could look at a raw idea and turn it into a TV show. He gave better notes on scripts than many a producer or network exec. But Bill wasn't good with younger agents: he was always giving them pop quizzes, asking, "What show has an opening for such-and-such director?" And even in the early days he'd take long weekends—later, they would turn into long weekends at his Paris home *or* his château in the Loire Valley. What's more, several times a year some minor issue would make him send us an overwrought letter of resignation announcing that he was going to go work with blind children or help save the bats from extinction. Bill just wanted to be heard and respected—to be courted a little—but Ron yearned to call his bluff.

We had poached Lee Gabler from ICM to be Bill's number two, in case Bill made good on his next threat to leave. Ron looked at Lee and saw Bill's replacement, but I didn't want to mess with our success. I wanted everything to stay the same, except that I'd get more. What I should have done for Ron was give him some of my own allocation of shares, and then figure out how to handle Bill. To really be his blood brother, I should have behaved as *his* agent.

Bill never had an inkling of Ron's animus. I was amazed at how well Ron hid his true feelings from someone he saw every day.

CHAPTER SEVEN

THE SECOND VALLEY

CAA HAD FOUR COMMANDMENTS: (1) NEVER LIE TO YOUR clients or colleagues. (2) Return every call by end of day (or at least have your assistant buy you a day's grace). (3) Follow up and don't leave people guessing. Every desk phone at CAA bore the message COMMUNI-CATE. After our Fred Specktor heard me use that word in every speech I gave, he stuck the plaques on Ron's phone and mine—and when we admired them, he stuck them on everyone's phone. It was our version of IBM's famous imperative to THINK.

The last commandment, and the hardest one to follow, was (4) Never bad-mouth the competition. Gossip was a tool of the trade. Other agencies routinely disparaged soon-to-be-released films by directors they hoped to sign. *The performances stink. The studio's pulling back on publicity. It won't make a dime.* The worse the buzz and the weaker the box office, the more open a director might be to changing representation. But if you were confident about your own work, why snipe? Why tear down someone you're hoping to be in business with? We built our company around positive thinking. We had no hierarchy, no titles, no reporting lines, no nameplates. We killed ourselves to take everyone's point of view in meetings, to make everyone feel empowered.

CAA had no formal business hours. If the partners' cars were in the garage at 8:00 in the morning, so were everybody else's. When I made my evening rounds at 7:00, 80 percent of our people were at their desks. The work was the thing. We even had a no-fly-by-day rule: if you flew to New York, you took the red-eye so you didn't waste a workday in the air. Ron and I would park our cars in the number one and number two spots and leave them there when we walked to business dinners, before coming back to retrieve them. We worked insanely hard, but we fostered the illusion of working impossibly hard. I believed momentum was everything—once a company relaxed, it was done for.

The lack of hierarchy was a myth, of course, a management tool. Nothing happened that Ron and Bill and I didn't want to have happen. We were democratic dictators. I thought of creating our corporate culture as akin to making a giant pointillist painting, dabbing in a million dots that, when you stood back, came into focus as a coherent picture. Each dot was a detail. For instance, we took great pains in our hiring: everyone we brought on had been interviewed by the whole company first, so we had across the board buy-in. And I wrote memos to everyone about everything: the advantages of Pan Am over Continental for flights to New York; the imperative need to look for "any post–1900 female biographical characters that have not been covered in the media" for our client Sally Field to play; specifications for the cake for Marty Scorsese's fiftieth birthday party ("Marty likes chocolate and is not averse to coconut"); even how to get Zegna suits at cost plus $200 so we'd all look sharp ("If you are interested, I will set up an appointment for my oldest friend Steve Stearns to come into the office with all of the fabrics for the fall line. If you are not interested, I do not care."). Sending out ten or more such memos every day, getting every detail just so, was extraordinarily time-consuming. But time was our nest egg.

Our corporate culture was American team sports boosterism mixed with Spartan military tactics mixed with Asian philosophy, all overlaid by the communitarian spirit of the Three Musketeers. That culture was a collective endeavor, and one that hundreds of people shaped and defined over the years. But among the partners I gave the most thought to what it should be. I scraped from an eclectic variety of sources, a businessman's version of Picasso's method. From law firms, I took our phraseology—Ron was a partner, and so were the people in the mailroom—and also the paramount importance of confidentiality. Our collaborative approach came from the way Magic Johnson ran his fast break with the Lakers. He'd drive it up the middle, have an open shot, and pass it up to feed an unguarded teammate. Who wouldn't kill to play with that point guard? At staff meetings and retreats, I began to talk about the philosophy of the Chinese general and military strategist Sun Tzu, whose *The Art of War* I'd read in college. We took his ideas on loyalty, on teamwork, and on how having complete information was the key to decision making. The book also resonated with me because it prioritized strength and toughness. Ron and Bill thought my emphasis on Sun Tzu was crazy, until they realized that it worked—that our team bought in. In truth, though, the Chinese general was always a bit of a prop. It wasn't so much what he said that inspired CAA, as the idea that we, a five-year-old company, were adhering to a philosophy from 2,500 years earlier. It gave us instant roots.

I was obsessed with the Spartan phalanx, the idea that you were only as strong as the colleague on your left. We'd go to meetings as a group, we'd go to screenings as a group, walking down the aisles together half an hour early, ten or fifteen strong, a show of power. I drove our people hard to sign at least two clients a week, and after we got up and running, our signing machinery was a thing of beauty. Let's say you were a promising screenwriter and I met you at a dinner at Morton's. I'd call you the next day for a quick chat—*not* about wanting to represent you, but about the virtues of your work (which three of our literary agents would have briefed me on). I'd casually toss in the names of a few well-known actors and directors who'd be a perfect fit with your sensibility. Ninety-nine percent of the time, you'd want to talk some more, and I'd suggest lunch or a drink. There we'd talk further about your work and your hopes and dreams. The killer move, as you got up from the table or were handing your parking ticket to the valet, was to say, "Why don't you come in and meet our crew?"

A few days later, when you drove in, one of our parking concierges (who'd been given a photo of you) would open your car door, greet you with a big smile, and say, "Mr./Ms. X, great to see you. Really hope you join the family!" or "Hope you have a great meeting!" (They switched up the patter to keep from going stale.) An assistant would escort you to the conference room, where five to ten poised, well-dressed agents would be waiting. They'd already have had a premeeting to script the ideas we'd be presenting, and now, for an hour, they'd pepper you with notions for developing your books and screenplays and shower you with the names of our clients who were eager to be in your films. At the end, we'd finally say, "We want to represent you." It was hard to resist. If you raised a serious issue—"I'd love to, guys, but I just signed with ICM for two years"—we'd always say, "Not a problem, we'll deal with it." We'd let ICM commission you for those two years as we packaged your work with our other clients, playing the long game.

Clients would often have five of our agents in their lives. Robert Redford, for instance, had Tina Nides as his literary agent, Sandy Climan providing strategy, David O'Connor as his daily point person, Jay Moloney routinely involved as my assistant, and me available when necessary. Usually clients would gradually gravitate to one agent for most conversations—though if that relationship soured, we had multiple backups ready to step in. Our point of differentiation was that a client got regular phone calls from not one but several agents—all coordinated among the client's team with the interoffice memos we called buck slips. You just can't beat five with one. All of our agents really did represent all of our clients. (Of course, this sometimes led to individual CAA agents feeling individually responsible for a given client's success, and claiming solo credit later. That wasn't how it was supposed to work—but it was an uptown problem.)

We told our agents that they were never not on stage, seven days and seven nights a week. There was no explicit dress code, but you knew you had to dress the way we did, and keep your private life as well as your business private. When we hired Rick Nicita from William Morris, he asked if he had to wear a suit; in those days you'd see other agencies' agents wearing corduroy blazers, and even an occasional suede elbow patch. "You don't have to do anything you don't want to do," I said evenly. Rick showed up in a suit. Only the music division dressed down—formality didn't play with their artists.

We had group meetings every day, and sometimes twice a day, to ensure that we were all on song. I also did rounds twice a day, like a doctor, carrying a sheaf of papers so it looked like I was going into a meeting—when actually I was gauging the general mood and taking note of anyone who seemed out of sorts. I viewed our people as my children, and for the first ten years I'd call every employee who didn't show up at work to make sure they were okay and to see if they needed anything, from chicken soup to a good divorce lawyer. I did it out of concern, but I also wanted them to know I was keeping a watchful eye. Our idea was to make everyone feel that our building was a comfort zone—and to balance that with a little anxiety should they step outside the building. We wanted the "Don't cross those guys!" message to be as obvious as a flashing sign at the border.

Yet our MO was to be attentive, polite, and well informed. I wanted worldliness to be one of a CAA agent's defining qualities—*Be able to talk knowledgeably about what your clients love. This will encompass pretty much everything*. I insisted that our agents have a reading list: one national newspaper, one international newsmagazine, and one special-interest magazine, such as *Golf Digest*. I had two hundred magazine subscriptions, and I'd skim the magazines as I was on the phone, everything from *Redbook* to *Road & Track*. I got a lot of flak about all this homework, but I remember feeling vindicated when Mike Menchel, a twenty-six-year-old agent, came with me to Aspen for the opening of a play Robin Williams was in. Mike walked up to Jack Nicholson and offered him a light, then chatted with him about golf and the Lakers—two of Jack's favorite topics.

I told our staff we should know about every news story days or weeks before it was in *Variety*. The trick was to find the hidden mother

lodes of information, and to do that we had to exploit a niche the rest
had overlooked. Ron and Bill and I began by handling studio executives' own employment contracts, as we'd long done for TV execs. We
took no fees for this; we were after something more valuable—an inside track. The vice presidents we handled would give us tips and take
a second look at our clients. Then we shared those tips with the most
powerful people in town. In the preemail era, when people were
flooded by phone messages, which calls did they return first? CAA's,
on the chance they might learn something useful.

Soon we represented so many executives that we could see the entire chessboard. The instant we sensed someone was unhappy we'd be
thinking about where to move them, and whom to move into their
place. We knew about openings before the executives themselves did.
That's how we helped move Les Moonves from Warner to run CBS,
Brandon Tartikoff from NBC to Paramount, and Marcy Carsey and
Tom Werner from ABC to their own production company, with a
CAA-brokered guarantee for several pilots from their former em-
ployer. I would often tell our agents to watch a space: "In thirty to sixty
days, something big will happen at Paramount." If I was quietly settling Frank Mancuso's dispute with Marty Davis about his severance
pay, and *Variety* ran a story that Frank was going to sue Marty, I'd
say "Don't count on it." I enjoyed seeming all-knowing, the great Oz,
but the real point was to signal our agents that we were working at
a level above their heads—that if they were planning to leave for a studio job, for instance, we'd know before they'd even discussed their
contract.

We drilled into everyone that they were rewarded by how the company did, and how they worked with their associates. The weakest link
broke the chain; being human and fallible broke the chain. It was a
tough business—Freddie Fields and the producer Ray Stark were
tough sons of bitches, and you had to be just as tough, or tougher, to
earn their respect. So I aimed for us to seem formidable. Regrettably,
we overshot the mark and became fearsome.

JUDY AND I PUT OFF HAVING CHILDREN WHILE WE BUILT
CAA. I was thirty-three in 1980, when Chris, our firstborn, arrived at
Cedars Sinai. As I giddily counted fingers and toes, my priorities
changed forever. Before Chris, I thought only of work. After Chris
came along—followed by Kimberly in 1983 and Eric in 1986—I still
worked weekends but I strove to carve out regular family time. I
wanted us to raise our children the way my parents had raised Mark
and me, with stable routines and rituals (and without the live-in grandmother). The big deals in Encino were Little League, backyard barbe-
cues at sundown, and street ball with my father and my friends. How
could we replicate that experience in Brentwood, with kids who grew
up around limos and private planes—and with a father who was
overbooked before he woke up? I didn't want them to feel entitled *or*
neglected.

After considerable trial and error, Judy and I came up with a system that seemed to work, more or less. On weekdays, we'd do whatever
CAA required—my lunatic daily scheduling, our evening entertain-
ing. But on weekends we'd revert to the '50s, with consistent parental
involvement. Save for an awards show or a formal dinner, we took
Chris with us in his baby basket wherever we went. He traveled to
Europe and Hawaii before his first birthday, and so did Kim and Eric
before theirs. The problem with this throwback arrangement was that
Judy ended up being largely responsible for raising the kids. She became the one in charge of feelings and emotions—of daily life—and I
was left as the planner, scripting where we should all be going.

I repeatedly told our kids that I didn't want them going into entertainment. For one thing, I didn't think they'd get a fair shake, given
the overhang of my reputation. For another, I privately worried
that they'd never achieve as much as I had: the kids of agents who followed them into the business never seemed to live up to their fathers'
reputations.

Each of our kids reacted to my growing public profile differently.

Chris had Judy's sensitivity and my fire; an excellent baseball player at John Thomas Dye, he expressed himself physically—I remember feeling stunned when I saw him hit a ball out of the schoolyard in sixth grade. Where did he get such easy power? But when his classmates made cracks about CAA or my success, parroting their parents, Chris would start throwing punches. That same sixth-grade year, his best friend's father and I got called in to the school because our sons had gotten into a fight with some kids who'd pushed them down. The vice principal told us that the school didn't tolerate violence. I said, "We agree. But what if someone is aggressive toward you first?" Calmly and methodically, point by point, we turned the discussion around until the vice principal let the matter drop. I thought, at the time, that I'd done a great job for my son.

When Chris was fifteen, I took him out for sushi to a little hole-in-the-wall place we liked called Asakuma. I was lecturing him about art, trying to interest him in it, and he was obviously just humoring me. Growing nettled, I said, "You know, your dad and his agency represent Michael Jackson and Madonna and Bill Murray and the Smashing Pumpkins. Your dad is actually kind of cool!" He looked up from his miso soup, smiling a little, and said, "Yeah, Dad, I got it." We both laughed. I was selling my son on me—selling him on the idea that I was contemporary and hip and that I knew exactly what he was thinking, which was totally untrue.

I was furious when Chris transferred his sophomore year from Brown University to UCLA, where his girlfriend was. My dream was that he'd get the Ivy League education I never did. He didn't have a dream—he had a girlfriend. I begged him not to go to UCLA; then I begged him not to go to film school afterward; then I begged him not to go to business school; then I begged him not to take a job as an exec at Paramount—the entertainment business, after all my warnings! I lost every argument. He had inherited my hardheadedness.

Kim was the most like me—inquisitive and no-nonsense and highly opinionated—except that she was female and an excellent horseback rider. She was entranced by fashion from an early age: when she was nine we found tear sheets from all the women's magazines buried in her closet, alongside her sketches for her own clothing line. She turned her back on all the entertainment-world hoopla, the movie stars over for dinner. When she was at NYU, later, she walked into the dorm one day and the security guard said, "Hey, did you see your dad was in the paper again?"—a reference to a front-page *New York Times* story about CAA and our work for MGM. Kim didn't say a word, but that afternoon she applied to transfer to Brown. She needed to find her own way, a trait I recognized and admired, even as it left me feeling forlorn. Was I driving her away?

When she was at Brown, I came to the campus to interview Martin Scorsese about creativity, and afterward, at a table with the school's trustees, I did what I always do—asked questions of everyone, getting them talking about themselves so they'd give me a clue or two that would enable me to pretend I knew of them, even if I hadn't the faintest idea who they were. Kim, who was at my table, watched these exchanges carefully. Afterward, she told me, "That was a great lesson—how you made everyone feel comfortable and important, while you were learning everything you needed."

Eric, our youngest, required the least maintenance. He used verbal judo to deflect any reference to what I did, and always seemed warm and self-confident. He had a quiet forcefulness. But he hated his school, Harvard-Westlake, and in tenth grade he came to me and insisted that we visit some boarding schools in the East, far, far away. He ended up at a school in Connecticut, and then at Northwestern University. He never liked CAA or the powerful, warping force field of the entertainment world, and was much happier thousands of miles from it. Where I always worked hard to seem unruffled by life, Eric was genuinely unruffled by it. I admired that about him—how did he end up so relaxed?

My kids all turned out well, but looking back I can see that my occasional impulse to treat them as clients was a really dumb idea. It was almost impossible for me to turn off my agenting impulses: "Here are your strengths, but here's what you could do better. Come here with me, meet these people, and that will set you up to do X and Y." I worked on my clients during the week, and my kids on the weekend.

WE DECIDED THAT ANOTHER ROYAL ROAD TO TALENT LAY through comedy. The focus of our efforts was *Saturday Night Live*, where producer Lorne Michaels had assembled the crackerjack Not Ready for Prime Time Players: Dan Aykroyd, John Belushi, Chevy Chase, Gilda Radner, and (in season two) Bill Murray. After the show's debut, in 1975, its stars became the Beatles of television. They could lift CAA to a new level if we could sign them. Unfortunately, a manager-producer named Bernie Brillstein represented Lorne and had dibs on most of the show's cast, including Aykroyd and Belushi. Chevy Chase, *SNL's* first breakout star, had his own manager and agent. Bill Murray, a free spirit, had no one, but we didn't yet represent anyone he trusted who'd vouch for us. So we stayed patient, waiting.

In June 1979, Michael Eisner invited me to a Paramount screening of *Meatballs*, a low-budget summer-camp farce with Bill Murray in his first lead role. The director was a Canadian named Ivan Reitman. *Meatballs* was the funniest thing I'd seen since *Animal House*, the fraternity farce Ivan had produced the year before. I introduced myself to Ivan and set a meeting through his lawyer, Tom Pollock. Ivan was a very desirable commercial talent: *Animal House* and *Meatballs* earned their budgets back thirty times over because he knew what audiences wanted. At our meeting, though, he immediately asked, "What can you do that I can't do for myself? I find my own material, and I don't need anybody to get me work." All my talk of strategy and positioning, all my promises of synergies with our team and other clients, seemed to fall on deaf ears. Afterward I told Tom, "Too bad—but thanks, anyway."

Tom said, "Ivan really liked you."

"Right."

"No, really!"

It turned out that Ivan was as good as I was at keeping his feelings hidden. After CAA signed him, we had someone to vouch for us with Bill Murray. Ron, our best closer, met with Bill in New York. But for some reason they didn't click; Bill was one of the few who remained uncharmed, unseduced. "We just kept walking around," Ron told me. "Why don't you take a shot?"

On my next trip to New York, I called Bill and said, "Where would you like to meet?"

He said, "Grant's Tomb at 11:00," and hung up.

It took me two cabbies to get dropped near a pillared mausoleum in Riverside Park. Bill was waiting there. Without saying much, he took off walking, destination unknown. I tagged along. It was clear he didn't want to be sold, he just wanted to see what I was like. So for seven hours we hiked through the city, with breaks for lunch and dinner. We talked about the Yankees and Bill's hometown football team, the Bears, about children and humor and life.

As Bill was assessing me, I was assessing him, and realizing that his fans had misread him. He didn't want to be a comedian; he wanted to be a great actor. Left to his own devices, he might have stuck to character roles in small quirky films. He was a free spirit who tried to make daily life into a movie scene, with the crucial difference that there was no script, so anything could happen. That afternoon he ordered a cup of coffee at a diner and said, "Good party," totally deadpan, and the server cracked up. Even crossing the street became an exercise in improv theater.

I was hardly Mr. Spontaneity, but I really warmed to Bill's random acts of curiosity, and for some reason he warmed to me, even after we started talking business about six hours in. Of all my clients, I was always most comfortable with the people in comedy, starting with Barry Levinson, and continuing with Robin Williams, John Belushi, Dan Aykroyd, and David Letterman. Perhaps it was because, like me, they were totally self-made and lived entirely by their wits. And of all of them, I was the most deeply, instantly comfortable with Bill Murray. He was extremely bright, startlingly well read, remarkably easy to talk to, and genuinely sympathetic.

I knew that *commercial* would be a dirty word to Bill, but I told him it was also a magic word. "Look," I said, "you need a couple of heavy-duty commercial movies first, to establish yourself in the marketplace, and then you can make anything you want." We followed that plan for fifteen years, setting up hits like *Stripes* and *Ghostbusters* and *Groundhog Day* while allowing Bill time to make personal films like *Mad Dog and Glory*. Sometimes we knocked heads. *The Razor's Edge*, based on Bill's favorite Somerset Maugham novel, had to be rammed down Columbia's throat. It was a complete downer, and I believed Bill's fans would be nonplussed. Bill was too young to be doing brilliant but esoteric work; there was plenty of time for him to get there, transitioning his audience slowly. But there comes a point where an agent must bow to a client's wishes, if he wants to remain that client's agent.

Ron told me I'd fallen in love with Bill—and he was right. Over the years, I helped talk Bill through two divorces, but he also became one of the very few clients I could unload my problems on. We usually hung out in Manhattan, meeting at a spot he chose at the last minute. Because he didn't like driving, we'd walk, me in a suit and Bill in some outfit like plaid shorts and a purple shirt. We'd stop at two or three restaurants for a drink so he could gauge the vibe before he chose one and settled in. He knew every doorman and maître d' by name, and tables always materialized. Once we joined a five-deep crowd outside a tiny place on Mulberry Street in Little Italy. Bill flagged down the owner and ordered wine for everyone waiting on the sidewalk. By the time they squeezed a table for us into the middle of the restaurant, people were having too much fun to care that we'd cut the line.

Around this time my son Chris, who was six, exhibited some worrisome neurological symptoms, and I took him to a specialist at Yale for tests. I was feeling anxious and low when Bill surprised me by showing up at my ratty New Haven hotel. He stayed for two days until the worst was ruled out. His compassion didn't stop with his friends. He passed out tens and twenties to homeless people as we walked and often knew their names. But he was nobody's patsy. On the Upper

West Side once, after we passed a man with a cup, Bill turned to yell, "Don't you fucking try to steal money from people who need it!"

The man said, "I'm sorry, Mr. Murray, I'm really sorry."

A few yards on, I asked, "What was that about?"

"He had two-hundred-dollar sneakers *and a clean cup*, and he's panhandling! I won't tolerate that. There are too many people on the street who really need it."

When I signed him, Bill was at work on *Where the Buffalo Roam*, a film about the gonzo journalist Hunter S. Thompson, who'd written *Fear and Loathing in Las Vegas*. After one of my late planes to New York, I headed to the Sherry-Netherland and downed two Sleep-eze and a shot of scotch. I hadn't slept the night before and was soon dead to the world . . . until I popped awake, heart pounding. The clock said 2:00 a.m., and my room door was open. Two men were silhouetted in the doorway.

A jauntily familiar voice said, "How you doing?" With charm and a twenty-dollar bill, Bill had cajoled an attendant into unlocking my door. "Let's go," he said. I pulled on my clothes and staggered out with Bill and his companion, a thin, balding guy in his midforties. I registered his pasty complexion and the sunglasses, which not many people wore indoors in the middle of the night—Hunter S. Thompson. As we barhopped through lower Manhattan, Hunter downed a prodigious amount of booze, expounded on contemporary literature and deer hunting, and proved to be bleakly funny, unremittingly intense, and deeply insane. The sun was up when I stumbled back to my hotel to shower, shave, and prep for my 8:00 a.m. meeting.

By then I'd grown close to Ivan Reitman. When Ivan pitched *Cheech and Chong Join the Army* to Paramount, Michael Eisner couldn't stop gushing. Ivan believed he had a guarantee to produce and direct three movies. But in a subsequent meeting, I realized that Michael was reneging. He indicated that Barry Diller had overruled him. The studio was now offering a basic development deal with no obligation beyond Ivan's first film.

Ivan at my side, I marched from Michael's office to a pay phone in the Paramount parking lot and called Frank Price at Columbia. A former television writer, Frank was the rare studio chief who could read a screenplay and give you surgical notes to improve it. He brought TV-style discipline to the movie business, giving you a prompt yes or no. Within five minutes, Frank and I had a verbal agreement to make Ivan's army project. He also wanted the two other films (one of which became *Ghostbusters*) as soon as we had working concepts. It was a much better deal for Ivan. I immediately told Michael that I'd sold the movie to Columbia—we had to demonstrate that if you broke a promise to a CAA client, there would be consequences. For once, Eisner didn't try to guilt me; he was just rueful that Barry had countermanded him.

I brought in Bill Murray to replace Cheech and Chong, and Ivan overhauled the script to reflect his new star; Bill's humor didn't need marijuana to lift off. Most of the rewriting was done by Harold Ramis, the Second City alumnus who cowrote *Meatballs* and who would co-star opposite Murray in *Stripes*. Lead actors usually arrive on the set a week or two early to rehearse, but Bill was incommunicado until the night before shooting. (He once disappeared entirely for two weeks before calling me collect from the Taj Mahal.) When Bill finally surfaced, he had yet to meet with Ivan, and I'd lay odds he had not read the script. But he showed up in makeup the first morning, on time and ready to go. If Bill liked the concept and had faith in the director, he didn't sweat the details. He ad-libbed his way through *Stripes*, and the loose, shaggy movie became a hilarious hit.

Frank Price had an exceptional feel for how a vague concept could become a commercial film. Another example was the *Karate Kid* franchise. I had met the producer, Jerry Weintraub, when I was twenty-three and he was booking Elvis Presley concerts through William Morris. Jerry's original idea was inspired by a feel-good local TV story about an eleven-year-old black belt, the youngest in the country. Jerry signed the kid to a management contract and asked me to help build a movie around him. Frank liked the idea but thought the boy was too

Me at age three, already on the phone.

Cub Scout pack 131 on the set of RKO Studios (I'm second from right).

Judy and me and our dog Sunny
in front of our house in the Valley the year we started CAA.

The CAA partners with our mentor Phil Weltman at Scandia restaurant.
LEFT TO RIGHT: Mike Rosenfeld, Ron Meyer, Bill Haber, Phil Weltman,
me, Rowland Perkins, Marty Baum.

One of our weekly red ads that rocked the business.

The team in David Letterman's new office at CBS after we closed his deal.
LEFT TO RIGHT: me, Robert Morton, Peter Lassally,
Jay Maloney, David Letterman.

With Tom Cruise and his first wife, Mimi Rogers,
at the opening of *The Color of Money*.

With Candy and Aaron Spelling
at a dinner honoring Tony Thomompoulos, who put us together.

snowmass
Christmas '91

Judy, Eric, Chris, Kim, and me with a typical CAA Aspen lunch crowd,
including Dustin and Lisa Hoffman, Michael and Jane Eisner,
Barry and Diana Levinson, Sean and Micheline Connery, Mark and Linda Ovitz,
Ivan and Genevieve Reitman, Chevy and Jayni Chase, Michael and Shakira Caine,
Sidney and Joanna Poitier, Sly and Jennifer Stallone, and Ron and Kelly Meyer.

The Hoffman and Ovitz families at our house in Aspen.

Movie talk over lunch in Aspen.
LEFT TO RIGHT: Ivan Reitman, Steven Spielberg, Michael Eisner,
Sylvester Stallone, Mark Ovitz.

Ron Meyer and me on the set of *Baywatch*
(or, more likely, Hotel Du Cap-Eden-Roc in Antibes).

Me and my neighbor Dustin Hoffman at Broad Beach, Malibu.

Me trying to convince
Danny DeVito of
something very
important that I
no longer remember.

Me trying to convince
Bill Murray of
something very
important that I
no longer remember at
the *Ghostbusters* premiere.

Judy, Chris, Kim, and me with Earvin "Magic" Johnson at the All-Star Game.

Chris and Eric playing video games with Tom Cruise on the set of *Far and Away*.

With Nick Nolte and Barbra Streisand on the set of *A Prince of Tides*.

With Martin Scorsese on the set of *The Age of Innocence*.

Ron and me in Italy with Ray Stark's lost dick.

With Bobby De Niro and Penny Marshall
at Marty Scorsese's surprise fiftieth birthday party.

Ray Stark, Judy, Chevy Chase, Ron Meyer, and Mark Canton
at Judy's surprise fortieth birthday party

Celebrating with Jerry Seinfeld and Shoshanna Lonstein after I renegotiated
Jerry's *Seinfeld* deal with NBC, getting him a record price per episode.
When I left CAA shortly thereafter, Jerry said, "I got the last Ovitz."

Sydney Pollack making dinner for my surprise fortieth birthday party.
Yes, we had a lot of surprise birthday parties.

A rare shot in which Robin Williams appears to be playing my straight man.

young. Make the hero a few years older, he said, and we could add a credible love interest and broaden our audience. The studio cast Ralph Macchio, then twenty-two and neither well known nor physically imposing. But as high school senior Daniel LaRusso, Ralph became a bubble-gum sensation. The studio made two sequels.

Stand by Me was a dark little drama about four adolescent boys (including a then-unknown River Phoenix) who discover a body outside their small town. Norman Lear financed the movie for director Rob Reiner, his protégé since *All in the Family*, and they came to us after several distributors turned them down. Unless their luck changed, Norman was out $10 million and nobody would see Rob's film.

Though we'd had nothing to do with *Stand by Me*, we felt an obligation to Rob, a CAA client, and to Norman, a good friend. We set up screenings with every studio and distributor who hadn't passed. To keep tabs, we had a mailroom trainee deliver the print and stay to see if people actually watched. His reports were revealing. The head of distribution at Fox told me he "didn't much care" for the movie—having slept through two thirds of it. Another executive gabbed on the phone throughout the eighty-nine-minute run time.

As a last resort, I called Frank Price. "I know you want these big films from us," I said, "and I make sure you get first crack at them. Now we've got a situation with one of our most important clients and a movie we think is terrific. You have the leverage to get it out there. We need this as a straight-out favor." I pressured Frank until it strained our relationship, and he finally gave in; Columbia paid Norman his investment and approved a decent ad budget. *Stand by Me* went on to gross more than $50 million. It was nominated for best adapted screenplay at the Oscars and best picture and best director at the Golden Globes. *Variety* ran a fascinating story on why everyone else had passed. The Fox executive said he was dying to buy this marvelous movie but could not come to terms with CAA. The phone yakker said the same.

If you believe what you read in the trades, the studios never make a mistake.

WE WERE LUCKY TO WORK IN A GOLDEN AGE OF COMMER-
cial film. People went to the local multiplex three times a month, piracy had yet to explode, and cable was in its infancy. With so many
movies being made, and with our increasing share of the talent, by the
early 1980s, CAA was poised for an explosive run. We'd grown big
enough to package movies with multiple clients, a common practice in
television but an uncommon one in film. Top agents like Charlie Feld-
man and Lew Wasserman (and later Sam Cohn) had sometimes paired
a filmmaker with an actor and then checked whether a studio had
something for them. But CAA was the first to orchestrate the entire
development process. We took an idea (a yet-to-be-published bestseller,
a magazine article, a news story), turned it into a script, and shoe-
horned as many artists into the project as we could. The primary difference with assembling a television show was that we didn't take a
packaging fee for films we put together, just our usual commission on
our clients' fees.

In the beginning we had been story-centric of necessity. Now we
had our share of big names, but the material still came first. We sat
with writers and floated screenplay concepts for our directors and actors, mixing and matching as we went. We had a story department, a
book department, and a development department, and we held a packaging meeting every week to stay in touch with the studios' needs.
Rather than pitch a ten-page treatment to a studio for $10,000, we'd
tell our writers to flesh out a first draft. Then we'd attach a name director and one or more actors and sell the option for $250,000. *Nothing*
went out unattached. If the movie got made, the writer earned $1 mil-
lion for a few extra weeks' work. Meanwhile, our CAA directors were
talking several times a day with their multiple CAA agents, which led
organically to the directors' casting more CAA actors. The process fattened our commissions and spared the studios the headaches and expense of development—though they had to pay a premium for our
talent. It was win-win-win.

The power of team agenting really struck me—"Hey, this is

working!"—on *The Natural*, which came out in 1984. Amy Grossman, one of our literary agents, represented the screenwriter Roger Towne (Robert's brother), who'd written a script based on Bernard Malamud's novel about a hard-luck baseball player. Amy had heard in one of our staff meetings that we were looking for a movie for Barry Levinson and Robert Redford to do together, so she brought the script to Rosalie Swedlin, who was on Barry's team. Then they both brought it to me on a Friday, when anyone could pitch me a project. After reading it over the weekend, I immediately called Barry, had him read it, and then flew with him to Sundance to meet Bob. Within a week both of them had committed to the film.

The Natural also clarified the advantages of packaging a movie *completely*, down to the character actors. We already represented Bob and Barry, and Bob's costar, Glenn Close, signed with us during the filming, but putting our clients Wilford Brimley and Kim Basinger into the film made it a different proposition. If we filled a movie with clients, and only with clients, we could present the whole package to the studios, giving them nothing to do except say yes or no. This was a crucial shift: we began to view studios as little more than banks and distribution vehicles—they'd finance the movies and get them into the theater, but the films were essentially *ours*. On *Rain Man*, a total CAA package, we even designed the marketing campaign. By shaping the package to win approval from the studio, we saved our clients from rejection anxiety. And by gathering all the conflicts we could under our roof, we'd have more knowledge, more leverage to get better salaries, and we could sort out whether a movie would be better suited to Ivan Reitman or Harold Ramis, to Stanley Kubrick or Steven Spielberg. Most of our actor conflicts were resolved simply and swiftly: by the director's preference.

In a humming economy, with cash there for the asking, what could stand in our way? Our numbers guru, Sandy Climan, refined our profit projections until they rivaled those of the studios. No longer were we bargaining blind. Our data allowed us to dictate our clients' fees, including shares of first-dollar gross no one else was getting. When Mike

Nichols came to us from ICM, his salary increased overnight from $2 million to $5 million. He called to ask how I'd done it, and I said, "That is our minimum price for a superstar director, and you are a superstar director." We needed all our top directors to have that leverage, so we needed to have all the top directors. The buyers' historical advantage was their stranglehold on distribution. At our apex, CAA matched this advantage with a near monopoly on keystone talent: we had forty-five of the fifty top-grossing directors. So we could tell the studios to take our package or leave it. They didn't pass too often.

I wouldn't claim that our movies were *better* than the studios' other films. We had our share of what we called shitburgers. In 1984, we packaged Sly Stallone and Dolly Parton in *Rhinestone*. In 1991, I put together a glittering package of Dustin Hoffman, Robin Williams, Julia Roberts, and Steven Spielberg in *Hook*, a sequel to the Peter Pan story. Great on paper; dead on-screen. Even our best packages, *Rain Man* and *Tootsie* and *Gandhi* and *Ghostbusters*, weren't high art—but they were artfully made and deeply satisfying. Our clients Ismail Merchant and James Ivory were born to do small, tasteful projects such as *A Room with a View*, but that model didn't work for bigger-budget films. We weren't in a creative medium; we were in a commercially creative medium. Our clients often glossed over that distinction so they could view themselves as artists rather than as talent for hire, but I always kept it in mind.

Yet I would argue that our movies were just as good as the ones the studios assembled, and that we were a more efficient assembly mechanism. We were better controllers than the studios, I believe, because we put the artists first. We had to, because in an important sense we had more at stake on every package than the studio did. All it could lose on a bomb was a lot of money, but we could lose a group of top clients. So we worked hard to assemble packages geared to clients' talents and needs, and to build their careers thoughtfully. In case after case, people's work took a leap after signing with us, from Barry Levinson to Sydney Pollack to Paul Newman. Our assault on the status quo made us less than popular with execs. But we worked for our clients. When a studio head reeled from sticker shock, we'd say, "We'd love you to have the movie, and it fits beautifully into your summer schedule. But it's up to you."

The first big step in our transformation into a quasi studio came on a romantic comedy about an actor who pretends to be a woman to land a role in a soap opera. The Michael Dorsey/Dorothy Michaels character reminded Dustin Hoffman of his youth, when he and Gene Hackman and Robert Duvall roomed together in New York and none of them could find work. He pulled in his friend Murray Schisgal to revise the script, and he gave the movie a new title, *Tootsie*—his mother's nickname for Dustin when he was small.

When *Tootsie* reached us, it had a second-tier filmmaker attached whom we didn't think was right. Frank Price at Columbia suggested Hal Ashby, the gifted auteur who'd made *Shampoo* and *Coming Home* and *Being There*. Hal's latest movie had tanked, and I'd heard stories of drug use and strange behavior. Still, I admired his work and took an open mind to our meeting at a Westwood hotel. Hal was on his game, and it looked like we had our director. But after the valet returned with my car and I was preparing to get in and roll away with Dustin and his wife, Lisa, Hal strolled over. He opened a gold cigarette case, grinning rakishly, and offered it to Dustin. Inside were a dozen joints.

I could feel Lisa bristling. "No, thank you," Dustin said.

As we pulled out, I said, "I love Hal Ashby, but we can't have him do this movie." The Hoffmans agreed. Why put Dustin, who had worked hard to leave pot behind him, in harm's way on a location shoot?

I called Frank Price. "As much as we'd like to, we can't go ahead with Hal."

"Why?"

"There's too much ancillary risk between him and Dustin." This was how we talked at such moments, using euphemisms the studio could pass on to the talent's representatives if necessary. Frank, well versed in such diplomacy, simply said, "Got it."

Columbia hired Larry Gelbart, who'd produced *M*A*S*H* for TV, for another rewrite. He came up with some superb bits, but we still needed a strong director to splice the various drafts together and find the deeper story. All we really had was a guy in a dress; we didn't know what he was doing or why he was doing it. I told Dustin, "You're going to think I'm crazy because the guy I'm suggesting has never done a comedy. He barely smiles. He is as heavy-handed a human being as you'll meet."

"Great pitch," Dustin said. "So?"

"I'm thinking you need someone who understands story and can get you a script. I'm thinking you need Sydney Pollack." I waited for Dustin to calm down. "At least you should meet him." So what if our director had no sense of humor? Dustin had plenty for both of them. Rock-steady Sydney could keep *Tootsie*'s radical concept from plunging off the rails.

And so it began. I invited Sydney to a dinner at my home and sat him next to Dustin. For three hours they talked about *Tootsie* like no one else was in the room. Sydney called the next morning and said, "There's no way I'm gonna do this."

"I understand completely," I said. "I didn't expect you to, though I think you should." Then I told him, "Look, put in five days on the script with Larry Gelbart and Dustin. They need your help." Sydney loved solving other people's problems. He agreed to hole up at Dustin's place in Malibu. Sparks flew. The script got better. At week's end he called and said, "I'm still passing."

Judy and I took Sydney and his wife, Claire Griswold, to dinner at the Palm. We ordered wine and the mandatory oversized steaks and lobsters. We ordered more wine. Sydney kept saying he wouldn't do *Tootsie* under any conditions. But I knew that Claire was remodeling their home in Pacific Palisades. I said to her, "Tell me what you need."

"Well," she said, "I need a brick driveway, but it's expensive."

"You got it. What else?"

"Let me see. . . . We're building a guesthouse. And we could use a new screening room."

"Done!" I said. It was my left-handed way of telling Sydney, *Just do this and take the money.* "So, Syd," I said as we left, "I guess we're going to do the movie."

And he said, "Why is that?"

"Because Claire needs a driveway."

"I'll think about it." I knew I had him.

Michael Dorsey was so hardheaded that nobody could work with him; playing a tomato in a commercial, he refused to follow the script and sit down because it was "illogical." To my chagrin, art imitated life. I flew to New York sixteen times in a twenty-two-week shoot because Sydney and Dustin could not get along. In Sydney's suite at the Sherry-Netherland, I found the floor piled with pages from seven writers and our director struggling to weave them into a coherent script. He was on a high-protein Pritikin diet, and as he made rib sauce in his kitchenette, he vented at me. Dustin was driving him berserk, he said, and it was all my fault. The shoot was so tense he'd had an arrhythmia. I doubted Sydney would quit the film, but I began to wonder if he'd survive it.

Yet the two were well matched. Dustin needed a manual transmission for his high-revving engine, someone who could say, *Stop here, this is good, no further.* When he worked with less assured directors, he rolled over them. Where Dustin was impetuous and demonstrative, Sydney was conservative and self-contained. Where Dustin was a born improviser, Sydney liked to follow the script. The film worked so well *because* the two principals fought every step of the way.

To help *Tootsie* at the box office, I asked Bill Murray, fresh off *Stripes*, to take a part that wasn't in the screenplay. For maximum impact, I suggested we write him in for a cameo with no billing and let him pop up on-screen. Eager to stretch into "serious" acting, Bill was all for it. Dustin said, "Let him be my roommate," which led to Bill's role as Jeff Slater, the wacko playwright. He would get a tiny fee and one point of the gross, which worked out great for him.

I escorted Bill to the vacant TV studio the producers had rented in Hell's Kitchen. They were shooting the reveal scene, where Dorothy Michaels shows herself to be a man. As we entered the glassed-in control booth, Dustin was shouting, "Well, I ain't fuckin' Robert Redford!" The veins in Sydney's neck bulged as he erupted in turn. Bill and I began backing out of the booth, but Dustin angled over and blocked the door: no exit.

I broke in. "Guys, I'd like you to meet Bill Murray."

Sydney glowered at Dustin. "Are you done?"

And Dustin said, "Well, no, I'm not!"

As we escaped, Bill murmured, "I don't know if this is such a good idea."

A day or two later, though, Bill was back in blue jeans and an old T-shirt. He said hello to Sydney and glanced around the stylish apartment where he and Dustin would ad-lib their scene. Then he began pulling books off the shelves, scratching up the furniture, piling the sink with dishes, and ripping up couch cushions with a butcher's knife. The crew froze—as I'd learned at Universal, no one messed with a hot set—as Bill tore the place apart.

When Dustin walked in, Bill turned to him and said, "Now *this* looks like the kind of rat hole you and I would live in." He was right. We needed more chaos, Bill's forte.

———————

WHEN THE TWENTY OF US WHO'D PUT THE FILM TOGETHER screened it at Warner, I almost burst with pride at how extraordinarily well it had turned out. We were all silent afterward, but I could feel Sydney and Dustin kvelling, too. They weren't speaking to each other—the war had continued in editing—but we all knew it was going to be a monster hit. I was so high on adrenaline I felt like I'd drunk ten espressos. That feeling of success, of having assembled the elements of a huge puzzle that everyone was going to love, was so exhilarating that it felt scary. It felt like a life killer. Because all I wanted, right then, was another hit of that feeling, and I knew I'd do anything to get it.

We had our industry screening at Grauman's Chinese Theatre, in front of the same people who'd told me I was a fool to give a comedy to

Sydney. I knew we were home free early on, when Bill Murray appeared and the audience hooted with glee. *Tootsie* was paced so well that each scene drew the hoped-for response. We were playing to a very tough crowd—industry audiences always want everyone else's films to fail—but they loved Bill and Dustin and Charles Durning and Jessica Lange and Teri Garr. They loved the romance between Dustin and Jessica and the reveal scene. And they *really* loved the screaming matches between Michael Dorsey and his long-suffering CAA agent, George Fields, played by none other than Sydney Pollack.

Though Sydney had cut his teeth as a TV actor in *Playhouse 90* and *Ben Casey*, he'd never had a real part in a film. He wanted Dabney Coleman for George Fields, but Dustin insisted that Sydney was the only one who could do it justice. Sydney demurred. Dustin sent him roses. Sydney kept resisting and Dustin kept badgering until I intervened and brought him around. He was drained by the double duty, but he made a pitch-perfect agent. He played it so grimly, so "Oh, my God, what now?," that you couldn't help grinning when you saw him. Sydney's on-screen fights with Dustin had an easy rhythm born of long, hard practice.

Tootsie grossed $177 million in North America, the second biggest movie of the year behind *E.T.* Sydney had his blockbuster. The film was nominated for ten Academy Awards, including Best Picture, Best Director, and Best Actor, a rare haul for a comedy (though it ran into an Oscar buzz saw called *Gandhi*—another CAA package—and only Jessica Lange won, for Best Supporting Actress). The film is now a comedy classic. Dustin was big enough to forgive my rash no-fee promise and pay us our full commission. And I even talked Columbia into picking up the tab for Claire Pollack's driveway.

OUR SUCCESS WITH BILL MURRAY LAUNCHED CAA IN COMedy, particularly among Bill's friends on *Saturday Night Live*. We signed Albert Brooks and Harold Ramis and, later, Chevy Chase. I met with Bernie Brillstein and said, "Let us handle your people on their film deals and we'll make you the executive producer. We'll get you paid and we'll put the movies together." Bernie agreed, as most people would when offered lots of money for no work. I started with Danny Aykroyd, the most normal abnormal guy I ever met, a strait-laced family man who was crazy about science fiction and the occult. A talented writer, he'd conceived the hit musical comedy *The Blues Brothers* for himself and his best friend, John Belushi.

John was a force of nature, a throwback to the physical comedians Sid Caesar and Art Carney. As Bluto Blutarsky in *Animal House*, he got laughs just by raising a bushy eyebrow. Offscreen, John might throw you to the floor and lick your face like a dog, or brood for an hour and never open his mouth. Wary around strangers, and inconsolably angry deep down, like most comedians, he could also be generous and big-hearted. He was a child in a man's body. His friends were fiercely protective of him. A number of dinners into my courtship of John, Danny finally gave me a wink and said, "John wants you to come to The Bar," an abandoned tavern they'd turned into a clubhouse. The three of us drove into deserted, pregentrified Tribeca, where they un-locked a battered door and switched on the lights. It looked like they'd decorated the place by setting off a hand grenade. The proud propri-etors broke out a bottle of scotch and poured it into grimy shot glasses. I knew it was an honor to be invited in, and hoped the scotch would act as a disinfectant.

By the time we signed Chevy Chase, CAA dominated the comedy world. Chevy was a solid leading man; John was reinventing slapstick; Danny was the idea guy; and Bill had extraordinary range. And comic actors were ageless: Jack Benny, Milton Berle, Bob Hope, and George Burns had all worked into their eighties. I envisioned a long run of hilarious and highly profitable movies.

We put together a comedy for Danny and John called *Neighbors*. Everyone liked the concept, based on a Thomas Berger novel—an up-tight suburban man driven crazy by his antic new neighbor—and the Larry Gelbart script. As we were in production, Universal released *Continental Divide*, a bland romantic comedy Bernie had engineered before John signed with us. John's fans, expecting the madman who yelled "Cheeseburger, cheeseburger, cheeseburger!," didn't buy him as Spencer Tracy. *Continental Divide* bombed.

Then Columbia chose a director for *Neighbors*, John Avildsen, who was best known for the melodramatic *Rocky*. Being new to movies, I wasn't confident enough to fight it. Avildsen cast against type by making John the quiet neighbor and Danny the obnoxious, dangerous one, and then shot a slow, dark film. When *Neighbors* previewed, less than 2 percent of the test audience rated it "excellent," and it, too, went on to tank.

But John was only thirty-three. The French director Louis Malle, who'd just made *Atlantic City* and *My Dinner with Andre*, wanted to cast him as a con man and Danny as an FBI agent in a takeoff on the Abscam bribery scandal. Then there was *Sweet Deception*, about a winemaker who, if he took even a sip of his product, went sideways drunk. I thought it could work for John if the script got a little edgier and a lot more physical.

Universal and Warner Bros. passed on *Sweet Deception*, but Michael Eisner was intrigued. We did barely any business at Paramount because Michael and his crew were so frugal. But they were adept at taking artists off of a flop or two and restoring them to their sweet spots—in John's case, commercial comedy. At a pitch meeting with John and Michael and Jeffrey Katzenberg, Eisner's number two, we framed the concept as "crazy winemaker," a grown-up Bluto Blutarsky, and the executives were sold. John would get $1.85 million, a record fee for him. John knew he needed help with the screenplay and brought in Don Novello, the writer-actor who played Father Guido Sarducci on *Saturday Night Live*. All systems go.

I had no real sense of John's drug problem until he popped up at my office in late February 1982. He brought along a reworked script, maps of the fictional vineyard, sketches for set designs, and a new title, *Noble Rot*. John was talking a mile a minute. We'd been out on the town together, but I'd never seen him like that. He was so shaky that two guys from our mailroom had to help him to his limo.

I called Bernie Brillstein, John's father figure. "John's having some problems, but he's working on them," Bernie said. I called Dan Aykroyd, who told me, "John's got some issues and needs help." I was troubled—who was going to get him that help?—but not frantically concerned. I hadn't had much exposure to the eighties drug culture and the damage it could do. You'd see cocaine around the movie business, but Hollywood was tame compared to New York's brazen club scene. And at CAA we were mostly boring workaholics who went home at night.

THE NEW SCRIPT FOR *NOBLE ROT* WAS A MESS. JOHN HAD strong comedy ideas but no sense of structure, and Don Novello was a sketch artist. After Eisner flatly told him the script wasn't working, John called me, in a state. I was more tactful. "You've done some really good things here, but there are issues with it playing as a film," I said. "Your character needs to be more sympathetic, and we need a cast-iron structural foundation to show off your talents." John hung up on me.

Eisner still wanted Belushi. He proposed shifting our pay-or-play contract (which locked in John's full fee regardless of whether the movie got made) to a project based on *The Joy of Sex*, the bestselling manual. Bernie was all for it. I thought the idea was banal and urged our team to turn up something better.

On March 4, the day before we had another big meeting at Paramount at 11:00 a.m., John dropped by CAA. He was jittering around, but he seemed under control. As he'd dismissed his limo, I offered to give him a ride to Morton's, where he was having dinner. As we drove, John chattered about his latest changes to *Noble Rot*. He said he'd come over to CAA the next morning to "warm up" before we went to the studio— a good sign, I thought. We reached Morton's and John opened the door. "Do you have any money?" he asked, sweetly. "I'm out of cash." I gave him a hundred bucks, and he thanked me. "See you tomorrow!"

When he hadn't appeared at our offices at 10:15 the next morning,

I called Bernie. John wasn't punctual, but I knew Eisner's schedule was tight. Bernie sent his brother-in-law to check John's bungalow at the Chateau Marmont. We were already late for Eisner when Bernie called back.

"John's dead," he said.

"Come on."

"No, John's dead." He was too shattered to say more. It would turn out that John's brain had basically exploded from a speedball, a mix of cocaine and heroin.

I called Eisner: "Michael, I have to cancel the meeting." I was barely keeping it together.

Before I could explain, he began yelling, "How could you do this to me? Everyone's here and ready and excited—what the hell is going on?"

"John's dead."

"Another of your agent tricks! Can't you come up with something better than that?"

At any other time his obtuseness would have been funny. "Michael, I'm serious," I said. I was able to maintain an even tone only because I knew he didn't really give a shit. "John's dead. I don't know how it happened, but there won't be any meeting."

IN 1979, TONY THOMOPOULOS, THE HEAD OF ABC ENTER-tainment, called to say that Aaron Spelling, the prolific producer of such ABC hits as *Charlie's Angels* and *The Love Boat*, was unhappy with William Morris, and that he'd told Aaron to consider CAA. (Tony took a risk for us—the other agencies would have killed him if they knew what he'd done—and when he was later forced out at ABC we got him a job at United Artists. He, in turn, took *Rain Man* from us when no one else wanted it, which worked out beautifully for everyone.) Ron and I met with Aaron and persuaded him to sign. That was huge for us, as we'd make more money from Spelling in the eighties and nineties than from any other client. We needed Bill Haber to head up the account, but he declared, "I refuse to handle Aaron Spelling!" He had half a dozen reasons why, dating back to obscure ancient history at William Morris. After Ron and I beat on Bill—*What happened to one for all and all for one?*—he grudgingly agreed to sit down with Aaron. In the meeting, he was charming and brilliant, a font of ideas, and soon he and Aaron were best friends. Quintessential Bill!

Yet representing Spelling, an eight-hundred-pound gorilla who needed feeding, wasn't always easy. We had a client named Lauren Shuler, a young producer who had put together a comedy called *Mr. Mom* from a script by John Hughes, another CAA client. Michael Keaton would play a husband who has to learn to do housework after he's fired and his wife takes a job—which, in the early eighties, seemed like a hilarious concept. We'd made it a CAA package, folding in co-star Teri Garr and director Stan Dragoti. Then Aaron Spelling heard about the project and demanded in. Ron was handling Keaton (who wanted Aaron in the mix) and Bill was handling Spelling, so they "should" have been the ones to talk to Lauren. But neither of them wanted the tough conversation.

So I convened the talent and their agents and hit Lauren with what I called the hard truth. I said, "Lauren, we want to bring Aaron in as an executive producer. He can help with the financing, and he can make a heavy contribution to the script, and the truth is the film will fall apart without him, so we have little or no choice." Knowing that her percentage on the back end would get cut almost in half, she resisted, politely, but I set up a meeting for her and Aaron. I still have the note I wrote to remind myself to convince "ASP" (Aaron Spelling Productions) that he "must do it with a smile." He smiled, he was charming, he made shrewd story points, and he took it for granted that it was a done deal. Seeing where the power lay, Lauren graciously agreed to the arrangement we'd forced on her.

I've thought about that conversation at least weekly since then, sometimes daily. Would the film have fallen apart without Aaron? No. Did he add to the film creatively? Yes, somewhat. And would it have caused CAA problems with our biggest TV client if we'd told him to butt out? Yes. By Hollywood logic the transaction shouldn't haunt me: Lauren Shuler got a great credit as the producer of a hit movie, and she made money on it. She went on to marry our director Dick Donner, and to become the powerful producer of such films as *Free Willy*, *X-Men*, and *Deadpool*. We've seen each other many times in the decades since then—and never spoken about *Mr. Mom*. Maybe it didn't bother her for long. But it was her very agreeableness about the whole extortionate process that stays with me. She was *too* nice. That meant that people had to be nice to us now; that we had the power to compel. No part of the transaction I muscled through was about helping talented people pursue or refine their vision. It was zero Creative Artists and 100 percent Agency.

I had become everything I detested in the sixties when I was a bleeding-heart liberal at UCLA—the very symbol of the establishment. I had become The Man.

WHEN JOHN BELUSHI DIED, IT TOOK THE HEART OUT OF our whole comedy gang. Danny was the hardest hit. He was more than John's best friend; he was his straight man and alter ego. For a while he couldn't even laugh, much less write. Then one day, some months later, Danny called and said, "What do you think about Bill Murray and me running around New York *Saturday Night Live*–style, chasing ghosts?" He'd come up with the idea earlier to revive John's career. Now he'd reconfigured it for himself and Bill and Harold Ramis. Ivan Reitman would direct.

Columbia snapped up the project. But the pre- and postproduction buzz on *Ghostbusters* was grim; people just couldn't envision *SNL* mixed with the supernatural. At the film's premiere, a black-tie fund-raiser for St. John's Hospital that Judy and I chaired, no one laughed. I already knew that you can't judge a comedy played to a tiny audience; now I learned that you can't show a comedy to a charity audience, as they're usually there under duress. On his way out of the theater, Warner Bros. CEO Bob Daly patted me on the back consolingly: "Don't worry— you'll get 'em next time."

He'd now deny that under oath. Because under Ivan's direction, the ghostbusters struck audiences as enjoyably workaday and nonchalant, like funny plumbers. Danny and Harold saved the best lines for Bill, who nailed them. In the mayor's-office scene, Bill predicts that the demon times to come will feature "Human sacrifice, dogs and cats living together, mass hysteria!"—unless, he tells the mayor with his most winning smile, he gives the ghostbusters free rein. And in that case, "Lenny . . ."—his picture-this expression is priceless—"*you* will have saved the lives of millions of registered voters." Danny's unselfish feeling for Bill was touching. I think he hoped Bill would be his new partner, but Bill was too mercurial to team with anyone for long. He made a bunch of great movies with Harold Ramis, culminating with *Groundhog Day*—and then Bill didn't speak to Harold for years. They reconciled only shortly before Harold's death.

Ghostbusters became the second-biggest film of the year, grossing more than $295 million worldwide, behind only *Beverly Hills Cop*. As our clients collectively got 30 percent of the gross, CAA got 3 percent of the gross; over the years, as TV and VHS revenues came in, we'd make more than $30 million from that film alone. The town had already taken notice that we got the new studio TriStar off to a flying start by teeing up its first two films: the fully packaged *The Natural*, and *Places in the Heart*, with our clients Sally Field and director Bob Benton. (It didn't hurt that TriStar was run by my old lawyer friend Gary Hendler, or that Hendler installed our client Sydney Pollack as the studio's "creative consultant." Favors come back around.) But *Ghostbusters* gave us real leverage. Early on, we'd always let the studio or network make the first offer—we didn't want to negotiate against ourselves, starting lower than they were willing to go. But by 1988 or so, we had so much clout that we were setting the price. We weren't negotiating anymore, we were just telling Warner Bros., say, "I have a package of A, B, and C, and it costs

X—you have twenty-four hours." If Warner Bros. hesitated, I'd already have Fox lined up, having told them, "You're in second position, but I have to know now: Do you want it?"

After *Ghostbusters* hit, I got a call from the agent who represented an actor named David Margulies, who'd played the mayor. The agent, a nice-enough-sounding guy at a small agency, wondered ingenuously if the studio, or my clients, would want to share a little of their largesse with David, given how much there was to go around. In my position, most agents would have said, "Hey, valid question, let me look into it," then called back the next day, after *not* looking into it, to say, "Gee, sorry, I couldn't get to first base with Columbia, or with the business managers for our clients here." Taking that extra beat would have placated Margulies's agent. Ron Meyer would have kept the guy on the phone for an hour and made a friend for life. But for the sake of brevity I'd adopted the habit of acting like a principal myself, like the guy who decided rather than the guy who pressured other people into deciding. So I said, "You've got to be kidding. Your client played his part, and he got paid! He was part of an ensemble beneath the stars—and no one in the world knows his name." I was brutal to this guy, who was in the same position I'd been in a few years earlier. I replayed the call in my head afterward, because it gnawed at me, and I had two takeaways. One, I was in danger of becoming a total asshole. And two, I really did want to be a principal someday.

In the early eighties, I'd begun collecting relationships. For instance, I reached out to Felix Rohatyn, the Lazard Frères banker who had almost single-handedly rescued New York City from bankruptcy in the seventies, and who was on the board of MCA and had Lew Wasserman's ear. I called and asked to see him, saying, "I need no more than ten minutes of your time." On my next trip to New York, I went to his office, shook hands, and placed my watch on his desk. Then I said, "I'd love to talk to you about how you saved New York, and also how you advise Lew—to learn from the Dean. And I'd love to be helpful to you in L.A. in any way I can." All to get him talking and to show that I knew what he'd done and that I admired it and wanted to learn from it. After ten minutes, I said, "Thanks so much," and stood to pick up my watch. Felix—and everyone else I used this stratagem on—asked me to sit back down. In this way I got to know Herb Allen, the head of Allen & Co., and Bob Greenhill at Morgan Stanley, and I'd always drop in on them when I was in New York—as well as on Mort Janklow and fifteen other book agents, a number of figures in the art world, and our clients Meryl Streep, Mike Nichols, Al Pacino, Sidney Lumet, Bob De Niro, and Marty Scorsese.

The relationships outside entertainment would prove useful to CAA in the plans I was beginning to develop. They'd be our bridges to a wider world.

THERE WERE PLANS FOR AN ANIMATED TV SPIN-OFF OF *Ghostbusters*, and the studio was pressing for a sequel—lots of deals to discuss. After *Meatballs* and *Stripes*, Murray's third straight winner had made him a box-office star. Because Danny was so business-oriented, I set up a "board of directors" for the *Ghostbusters* property, encompassing the two of us as well as Ivan, Harold, Bill, and Ray Kurtzman, CAA's top lawyer. I sent a memo to them all in April of 1987, hand delivered in a big envelope, addressing them as the "Board of Directors," and telling them that we had to talk about a sequel, and that "it is imperative that we do this meeting in L.A. in the next two weeks." It wasn't really imperative, but they needed guidance and structure, so I created a protocol and a sense of urgency. We kept minutes and followed *Robert's Rules* as well as you could with a pack of anarchists.

By our second board meeting, Coca-Cola, which owned Columbia, had replaced Frank Price as chairman with David Puttnam, an upper-crust Englishman. Puttnam viewed American studio executives as over-spending morons, American directors as clumsy rubes, and American actors as ill-behaved adolescents. After he denounced Bill Murray on the front page of *Variety* as a "taker" and the poster child for Hollywood selfishness, I immediately counterattacked to defend my client (as well as CAA, as Puttnam was taking an indirect shot at our pricing). I called Dick Gallop, Columbia's CEO, and Herb Allen, the most influential board member at Coca-Cola, and I told them Bill Murray was Columbia's biggest star and had attended every single press and PR event he was asked to do, and that Bill was the most *un*selfish man I knew. I mentioned just a few of Bill's many acts of generosity. Then I said that this attack was beyond unacceptable to me and to everyone who knew Bill, most of whom were also clients of CAA.

"What can we do to fix this?" Dick asked.

"Short of getting rid of David Puttnam, I can't think of anything," I said. "Bill is beside himself. Our response will not be direct—we have too much respect for you both to attack you in the media—but it will be consequential." Columbia owned the *Ghostbusters* franchise, but no one could stop us from sitting on it. At that second board meeting I moved that we shut all projects down—seconded, carried. Only after Puttnam was fired, after just sixteen months in the job, did Ivan and company begin making plans to return to work. That's why there was a five-year gap between the first movie and the sequel.

In the interim, Ivan Reitman led us to a new economic model. For his 1988 film *Twins*, neither Ivan nor the stars, Arnold Schwarzenegger and Danny DeVito, made a penny up front. Instead, they took healthy percentages of the gross. When the movie earned more than $200 million worldwide, it was a bonanza all around. From *Meatballs* and *Stripes* through *Dave* and *Junior*, Ivan was extraordinarily consistent in a hit-and-miss genre. And the wait for *Ghostbusters II* had only made the studio more eager: we were able to negotiate Ivan, Bill, Harold, and Danny big up-front fees and 30 percent of the gross, rising to 35 percent once the film had earned two and a half times its negative cost (the point at which the studio covered its expenses).

The movie had a blowout preview in Seattle. The approval rating was in the nineties—Columbia wouldn't ask Ivan to change a thing. On the plane back to Los Angeles, he flipped through the viewer comments that directors used as the basis for further editing or possible reshoots. They made for pleasant reading. Then he set the cards aside and said, "It's not crisp enough." He showed me a page of notes on the cuts he planned. Most directors are wedded to every frame, but Ivan wanted faster and funnier and left blood on the floor to get there. On *Ghostbusters II* he trimmed another five minutes. The film grossed $215 million around the world, and further demonstrated our thesis that when CAA called the shots, everybody made out well.

CHAPTER EIGHT

P.L.

WHEN I WAS IN COLLEGE, NO ACTOR WAS BIGGER THAN Paul Newman. He epitomized cool.

Paul always had top-shelf representation, from Lew Wasserman in the 1950s to Freddie Fields at CMA after that. The sixties and early seventies were great years for Paul: *Hud, Harper, Hombre, Cool Hand Luke, Butch Cassidy and the Sundance Kid, The Sting.* After CMA sold to Marvin Josephson in the merger that created ICM, in 1975, Paul chose to manage himself. And he struggled. *Buffalo Bill and the Indians*, an antiheroic western from Robert Altman, did poorly. *Slap Shot* was a cult phenomenon that made no money. Paul returned to Altman for *Quintet*, a total failure. A volcano disaster film called *When Time Ran Out . . .* grossed less than $4 million. A big star could withstand two straight duds, maybe three. But four was definitive. Paul's last commercial success had been *The Towering Inferno*, an ensemble piece, and by 1980 that was six years ago.

And in 1978 his only son, Scott, had died of an overdose, taking the heart out of him.

Joanne Woodward, Paul's wife of more than twenty years, had become a client when Marty Baum joined us, and she asked Mike Rosenfeld and me to meet her at Yamamoto's in Century City. I had always found her intimidating: she was polite enough, but something in her manner suggested she had judged me and found me wanting. At this meeting she wanted advice: Paul was in a funk; could we help? When I followed up a few days later at their home in the flats of Beverly Hills, I found Paul to be quiet and self-deprecating. He talked about what he wanted to do—more movies with Bob Altman, for example. Fine, I said, as long as he also did projects with mainstream appeal. *Fort Apache, The Bronx*, his current film, was a step in the right direction. (At the agency, our rule of thumb was two commercial films for every noncommercial one.) We needed to develop material for Paul rather than taking what the studios dished out, which by then was leftovers. Choosing my words carefully, I said, "I want to put together some movies that people want to see and that you can be proud of." He nodded, hopefully.

A few weeks later, he invited me to meet him for lunch in New York, where he was shooting *Fort Apache*. I took the red-eye and got in at 5:30 in the morning. After showering, shaving, and changing, I met him at a booth at the Grand Central Oyster Bar for an 11:30 lunch. Paul ordered four dozen littleneck clams and began scarfing them down. He loved eating clams, talking about clams, exploring every nook and cranny of the vast and fascinating culture of clams. I happen to hate clams. But if Paul Newman loved clams, then I loved clams. In full chameleon mode, I mimed tossing some back and then slurping up the liquor, the liquid residue in the shell—when in fact I was dumping the whole mess beneath the table. An hour later, after a good chat, we shook hands and parted. I raced to the nearest deli and got myself a nice, safe tuna salad sandwich.

The agency found Paul a script about an honorable liquor salesman and a reckless reporter—a natural for him, as he felt abused by the media, which had attacked *Fort Apache* as racist for the way it portrayed the South Bronx. I brought the script for *Absence of Malice* to Sydney Pollack. The lead character was the Italian American son of a deceased mob boss, and Sydney wanted Al Pacino (who was not yet with CAA) to star, but I pushed Paul to the head of the line. A great actor like Paul didn't need fixing; he just needed a change of pace away from Bob Altman, who had made only one real hit, toward Sydney Pollack, a commercial director with credibility who would push Paul as an actor.

To encourage Paul and Sydney to commit, I persuaded them to spend a day revising the screenplay, which had been developed by Paul's pal George Roy Hill, who'd directed him in *Butch Cassidy* and *The Sting*. Sydney went over to Paul's house in Beverly Hills and they spent more than ten hours at Paul's dining room table making changes on every page—with me sitting there, soaking up an extraordinary education in how a star and a director can home in on their mutual sweet spot. They transformed the main character so he was less Italian and more American, and built in the ironclad three-act structure that Sydney demanded. Sydney excelled at development and Paul was a director in his own right—but the meeting was as much about chemistry as structure. They hit it off right away: two guys' guys who loved small planes and fast cars. My only contribution that day was to suggest Sally Field, a client of ours who'd been my high school classmate, as the journalist who investigates—and of course falls for—Paul's character.

A few weeks later, Sydney chartered a Learjet 35 to fly us to Sears Point in northern California, where Paul was test-driving his race cars. On the way home, after a few drinks, Paul yelled to the young pilot, "Hey, can you do a barrel roll?" Which was illegal for a charter and appalling to me.

"You know better, Paul," Sydney said sternly. "He can't do that." Returning to my beer, I missed Sydney giving the pilot a wink. The next thing I knew, I was staring at my upside-down glass. As Paul and Sydney cracked up, I visualized the headline: PAUL NEWMAN, SYDNEY POLLACK AND FRIEND DEAD IN CRASH.

Sydney screened his rough cut of *Absence of Malice* at Columbia for a group of us, including his stars and some Columbia execs. Rough cuts are tricky: without final music, or the buoying response from a full theater, it's tough to envisage how the finished film will play. Famously, after Spielberg screened his rough cut of *Jaws* for Universal, the studio said it wouldn't release it. As we walked out, Sydney glanced anxiously at me, and I glanced anxiously at Paul. Paul glanced at Joanne. And Joanne said, "Paul looked as bored doing the movie as I was watching it."

My heart began to race. I said, "Joanne, I'm sorry you feel that way. Let's run it in front of real people and see where we are." She had a gift for making me feel crass and stupid, just another agent. Paul and I were by now drinking beer and hitting racetracks together, and I felt he was beginning to see me as a kind of surrogate for his lost son. For a personable movie star, Paul had almost no close friends, yet I was becoming one. But the only person he really trusted was Joanne. If the first project we'd put together for him turned out to be a turkey, we could lose my flagship director and my new big star in one go. That evening I called Paul and said, "I have to tell you, I love Joanne, but I thought you were awfully good in that movie. I don't agree with her."

"Well, I don't know if I do, either," he said, thoughtfully. "I know she's critical of my work. But we're open with each other, and I trust her." Joanne's scorn kept me churning until the film was released—to strong reviews. Paul's understated performance earned him an Oscar nod, and we could feel his fortunes turning.

Our next Newman package was *The Verdict*, the David Mamet courtroom thriller directed by Sidney Lumet. The producers had originally cast Robert Redford as the alcoholic ambulance chaser Frank Galvin. But Bob, always sensitive about his image, balked at playing a loser who punches a woman in the face. As Paul was eager to display a darker side, I slid him into the role. The film played beautifully, earning him another Oscar nomination. He was back.

REDFORD AND NEWMAN LOOKED OUT FOR EACH OTHER. Paul went to the mat for Bob on *Butch Cassidy and the Sundance Kid* when Redford was a young unknown, and Bob returned the favor on *The Sting* four years later, when he was the hot one. For fifteen years I tried to find a third buddy picture for the two of them. The closest I came was *Lethal Weapon*, but Bob hated the script.

They were fast friends but very different people. Paul was gregarious, while Bob kept the world at arm's length. Paul was punctual; Bob was always two hours late, running on Redford Standard Time. When I signed Bob, Claire Pollack, Sydney's wife, told me, "I'm going to give you some great advice. Meet Bob only in your office, and if it's in his office, call before you head over to make sure he's there."

Redford and Sydney Pollack had a complicated relationship. True friends who did magical work together, they also bickered constantly. I was once having dinner with Redford at a restaurant in Santa Monica after they had squabbled on the set of *Out of Africa*. When I told Bob that Sydney had just come in, Bob immediately made us sneak out the back.

In Utah, where Bob founded the Sundance Film Festival, and where he could eat out undisturbed, he was a totally different person. He was loose and relaxed and great fun to be around. And when he became a director, later, he saw it as a high calling and rose to its demands. Actors like Brad Pitt and Donald Sutherland all told the same story: Bob the director was easy, understanding, generous, and supportive. He held nothing back. When I visited his sets, they were happy places. The entire cast of *The Milagro Beanfield War* adored him. As a director, Bob became the person he wanted to be.

Unfortunately, most of my dealings were with Bob Redford the actor. On the first day of shooting for *The Natural*, the thirties-era baseball movie we'd packaged, I arrived at the set in Buffalo, New York, at 8:45, fifteen minutes early. Bob rolled in after 10:00. Wearing a sheepish smile, he told Barry Levinson, the director, that he'd forgotten to reset his watch after flying in from L.A. the night before. Uh-huh. When the actors were sized for their baggy period uniforms, Bob decreed that his would be tailored and tapered, historical accuracy be damned. He did look amazing in the movie. But he behaved like a dick off camera. When Glenn Close, his costar, asked whether she should sign with us, he counseled her against it: "They're too big." She signed with us anyway because, she told us, "I asked him, 'So, are you leaving?' And he said, 'No.'"

David O'Connor, who serviced Redford day to day, liked to tell people the story of how Bob called him to say that he was tired of me, and that he was going to phone me to suggest that David be his lead agent. A little while later, David's story went, I summoned David to my office and said I felt that he was ready to finally handle Bob Redford himself. Now, it's true that I liked to seem all-powerful, as if I'd foreseen and ordained everything under the sun. It was a weakness of mine, and Bob knew that. But what really happened was that I'd called Bob to say that maybe David should take him over (because Bob was such a pain in the ass). Bob had agreed. And then he'd immediately called David to pretend the shift was his idea—knowing that the resulting crossed signals would stir up strife.

He hated the constraints I put on him; hated that I insisted he read the scripts he was sent and respond quickly. The real problem was that he hated being a movie star, hated being fawned over and treated like a rare and valuable commodity. He'd once been a painter, and he would have been much happier if he'd kept doing that. Sydney Pollack told me that Bob was, at heart, deeply embarrassed by acting. All of which was entirely human and understandable. But instead of choosing another profession, he took his unhappiness out on the people around him.

He was one of our most difficult clients. But he was so talented we never once said to each other, "It's not worth it."

––––––––––––

PAUL FOLLOWED *THE VERDICT* WITH A PASSION PROJECT called *Harry & Son*, about a construction worker cut off from his two grown children. It was his way of working through his grief and guilt over his own lost son. Though he directed and starred and assembled a strong cast, he didn't have a prayer at the box office.

But I had a plan to help him, and us. Paul was always looking for tips on recent movies. When I touted Martin Scorsese's *Raging Bull*, he watched it and called me all revved up: "It's one of the best things I've ever seen!"

"You should work with Marty," I said instantly.

"What do you have in mind?"

"I don't know yet, but I'll find something. In the meantime, write him a fan letter." People still wrote letters in longhand then, and their impact was underrated. I often sent out more than a thousand letters a year, commemorating every opening of a film (I'd send along a lucky horseshoe from our gift office), award nomination, or award—and those were just the rote letters. The ones that really had an effect were the personal ones, the ardent ones, wooing and praising and letting people know: *I saw what you did and it was terrific.*

Paul said, "You're kidding."

"No, he has enormous respect for you." I wasn't sure this was true, but how could it not be? Everyone had enormous respect for Paul.

I dropped Paul's letter by Marty's office. When I saw him light up as he read it, I sensed my opportunity. I'd been an admirer of Marty's since *Mean Streets* and *Taxi Driver*. If I could bring him to CAA, he'd be a force multiplier. Every actor worth representing wanted to work with Scorsese. Like Dustin Hoffman, he'd be a reference client for us, someone who'd humanize us with the very top talent.

Marty's longtime agent, Harry Ufland, was moving into film production. To edge my way in, I had spent a lot of time sympathizing with the director over *The Last Temptation of Christ*, his embattled adaptation of the Nikos Kazantzakis novel. Marty had somehow swung a development deal with Paramount even though no one thought the project even faintly commercial. But four weeks before the shoot, a group of evangelical nuns had barraged the studio with outraged letters, and Paramount's parent company, Gulf & Western, had pulled the plug. It was devastating for Marty, who'd spent a year in preproduction and the ten years before that obsessing about the film.

Our agent Tina Nides had passed me the galleys for *The Color of Money*. It was a pool hall novel by Walter Tevis, a quasi sequel to his *The Hustler*, featuring a middle-aged Fast Eddie Felson, twenty-five years on. When we asked Paul to option the book for development, he was reluctant. Fast Eddie was one of his signature roles. What if the new film—or his performance—didn't measure up? Old-style movie stars neither did sequels nor optioned projects. So we optioned Tevis's book on spec for $75,000, a sizable sum for us at the time. Agents didn't option projects, either, but I considered it an investment in the Marty Scorsese business.

Marty read the galleys overnight and came to my house the next morning. He was sweet, tightly wound, and anxious about his future. He poured out his worries amid a torrent of creative ideas. Then we addressed his finances, which were a mess. Marty's business manager hadn't paid his taxes. Two of his last three features, *New York, New York* and *The King of Comedy*, had been inspired works that never found an audience. He was lost and needed a champion. You didn't sign Scorsese for the commissions, because he hardly cared if his movies made money. The rub was that he worked in a pricey medium. My plan was to nudge Marty toward the commercial side, alleviate his financial woes, and free him to make whatever he wanted. Marty liked my business background and my willingness to take a stand with the studios. He became emotional when I said I'd revive *Last Temptation*. I had no idea how to do it, but I promised to find a way. By the end of the conversation it was understood that we'd represent him.

Though sequels didn't appeal to Marty, either, directors my age worshipped the same stars I did. Marty wanted to work with Paul Newman as much as Paul wanted to work with Marty. When I put them together, they seemed an odd couple, the rugged sportsman and the jittery aesthete. But they were opposites who attracted.

We brought in Richard Price, one of CAA's top novelists, to help Marty with the script for *The Color of Money*. They found a middle ground between their darker take on Eddie Felson and Paul's sense of what his fans could accept. But even with Marty and Paul attached, it was no easy task to find the film a home. We thought we had a deal at Fox until the studio chief lost his job. The same thing happened at Columbia. Others passed because the movie sounded esoteric. It wasn't a high concept you could pitch in two sentences, and you couldn't actually market it as a sequel, because no one under thirty-five remembered *The Hustler*.

As a last resort I asked Marty to write to Jeffrey Katzenberg at Disney's Touchstone Pictures, part of the Disney empire that my old friend Michael Eisner had been appointed to run in 1984. Disney never bought from CAA. They didn't believe in paying up for our packages, which Eisner claimed were essentially vehicles for extorting the studios. Furthermore, Touchstone was best known for family comedies such as *Splash*. But at that moment Disney was hungry for a star vehicle, particularly one that could be made—at their insistence—for only $14 million. For Marty it would mark a return to guerrilla filmmaking in the tradition of *Mean Streets*, only with stars. Given his habit of going over budget, he needed to prove that he could deliver a big picture with big names for a price.

To bridge the movie to younger viewers, we had someone special in mind for Fast Eddie's protégé: Tom Cruise. CAA was known for poaching clients after someone else had developed them. We had no compunction about it. Given the time and effort we invested in our artists, it made sense to sign people with track records, or at least with demonstrated potential. But we nurtured some young talents from the beginning. Barry Levinson was one case. Another was Tom, who came to us on the recommendation of Stanley Jaffe, the producer of a low-budget drama from Columbia called *Taps*. Stanley called Paula Wagner, who covered Columbia and was one of our best young agents, and said, "You guys should take a look at some footage of this kid. He's incredible." (Like most people who made this sort of recommendation, Stanley was looking to ingratiate himself and to get a chit, so that the next time a project came up we'd think of him.) Tom was eighteen, and he'd gotten just $50,000 for *Taps*. Knowing Stanley's superb taste, we checked out the dailies, and Paula became completely convinced that Tom was the next big thing.

We set up a meeting, and Tom was polite and engaging, all "Yes, sir," and "No, sir." He must have been nervous, but he didn't let us see it. He wasn't one of those great-looking guys trying movies on a lark. He was rigorously trained, and you could tell that he was not only passionate about his craft but fanatically determined to become a star. "I *want* guidance," he said. When I said, "It's going to take guts for you to put your complete faith in us," he nodded vigorously and said, "Yes, sir!" That was another one of my vaccinations—I was inoculating him against all the other agents who'd take a run at Tom once he got going.

We jotted down the names of the directors and actors we thought he should work with: Ridley Scott, Tony Scott, Roger Donaldson, Barry Levinson, Marty Scorsese, Oliver Stone, Rob Reiner, Stanley Kubrick, Paul Newman, Dustin Hoffman, and Robert De Niro. Then we promised that he'd work with every one of them if he came to CAA—by then, we could make such promises. And Tom did work with them all, eventually, except for Robert De Niro. Every time he crossed a name off his list, he'd call to remind us that he was getting closer to zeroing it out, and to thank us.

Now it was two years later, after we'd helped Tom break out in *Risky Business*. He was about to blow up in *Top Gun*, so his days in supporting roles were numbered, but we knew he'd leap at a chance to work with Paul and Marty—two of the names on his list, in one film.

Heading into the shoot, Marty came by my office with a loosely bound script. Scrawls of semilegible notes crowded the margins. The left-hand pages were filled with hand-drawn production setups, three or four per page, with stick figures for the actors. Marty precut his movies in his head, down to the camera placements. There were close to four hundred setups, and he knew exactly what he wanted in each one. Any director would put the camera directly over the pool table during a tense match, but only Marty thought to put the camera in the upper corner of the room, to show the tension from a 45-degree angle. I admired that shot enormously, knowing that I wouldn't have thought of it in a million years.

The shoot was an on-budget dream. On set in Chicago, I saw what made Marty unique. He came fastidiously prepared, but he'd change his plan on the fly if someone had a better idea. He gave his actors maximum latitude but reined them in if they went too far. As Paul said, "He watched me like a hawk." Every movie star has a screen persona: Paul's was the devil-may-care rogue who lit up the screen in *Cool Hand Luke* and *Butch Cassidy* and *The Sting*. The audience expected it and the studios made mounds of money from it. But Marty never let his actors coast through their comfort zones. In *The Color of Money*, Paul became someone else—brooding, touchy, corrupt, yet somehow principled underneath. Years later Marty did the same thing with Leo DiCaprio in *Gangs of New York*, which is why Leo has worked with him on four more films. It's a Scorsese specialty, grinding movie stars into artists.

I BORE JOANNE WOODWARD'S SLAM OF *ABSENCE OF MALICE* in the pit of my stomach for years. I worried about *The Color of Money* until Paul swept the early honors for Best Actor. By that point, having lost all six times he'd been nominated for an Oscar, he'd sworn off attending the Academy Awards. He'd been embarrassed to have to settle for an honorary Academy Award the year before (via satellite hookup from Chicago, he'd said, "I'm especially grateful this award didn't come wrapped as a gift certificate to Forest Lawn"). Yet Scorsese's prestige helped, and voters finally seemed ready to reward Paul for being so good for so long. When his name was read out—and his good friend Robert Wise, the director of *The Sound of Music*, went up to accept the statue for him—I rushed to the lobby to call Paul at home. "So I'm one for seven," he said. "Better than a kick in the ass." But he sounded pleased and proud.

I was, too. But I privately worried that Paul hadn't yet signed for a new film. Ron and I had a rule that if one of our actors was nominated for an Academy Award, we had to sign him to a film fast, because experience had shown us that if he won, suddenly he would feel all sorts of new pressures and expectations, and no project would look quite right. And, indeed, it would take three years before Paul next appeared on-screen, in the unmemorable *Fat Man and Little Boy*.

The year after his win, Paul was asked to present the award for Best Actress, as was traditional. Knowing that I disliked the ceremonies as much as he did, he agreed to present on the condition that I go with him. I took him to Spago for Swifty Lazar's Oscar party. Forty-five minutes before he was scheduled to go on, we stepped into a limo and shot down to the Dorothy Chandler Pavilion. We stepped through the back door and into the greenroom, where Paul was pleasant to everyone if not exactly sociable. He walked onstage, did his thing, walked off, and said, "Let's get out of here." We went back to Spago for the rest of the evening.

Once our relationship became more than agent-client, I joined his friends in calling him P.L., for Paul Leonard, his first and middle names. We'd race go-karts together at a slick track in Los Angeles, or I'd meet him near his home in Connecticut for beers. One night he drove me back to New York in his souped-up Volkswagen—a white-knuckle ride because P.L. was aiming to beat his personal best of around fifty minutes.

He was always on me to take more vacations. When I told him about an upcoming family trip to the Kahala Hilton in Honolulu, he said, "It's about time." One balmy afternoon I went to our suite there and turned the key. The door swung a few inches and stopped dead. I craned my neck to look inside and saw cases of Budweiser stacked to within two feet of the ceiling. Having scored Paul a Bud promotion deal to help finance his race-car team, I knew the guilty party even before I saw the note: "Relax, P.L."

Unlike most film royalty, Paul understood the trap of stardom. He told me, "You know, I've been a movie star for a long time. And no matter how hard I try to tell myself I'm just a normal person, I keep hearing how wonderful I am. It gets to the point that you start to think you're something you aren't."

He enjoyed the occasional reality check, such as the one that happened when we met to watch Marty edit *The Color of Money* at his New York office. A middle-aged woman stepped into the elevator, gasped, and told Paul how much she adored him in *The Towering Inferno*.

He flashed his grin. Then she started calling him "Steve," as in Mc-Queen, his costar. Paul played along, but I could see he was about to crack up. When we reached the woman's floor, she said, "Steve, it was so great to meet you."

And Paul said, "You should take a better look at my costar, Paul Newman. He's a fine actor and a really good guy."

THE COLOR OF MONEY GROSSED MORE THAN $52 MILLION IN North America, nearly four times its cost. Disney was ecstatic; Marty was giddy with relief. "You know, Marty," I told him, "you could actually get paid for being a film director." Before we signed him, his price was in the low six figures and he'd never shared in his movies' profits; we would raise his price to $3 million. (By the mideighties, we'd made all our directors three-million-dollar guys—there weren't any women directing then, unfortunately—and five years after that we established our top directors as five-million-dollar guys.)

It was CAA's first hit package with an auteur director and two big dramatic stars. However, I still owed Marty *The Last Temptation of Christ*, an unpackageable disaster in the making. It was tainted by incendiary content, weak curb appeal, and the stigma of Paramount's rejection. Yet Marty wanted to make *Last Temptation*, he told me, "more than anything in the world." I shared neither his passion for it nor his belief in it, but just getting the thing released would make CAA look heroic.

Marty offered to cut the budget in half, to $7 million, by switching locations from Israel to nonunion Morocco, paying the actors at scale, and slicing his own fee to the bone. Before going to the studios, we created a financial model for the film, a matrix of expenses and revenue streams (domestic, foreign, video rentals, network, and cable TV prebuys). We projected *Last Temptation*'s worst-case loss—with zero ticket sales—at $20 million. A medium scenario cut the loss to $5 million.

So who owed us a seven- or eight-figure favor? Twenty million dollars sounds like a hugely expensive good turn, but it's all relative. Two years earlier, MCA/Universal had fattened on two CAA packages, *Back to the Future* (a $350 million worldwide gross on a $19 million budget) and *Out of Africa* ($266 million worldwide). It was time for them to reciprocate by taking *Last Temptation*. Because Marty needed a permanent office where he could cut his films by hand with his longtime editor, Thelma Schoonmaker, we'd ask for that, too—all of Marty's needs in one big favor package.

In October 1986, MCA named the entertainment lawyer Tom Pollock chairman of Universal Pictures. It seemed like a radical choice, but Tom was a discerning reader who knew film economics cold. He'd made creative deals as early as 1973, when he negotiated George Lucas 20 percent of the net in lieu of a salary on *American Graffiti*. Tom's handiwork financed the *Star Wars* trilogy and made Lucas's career. We loved Tom because he made development deals with a number of CAA directors, including Ivan Reitman, Bob Zemeckis, John Hughes, and Ron Howard and his producer Brian Grazer. Universal under Pollock was a throwback to the old Hollywood system, only with an agency in the middle. I knew the studio would work to land a talent magnet like Marty, just as we had; an enterprising guy like Tom could be persuaded to see *Last Temptation* as a loss leader.

I pitched the movie as part of a broader deal for Universal to get first look at all Scorsese projects. Later I wove in the other goodies we wanted—the overhead to run Marty's company out of the MCA building in New York, edit facilities, and a screening room. Tom hedged his bet on *Last Temptation* by bringing in a financial partner, Garth Drabinsky's Cineplex Odeon chain, but he agreed to bankroll the film even before Marty signed to do something more commercial.

There was one last loose end. Because *Last Temptation* had gone into turnaround at Paramount so late in development, more than the usual sum had been sunk into sets, costumes, props, and location costs. Frank Mancuso, Paramount's studio chief, had already waived $3 million. When I asked Frank to forgive the last million on the books, as Universal was demanding, he let it go without a fight, remembering that he'd just had *Top Gun* from us. The business in those days was more like a family. Everybody bitched and groused, but we all took care of each other, confident that the favors would come back around.

The smooth sailing lasted five minutes. Then Universal resisted Marty's choice of Brooklyn-accented Harvey Keitel to play Judas. Harvey was one of Marty's boys, along with De Niro and Joe Pesci, and we told Tom Pollock it was futile to fight it. They had to let Marty do the movie his way. *Last Temptation* was more than a movie for him; it was a profession of his faith, and he doubted he could do it justice. I called him every other day in Morocco as he battled the worst angst of his life.

By the time the eight-week shoot wrapped on Christmas Day, the religious right was beginning to rumble. I wasn't troubled by the small, early protests, or by the offer from Campus Crusade for Christ to buy the film for $10 million so it could burn all the existing prints. Maybe the local news would pick up the story, I thought. (I was a sucker for free publicity.) I was naive. In July 1988, a few weeks before it opened, *Last Temptation* landed on the cover of both *Time* and *Newsweek* as a brewing controversy. A so-called reverend denounced "these Jewish producers with a lot of money." There was fundamentalist street theater outside Lew Wasserman's home in Beverly Hills, with the guy playing Lew planting his foot on Christ's back. As the FBI logged assassination threats from the Aryan Nation, a bloody pig was delivered to Wasserman's number two, Sid Sheinberg.

Lew didn't scare, but Sid came unglued. He called me from his home one morning and said, "Mr. Ovitz?" We were friendly—I was friendly with anyone who ran a studio—but he always addressed me and everyone else as "Mister." A gangly, six-foot-two exec with a pock-marked face, Sid was Lew's longtime whipping boy. Knowing he was never going to get Lew's job, he took his rage out on others. But there was a purity to his animus. When he compared me to an agent for Mossad, the Israeli intelligence agency, I took it as a compliment.

"Yes, Sid?"

"Mr. Ovitz, I would like to inform you that a hundred people with placards are marching up and down in front of my driveway, and my family is quite frightened."

"Sid, I'm really sorry. Should I come over?"

"You won't be able to get through."

It was my job to anticipate public opinion, and I felt I'd failed. I worried about Marty's future. Could I even have cost Tom his job at Universal?

As the frenzy peaked, Marty asked me to join him for the film's debut at the Venice Film Festival. Judy and I left early for a weekend on the French Riviera. Our first morning there, out for exercise on a racing bike, I headed down a steep road by the hotel. A mile or so out, a sports car cut me off, and I swerved onto the cobblestone shoulder. My bike jackknifed and I flew into a low rock wall.

I woke up in the hospital in the worst pain of my life. I had four broken ribs, a punctured lung, and a concussion. Hours later, in a medication fog, I called Marty to tell him Venice was out. He was nice about it, though he kept saying, "Are you sure you can't come? It doesn't sound so bad."

The rest was anticlimax. The movie ran largely without incident and grossed about $8 million. Universal broke even. Jon Avnet, Marty's producer on the film, later credited me with having "made that film happen," and said I "willed it into existence." I appreciated the salute. But the best thing about *Last Temptation* was the day it was behind me.

———————

ONCE MARTY JOINED US, I KNEW THAT BOB DE NIRO, who'd starred in five of Scorsese's films, was sure to follow.

I had never bought the Agenting 101 rule that representing two similar stars is a conflict of interest. Instead, I preached, "No conflict, no interest"—we wanted all the conflicts because that gave us leverage; the studios couldn't threaten us that they'd opt for a similar piece of talent at another agency. Three guys competed for roles in Bob's category of the character-actor leading man: Bob, our client Dustin

Hoffman, and Al Pacino. Dusty's fee in the mideighties was $6.5 million, about the same as the other two—and as Newman and Redford, pure leading men who played versions of themselves. The only actors who earned more—a lot more—were the action heroes, Stallone and Schwarzenegger.

Also, and crucially, the conflicts were always more apparent than actual. I canvassed our files, and there wasn't one film Dustin had done in the previous five years, from *Kramer vs. Kramer* to *Tootsie*, that De Niro would have wanted. After making the same point to Dusty, who agreed with the logic—that he wouldn't have wanted to be in *Raging Bull* or *The King of Comedy*—I pitched De Niro on the idea that it was better for everyone if CAA cornered the market on leading men. All the best parts would flow into our agency and be parceled out to whoever fit them best. In the unlikely event that two stars wanted the same role, we'd talk it out. (It never happened.)

Using the same logic, we would sign Al Pacino a few years later (after he stopped asking us to cut our commission to 5 percent). All three stars thrived at CAA at the peak of their popularity, and we got better deals for all of them. Though the studios always tried to pretend that if De Niro didn't take a role at their price they'd go to Hoffman, we already knew Hoffman didn't want it. We even packaged Pacino and De Niro as dual leads in *Heat*, a big hit by the brilliant director Michael Mann.

Of all our clients, De Niro was the most private, even more private than Redford. He didn't act like a movie star and couldn't stand being treated like one. (Meryl Streep, who lived down the street from us in Brentwood and who took her turn in the school carpool, was the same way.) Shortly after Bob signed, I met with him at Matsuhisa, the yet-to-be-discovered Japanese place on La Cienega. It was a hole-in-the-wall, but Nobu Matsuhisa's cooking was fantastic. And he'd converted a studio above an adjoining garage into a private room you could secretly enter from the parking lot—perfect for Bob.

As Nobu's gracious wife served us one knockout dish after the next, Bob kept glancing over my shoulder or through the small window. A four-star meal in Los Angeles in total anonymity—he couldn't believe it. He went back three times in ten days before I joined him again and introduced him to Nobu. They had a passionate conversation about food and New York, beginning a friendship that would later lead them to become partners in Nobu's restaurant in Tribeca, Bob's home neighborhood.

Like Paul Newman, Bob had made some iffy choices as an actor for hire. I explained to him how our clients controlled their own projects, and Bill Haber suggested putting the producer Jane Rosenthal into his life. Jane worked with us to develop strong roles for Bob in *The Untouchables*, *Midnight Run*, *Awakenings,* and *Backdraft*. She and Bob cofounded the Tribeca Film Center, and still work together today.

It's hard to believe, now, that some of the films we assembled at CAA ever got made. *Goodfellas*, adapted by Marty Scorsese and our client Nick Pileggi from Nick's book, was a textbook risky idea. It was the true story of Henry Hill, a cocaine-addicted stool pigeon who beats his wife and pistol-whips an unarmed man even as his mobster friends casually shoot people in the head. On paper, at least, Henry was wildly unsympathetic. Nine years before *The Sopranos* aired, we had no way of telling if the movie could be commercial.

After Universal passed, I brought it to Bob Daly and Terry Semel at Warner Bros. They wanted the running time held to 140 minutes, max, and they approved a lean $25 million budget. Our first clash came over casting. Warner was a star-driven studio, and *Goodfellas*'s lone star was De Niro in a supporting role. Ray Liotta had wowed De Niro in *Something Wild*, and Marty decided that Ray should be Henry Hill. The studio tossed out bigger names, from Tom Cruise to Eddie Murphy (a classically terrible studio idea that would have led to some extremely acrobatic story changes), and it was prepared to raise the budget to accommodate a star. But Marty thought too much star power would overwhelm the story. So I held firm, which made De Niro appreciate how I'd fight for what he wanted.

Today it's impossible to imagine anyone but Ray Liotta as Henry Hill. He had to play four distinct characters: the wannabe wise guy, the mature wise guy, the out-of-control addict wise guy, and the schnook in the Witness Protection Program. *Goodfellas* inspired the performance of his life.

———————

I'D READ ALL THE GREAT BOOKS ON HOLLYWOOD'S HIS-tory and seen every Oscar-winning film going back to 1929. But I didn't *get* movies until I started watching them with Marty in the late eighties, when he rented a one-bedroom apartment in my building in Manhattan on West Fifty-seventh Street. After getting in from L.A. at one in the morning, I'd drop my bags at my place, rap on Marty's door, grab a plate of food, and sit in front of whatever was playing that night on his projector. Marty was a walking film encyclopedia, and the fare ranged from Michelangelo Antonioni to obscure Czech and Polish directors from before World War II. He adored the work of Michael Powell, the husband of his editor, Thelma Schoonmaker, and screened *The Red Shoes* over and over. There was nothing better than walking into a dark room with a projector flickering, showing an old movie I'd never heard of but that might one day influence Marty's own work. That dark room became one of the few places, in my increasingly busy life, where I felt at home.

My schooling continued on the set of *Goodfellas*, where Marty let me shadow him. I learned the importance of detail and how planning and inspiration could coexist. I took a master class in the film's soundtrack, one of the best scores anywhere, ever. When Henry Hill runs from the narcs to Harry Nilsson's "Jump Into the Fire," Marty used no dialogue. Music was all he needed to propel the action.

Warner's main concern was the film's graphic violence. When we screened Marty's 175-minute rough cut for the execs, two scenes particularly troubled Bob Daly. The first occurred right after the opening credits, when you could hear Joe Pesci's character's kitchen knife carving through a hog-tied gangster. The second came when Pesci shoots and kills Spider, the young man waiting on the wise guys at their poker game. (Spider was played by Michael Imperioli, who went on to star as

Christopher in *The Sopranos*.) Marty thought the action was funny and revealing, but Warner Bros. found it gratuitous.

I moved like Henry Kissinger between studio and client. After half the audience fled a *Goodfellas* test screening in Burbank, it was touch and go. Fearing the film might be canceled, I appealed to Marty to modify the stabbing, saying it really was too much, and also to cut some time so *Goodfellas* could play twice a night and have a chance at earning out. Passionate as Marty was, he was open to a good argument. He shortened *Goodfellas* to 145 minutes and made the first scene crisper and less gory. In return, I backed Marty in his determination to keep Spider's death intact. That scene exemplified his characteristic tone of savagely funny realism; to tamper with it would have been like telling Degas he couldn't use blue.

The Warner Bros. executives were half an hour late for the next preview in suburban Orange County, and the audience was fidgeting before the lights went down. There were Pesci and De Niro butchering the hapless gangster—but no audio! The lights came back up and after a delay, the projectionist tried to sync picture and sound—and failed again. Marty was going nuts. No picture could get a fair screening after a long delay and two false starts. I hustled him across the street to a coffee shop. Bob Daly and Terry Semel followed. Seconds before they caught up, I whispered into my assistant Jay Moloney's ear. I heard Bob and Terry out as they pleaded for another try, and at last I said, "Okay, go ahead. But we won't participate." Marty shook his head violently, feeling betrayed. I led him to my car for the drive back to Los Angeles.

He said, "Aren't we going in for the screening?"

"Nope."

"Why not?"

At that instant my car phone rang. I put it on speaker, and heard a frantic Warner's executive wanting to know where the print was: they couldn't find it anywhere. Marty looked horrified. I said, "Oh, no! I can't imagine what happened!" After I hung up, I explained to Marty that I'd told Jay Moloney to secure the film canisters and drop them in my trunk. Marty burst out laughing and could not stop.

The next preview was glitch-free. *Goodfellas* came out that fall to near-unanimous acclaim and went on to earn six Oscar nominations.

FOR MONTHS IN 1989 I PUSHED MARTY TO COMMIT TO *CAPE Fear*, a remake of a noirish film from 1962 about a psychopathic ex-con named Max Cady (played by Robert Mitchum) out for revenge. It was commercial, it would fulfill Marty's deal with Universal, and I knew he'd nail it. "It's a remake," he kept saying. "I don't do remakes."

That's what he'd said about sequels. It was an edict I knew I could work around. But there was a further problem with *Cape Fear*: Steven Spielberg, not Marty, controlled the rights. At the time Steven had no agent, though I was working hard to rope him in. He'd caught wind of a script that Scorsese controlled, *Schindler's List*, and he couldn't stop thinking about it. Based on *Schindler's Ark*, a novel by Thomas Keneally, it told the story of a German industrialist who saved a thousand Jews from the Nazi gas chambers. Steven saw Schindler's story as the ideal vehicle for an accessible movie about a monstrously difficult subject.

It seemed to me that the wrong people were matched to the wrong projects. Steven needed a more culturally relevant film to broaden his profile: to get bigger he had to go smaller. So I did what I always did— I represented the client before I actually, technically, represented him.

"You know," I said to Marty, "I understand why you want to do *Schindler's List*. But you don't *need* to do it. Steven doesn't need another picture like *Cape Fear*. Why don't the two of you swap?"

Marty was unconvinced. I tried again: "Look, you can cast Bobby in the Mitchum part and have a field day." Working with De Niro always appealed to Marty. But it was never easy to talk him into or out of anything—he had to work his way through it. He was as deeply Catholic as Steven was deeply Jewish. Religion permeated his movies and he was eager to explore another faith. It would be wrenching for him to part with *Schindler's List*.

From countless nights with Marty and his 16mm projector, I knew of his passion for genre movies, from horror to obscure Asian pictures, the bloodier the better. (Years later, the Hong Kong drama *Infernal Affairs,* which he'd shown me in the eighties, would inspire his Oscar-winning *The Departed*.) "*Cape Fear* could be something you've never achieved before—a Scorsese-style film noir," I said. "You'll create a truly sinister villain!" Marty loved the dynamic in the original between the Mitchum character and the budding-but-innocent girl played by fourteen-year-old Lori Martin. He'd created a similar vibe in *Taxi Driver* between De Niro and Jodie Foster, who was thirteen at the time.

Five or six bruising conversations later, Marty was finally ready. I called Steven and said, "Marty has a terrific take on *Cape Fear*. You guys should talk."

I set a call between Steven and Marty. They'd never had a business conversation, but given their shared intrepid spirit, I wasn't surprised to hear that they had hit it off. Hesitantly, Marty joined Steven in asking me to put the switch together. Within a week they had an understanding. Steven agreed to produce *Cape Fear*, with Marty directing on a generous back-end deal, and Marty passed *Schindler's List* to Steven.

In the midst of this statecraft I took a call from another client. Stanley Kubrick said, "I hear that Marty's doing a Holocaust project."

"That's not quite true," I said. "It looks like he might be trading with Spielberg."

"Because, you know, I've got one, too." Stanley had grown up during World War II in a Jewish family in New York. He'd been thinking about making a Nazi Germany picture called *The Aryan Papers* for years; he made so few films because he treated each one like a doctoral thesis, nailing down every detail. It had stalled on his development list, until the rumors about *Schindler's List* rekindled his interest. Now he wanted me to read his first-draft screenplay and help me decide his next move.

Because Stanley didn't send scripts out, and because he hadn't flown in twenty-five years, I went to see him in the English countryside at Childwickbury Manor, his enormous house in Hertfordshire. First, a messenger came to my hotel with the *Aryan Papers* script, sat outside my door as I read it, and collected it when I was done. It was tense reading because I knew there was room for only one Holocaust film; two would dilute the box office and spark unfortunate comparisons. Soon I'd be advising a hall-of-fame artist to surrender a passion project— either one of our most venerable clients or the director we most hoped to recruit.

It was even more ticklish because the two directors formed a mutual-admiration society. Stanley vocally admired the younger director's work, and Steven felt the same way about *The Shining* and *2001: A Space Odyssey*. They had hours-long phone calls, and Steven dropped by Stanley's house whenever he went to London. But Hollywood friendships had often been wrecked by lesser conflicts.

I drove to Stanley's estate bearing bad news. *The Aryan Papers* wasn't as good—or as commercial—as *Schindler's List*. It had no complex protagonist, no Oskar Schindler, for an audience to engage with. And because Stanley took longer than Steven in development, plus forty weeks or more to shoot (roughly twice the norm), he'd be in theaters second, putting him at a major disadvantage.

We sat at the wooden picnic table in Stanley's kitchen. I told him *Aryan Papers* was too similar to *Schindler's List* and too derivative of *Sophie's Choice*, the acclaimed film from eight years earlier. "It's just not Kubrick to be unoriginal," I said. Seeing that he was still uncertain, I lowered my voice and added, "Plus, in all candor, we just killed ourselves switching scripts between Marty and Steven." I only used the help me-out-for-once card because I knew that what I wanted, in this case, was also what was right for Stanley.

"I get that," he said, gravely. The following week, he called Steven to tell him he was letting *Aryan Papers* go. His act of generosity brought the directors even closer, and they remained intimate friends until Kubrick's death in 1999. Two years later, Steven completed Stanley's unfinished *AI: Artificial Intelligence*, and dedicated it to Stanley.

Cape Fear would gross $182 million worldwide, more than three times Marty's record, and seventeen-year-old Juliette Lewis would earn an Oscar nomination for her not-so-innocent flirtation with De Niro.

Schindler's List would win seven Academy Awards, including Best Picture and Steven's first Oscar for Best Director.

Marty was happy. Steven was happy. Stanley was not unhappy.

This was extremely unusual.

———————

IT TOOK STEVEN SPIELBERG THREE YEARS AFTER HIS SWAP with Marty to finish *Schindler's List*. Universal was in no hurry to get it done: *Schindler* struck the studio's execs as a more expensive *Last Temptation of Christ 2*, a hot-button topic that would repulse moviegoers. If Steven hadn't been Universal's meal ticket—and hadn't worked on their lot, where they had to see him every day—they probably wouldn't have warily backed it in the first place.

Steven felt he had to shoot in Poland, where the events took place, but Sid Sheinberg said that was too expensive. After Steven won that round by accepting a bare-bones budget, the studio objected to his plan to film in black and white. Tom Pollock begged for color for the video market with a transfer to black and white for the theatrical release. Steven held firm. Color shoots, he said, made a transfer look pink and white. The dispute dragged on for weeks. Because Sid and Steven were like family and it hurt them to fight, I had to jump in. I said that Steven had an unambiguous vision of the Holocaust as "life without light." Black and white was essential to that vision—case closed.

Schindler's List was filmed in Krakow in the dead of the Polish winter. As I flew over to meet Steven there on other business, I began to feel jittery. I grew up with kids calling me a kike and was pummeled more than once when I fought back. But all my life I had avoided thinking about the Holocaust because it enraged me that so many Jews had been so powerless, and that the world stood by and let the atrocity happen.

I arrived in the morning for a quick tour of the sets, including the death camp exteriors thrown up outside Auschwitz-Birkenau. One hour into the liquidation of the Krakow ghetto, with stone-faced men in Nazi uniforms everywhere, I felt like I was living in 1941. Steven wanted to make the scene almost unwatchable, and he succeeded. As the Nazis raided a home and machine-gunned two Jews wedged between a mattress and a bedspring, I thought to myself, *Six million were killed, and I could have been one of them*. I felt so nauseated I almost threw up.

I spent that day in a walking stupor. As a boy, I'd asked my immigrant grandmother, "Why didn't the Jews fight back?" Now I felt that I understood. The Jews didn't fight because they couldn't move; they were terrorized into paralysis. I had the same sense of paralysis on that set.

That night I joined Steven and Kate Capshaw and his stepdaughter, Jessica, at their rented house nearby. I came with a proposal that we'd been working on for a year: an expansion of Amblin Entertainment, Steven's production company, into a full-service studio. CAA would shepherd and commission Amblin's productions for a monthly consulting fee. The potential seemed limitless—and, of course, we'd finally land Steven as a client.

Shaking off my existential dread, or at least compartmentalizing like crazy, I gave it my best pitch over dinner. I was pitching Kate as much as Steven because she was strict about family time; I always asked her permission before calling her husband after six p.m. As I spoke, I could see Kate shaking her head. She didn't want her husband toiling like Jeffrey Katzenberg, Eisner's studio chief at Disney. "That man does nothing but work," she said. "That's his whole life." My shiny idea was dead on arrival.

A year later, with Katzenberg and David Geffen, Steven founded DreamWorks SKG, the first new full-service studio in L.A. in seventy years. Kate gave it her okay because Jeffrey was one of the partners. She figured he would log the long hours while Steven just made his films. And for as long as DreamWorks lasted, that's pretty much how it worked out.

After *Schindler's List* was released, CAA gave a million dollars to the Shoah Foundation, which Steven had founded to preserve video testimonies by Holocaust survivors. It was more than our combined commissions on the film. I felt good about the donation, but my experience on the set highlighted the underlying problem with my life. Because as soon as I got back to Los Angeles, I suppressed all the feelings that being on the set of the Holocaust had stirred up in me and went right back to scorching the earth for my clients.

Yet every time I saw the film—and we previewed it a lot—the experience hit me fresh again, and I took a beat to remember how lucky I was, and to remember the fate of all those who weren't so lucky. That's what movies can do.

CHAPTER NINE

NO PRESSURE

I GREW UP IN AN ENVIRONMENT WITHOUT PAINTINGS AND sculpture. They didn't teach art at my high school, and my parents had no interest in it. The first time I saw art worth mentioning was when I drove to New York before starting at UCLA and went to the Metropolitan and the Museum of Modern Art. The sheer visual stimulation was so emotionally shocking that I felt like I was hallucinating. Art was everywhere in New York, in parks and squares and the lobbies of apartment buildings. It was only a three-day visit, but I would never be the same. In my second year in college, I enrolled in the first of many art history courses, one of those slide-show surveys that range from caveman drawings to Jackson Pollock. It was the one class I'd literally run to.

At William Morris, I began to collect young California artists such as Laddie John Dill and Chuck Arnoldi. I wasn't systematic; I bought what I liked and could afford. The next leap came after we started CAA and I began going to New York regularly. In the late 1970s, before Chris was born, I'd be in the city two or three Saturdays a month. After work I'd squeeze in a few hours at the galleries and museums, often with Judy at my side, loving what I was seeing, though for the most part I had no idea what I was looking at. Minimal art in particular left me nonplussed. (My tastes have changed; I now collect extensively in that area.) But I didn't need to understand a piece to be moved by it. Art nourished me. The Museum of Modern Art became my home away from home. I could always find something new and exciting there, even in works I'd seen a dozen times before.

Around this time I met a close friend of Bill Haber's, a TV exec named Barry Lowen who was assembling the most interesting collection of contemporary paintings and sculpture in Los Angeles. Barry was smart, curious, engaging, and involved. He was a founder of the Museum of Contemporary Art in downtown L.A. and a key supporter of the Los Angeles County Museum of Art. And he was one of the warmest guys I've ever known. Cultured and soft-spoken, he had an extraordinary eye for young artists, such as Ellsworth Kelly and Cy Twombly, who could go the distance.

We talked every other day, more about art or life than business, often over dinner at my house or his. After Barry became ill with AIDS, I stayed in touch daily to try to lift his spirits. He made me the executor of his estate and left me his vast art library, the core of my library today. Barry died in 1985 at the age of fifty. Every now and then I'll slide a book off the shelf and a slip will fall out with his name on it—a note about a picture he wanted me to look at. These visitations are poignant, but they always make me smile.

———————

MY FIRST BIG BUY, IN 1976, WAS A JASPER JOHNS GEMINI print, *Periscope I Red, Yellow, Blue*. It cost $600, and I felt trepidation as I wrote the check. Knowing that I needed guidance, Mort Janklow later set me up with his friend Arne Glimcher at the Pace Gallery. I strolled through Arne's showing room, feigning savoir faire, wide-eyed at the price tags. He said, "I have something to show you." A minute later I was staring at a Matisse. "A real bargain at seven hundred fifty thousand," he said.

The number seemed so surreal I didn't know what to say. Afterward, I called Mort in a fury: "Who the hell has seven hundred fifty thousand dollars?" Arne, I complained, was a snob who'd made me feel like a rube.

Mort chuckled and said, "Give him another try."

So I did. After Arne put in the time to guide me and help me to see the nuances of the works in front of me, I finally bought a major Brice Marden from him for $60,000. Our phone calls were a welcome break from my work, and the guy I had written off became a close friend. When we traveled to Paris with our wives, Arne showed me an artist's-eye view of the city. He expanded my collecting into different mediums and periods. After he took me to "Primitivism" at the Modern, which revealed how African masks inspired Picasso's Cubist portraits, I returned thirty times. Today a room in my house is dedicated to Picassos and African masks. I feel a little charge of strangeness—which is what Picasso does to me—every time I go in there.

My growing art collection made me feel I'd escaped the Valley at last. But escape is never painless. One day my dad came to our house in Brentwood and saw my first Picasso, which I'd bought for $100,000. He looked at it, looked at me, then looked away. Neither of us said anything.

I bought my parents a large condo, and my dad was grateful, if a little embarrassed, that I was now taking care of them. My mother was grateful in a general way, but she complained that I never spent enough time with her: she was a guilt expert. She increasingly reminded me of a demanding client, the kind you can never satisfy no matter what you do. Families always want you to stay the person they think you were.

———

A FEW YEARS LATER, I SAW MICHAEL MANN'S *LAST OF THE Mohicans*. The film overwhelmed me; it was like a 112-minute oil painting. I called Michael from my car and said I had three words for him. The first was *brilliant*. The second and third were *Albert Bierstadt*, the nineteenth-century painter of luminous landscapes of the American West.

Michael was surprised and pleased: "How did you know?" He said Bierstadt was an inspiration for him to make the movie.

I felt happy, hearing that, because it ratified an idea I'd had for some time. As I'd become more involved in the New York art scene, I'd begun to see parallels between art and fashion and movies and television—a connection among all things creative. The more deeply I understood painters and sculptors, the better I related to film artists. Art deepened my feel for writers, in particular. When one of them pitched me an idea, I had a stronger visual sense of its possibilities than before. I could *see* how it might work on the screen (or not work). I had a frame of reference for production design, even lighting and costumes. I could be a more useful part of the conversation.

My affinity for Scorsese's work came from deep in that place. If you froze Marty's films, you could mount the individual frames.

WHEN CHRIS, OUR FIRSTBORN, WAS LESS THAN A YEAR old, he got terribly sick with a systemic infection. It took awhile for the doctors to diagnose him, and Judy and I were scared to death. Chris was still struggling when we ran out of his antibiotic at our weekend home in Malibu, where no drugstores were open on Sunday. I drove at top speed to Saint John's Health Center in Santa Monica in my T-shirt and cutoff jeans and flip-flops. I rapped on the glass and told the druggist what I needed. Then I realized I'd forgotten my wallet.

"Look," I said, "here's my number, call my wife, she'll verify who I am!" I must have sounded crazed.

The man held up his hand and calmly said, "Take the scrip and bring me a check tomorrow."

The next day I returned with two checks, one for the prescription and one for a substantial donation. When I couldn't find anyone to take the second check, I called a board member listed on the hospital's brochure—Glen McDaniel, the Litton Industries general counsel. Six months later, I joined the board myself and began working with Glen on the Saint John's Health Center Foundation. With Judy in charge, we organized an annual movie premiere around big CAA packages such as *Ghostbusters* and *Out of Africa*. We raised at least $2 million each time.

As UCLA graduates, Judy and I later gravitated naturally to helping the university's medical center. It had no board at the time, just a doctors' society that raised about $65,000 a year. We assembled a board of prominent people to engineer a kickoff fund-raiser for 1,500 people at Fox. We enlisted CAA clients Chevy Chase and Crosby, Stills & Nash to entertain and raised another $2 million. I worked hard for UCLA in part because it proved extremely useful for CAA to be able to get our clients or potential clients the best medical care with one call—but even more because I believed in its mission and liked the idea of helping people, saving people.

———

BY 1985, WE HAD ABOUT SIX HUNDRED CLIENTS. WE'D gradually become a corporation, with buttoned-down execs running large fiefs of our expanding empire. I'd gotten to know Ray Kurtzman at William Morris; by the time he replaced Sam Sacks as the lawyer who headed its twenty-five-man group, he had already headed up both Columbia Pictures and the Mirisch Corporation (and produced such classics as *The Guns of Navarone* and *The Magnificent Seven*). Ray's office was next to mine, and we were friendly. He was short and soft-spoken and nondescript, but he wasn't afraid to raise his voice when someone was doing something shady or unprofessional. When our Gang of Five left to form CAA, it fell to Ray to collect the commissions we owed William Morris from preexisting contracts—a sizable sum. The awkward circumstances kept us in touch.

One day in 1978 I told him, "I can't offer anything close to what you're making, but we want you to come with us." Ray was in his forties, with three kids and a Beverly Hills mortgage. Leaving powerful William Morris for our start-up was a gutsy risk; he'd be taking a 75 percent pay cut, to $120,000, and we had no legal department other than him. But he didn't like the leadership at WMA, and he was ready for a gamble. He built our business affairs and legal departments from scratch and closed thousands of deals for us—our agency turned over more of the details of contracts to our lawyers than other agencies did, so the agents could devote their hours to developing new business— but, most important, he served as our grown-up. He was our fifties-sitcom dad who lays down the law. Ray became the conscience of the agency, a personal mentor, and a close friend. I find it quietly pleasing that his son works at CAA today.

Bob Goldman was my personal accountant before he became CAA's chief financial officer. Even quieter than Ray, he was equally professional and ego-free. He handled our real estate investments and tax matters, keeping our money safe. He and Ray helped keep CAA grounded and stable while the rest of us flung zip lines into distant treetops.

The first ten years at CAA were the best ten years of my life. And it seemed, for the first few years after that, that everything just kept getting better. By the late eighties, CAA had become a story factory. Hundreds of scripts, treatments, articles, and novels poured into our office each month. Ten full-time readers generated three- or four-page synopses for our agents, who read the most promising material in full and brought it to staff meetings for review. On Friday, any of our agents could pitch me one-on-one, so each weekend I plowed through several scripts they'd recommended. Our packages were in full swing. ICM or William Morris might package half a dozen multiclient projects a year in TV and film; we assembled thirty or more. As a rule, we loaded artists into a film until their aggregate share of the producing studio's gross totaled 20 percent to 30 percent. If the film returned $100 million to the studio, our clients earned $20 million to $30 million. Ten percent of that was a handsome payday for CAA—$3 million in 1985 is the current equivalent of more than $7 million.

We busted a gut for the money. We scrutinized the film's budget, gave notes on every rewrite, sat in on screenings, broke the news to the director if revisions were needed, then reviewed every ad for the finished picture. We trained our young agents in how to read by giving them a 1978 *Esquire* article by Aaron Latham, whom we represented, about a honky-tonk bar with a mechanical bull. The brightest of our up-and-comers could envision the article as a movie, which we'd made in 1980—the hit *Urban Cowboy*, written by Latham and director Jim Bridges and starring John Travolta and Debra Winger. We put the same inspired hard work into our television and music projects. When the *Wall Street Journal* interviewed Aaron Spelling about *Hollywood Wives*, a Jackie Collins miniseries, and other series that we'd packaged for him, he called us his extramural "creative staff."

The joke around the industry was that our agents were like the Stepford Wives: well paid, affable, driving shiny new cars, living the American Dream. They were young, on average in their early thirties: ten years younger than agents at our biggest rivals. And they were happy because it was all working—or at least as happy as agents can be. As the famous talent agent Swifty Lazar put it, "There hasn't been a phenomenon such as CAA since 1947, when Lew Wasserman and MCA dominated Hollywood. Comparing CAA to its strongest competition is like comparing Tiffany's to the A&P."

I was beginning to have personal leverage, and it was a great feeling: it was like putting your foot on the gas pedal of a Ferrari and feeling the chesty rumble. When Wolfgang Puck opened Spago on the Sunset Strip in 1982, he introduced Los Angeles to a lighter California cuisine: smoked salmon pizza, squab on peaches, goat cheese galore. Judy and I became devotees of the place. Wolfgang made such great food, was such a charmer, and had such a disarming accent that I thought he deserved a larger audience. So in 1986 I took the president of ABC Entertainment, Lew Erlicht, to dinner at Spago with his wife and Judy. I called Wolfgang beforehand and told him to cook the meal of his life, and to pay particular attention to Lew. The food was excellent, Wolfgang was witty and engaging, and Lew personally polished off at least two of the three bottles of carefully chosen red wine that Wolfgang sent out.

When Lew was good and hammered, I said to him, "Listen, you've got Julia Child doing cooking segments on *Good Morning America*. She's great, but why not give Wolfgang a trial of three appearances so you can bring in some younger, hipper viewers? As you can see, he's a natural. If he does well, he'd be a great regular contributor." Lew said: "You write it up and I'll sign the contract." At that point he would have agreed to pretty much anything. "Great!" I said. I pulled out a pen, drew up my plan on a napkin, and had Lew sign it.

He called the next day to thank me for dinner, and after some chitchat I asked when Wolfgang could expect to go on the show. Lew said, "What are you talking about?" He had no memory of that part of the evening. I said, "I'll send the contract over." I had a kid from the mailroom drive to ABC's offices in Century City. He was immediately ushered into Lew's office. The kid opened his sports jacket and there, safety-pinned to his shirt, was the napkin Lew had signed.

"Give me that," Lew said, reaching for it.

"I'm sorry," the kid said, closing his jacket and backing away. "Mr. Ovitz told me to let you view the contract you signed, and then return it to him."

Lew wasn't too happy about it, but Wolfgang got his shot on air. The day before he went on, I sent around a memo telling everyone in the agency to have their relatives call ABC's switchboard the following morning, after Wolfgang's appearance, to say how much they loved the new chef. Switchboard calls were the networks' way of measuring heat in the mideighties, an early version of Twitter followers. ABC was blown away. I never pulled that trick again; it's something you can only do once. But it was all to help a genuine talent who would have made it as a TV personality on his own—just more slowly. And ABC could hardly complain that I'd pulled a fast one, as Wolfgang remains a regular on *Good Morning America* to this day.

With my growing leverage it became increasingly easier for me to help our artists expand their footprints into related fields. I knew that Steve Ross at Warner Bros. wanted to build an empire in which the right artist could excel in every facet of the business. Now we found ourselves representing just such an artist: Madonna. After discussing her future with her manager, Freddy DeMann, and her lawyer, Allen Grubman, I told Steve that we had a client who could simultaneously showcase her talent and his company. "She's doing huge business on your record label," I said. "She's big in personal appearances. She was really good in *Desperately Seeking Susan* for Orion. She wants to write a book—and you own an imprint. Why don't you and I figure out how to cover all the things she can do?"

Steve was game, so Freddy and Allen and I went to work. First we had to enlist Time Warner's division chiefs, who had considerable autonomy. Madonna was Warner Music's hit machine, and Mo Ostin, the label's president, didn't want her distracted. Somehow we cajoled him into a meeting in New York. The toughest sell was Bob Daly, who didn't need Madonna in his movies. But he agreed to come, too. So did Larry Kirshbaum, who ran Warner Books.

Sometimes stardom happens by accident. You're Peter Frampton and everybody starts buying your live album just because. You sell sixteen million units, then you fade away. But Madonna was no fluke. I met her when she was nineteen and Freddy DeMann brought her to our Century City offices. She took the whole meeting with her head on the table, like a bored teenager—but she absorbed every word. She called me "Mr. Ovitz," then and later, seeing me as a suit-wearing grown-up. Yet of all of CAA's clients, she was the best at expanding her brand. Despite her extreme persona, she was disciplined, focused, and cultured.

When we met with Steve and his chieftains, Madonna sat at the circular table and studied a lengthy outline she'd written in fountain pen. As we got started, one of Allen Grubman's partners spilled his water glass all over Madonna's notes, rendering them illegible. Though obviously upset, she composed herself and spoke off the cuff. She talked about movie development and TV production, and how they could play off her music and vice versa. She pitched a sex book. She pitched every aspect of her brand working for Steve's empire. He was so impressed that we signed an unprecedented omnibus deal. Some of Madonna's ideas worked out great—her sex book, with its metallic cover, sold half a million copies in one week—but she never made it as an actress. No one can do everything perfectly.

I WAS NOW ABLE TO PUT EXECUTIVES IN PLACE AT THE STU-
dios and then sell our projects to them, controlling both supply and
demand. By 1984, after Michael Eisner wasn't chosen to succeed Barry
Diller at Paramount, he knew he had no future there. Fortunately, another studio needed new leadership. Disney was hurting in film and
TV and hurting even worse in merchandising. Its overseas business
was next to nonexistent. CEO Ron Miller, Walt Disney's son-in-law,
left for the day at two o'clock. Michael and his running mate, Frank
Wells, campaigned for the job with every board member they could
find. But they had no entrée to Sam Williams, the state bar chairman
who headed Disney's search committee. Sam practiced at a downtown
L.A. law firm whose senior partner, Seth Hufstedler, was my personal
attorney. In those days the Los Angeles business community was split
between downtown and West L.A., and one had little to do with the
other. The lead contender to replace Ron Miller, Dennis Stanfill, was
a downtown favorite. He looked like a shoo-in.

At the eleventh hour I set up a secret rendezvous in Orange County
so Frank and Michael could meet with Sam Williams. They wowed
him. Later I prepped Michael for his first meeting with Sid Bass, the
art-collecting oilman who was about to become Disney's largest shareholder. To keep Michael from coming off as a one-dimensional entertainment guy, I briefed him on every painting in Bass's home. Disney
offered Wells the top spot as chairman and CEO, with Eisner as president. Michael told Frank he wouldn't serve as his number two, and the
jobs were flipped.

Boy, do I wish Frank had told Michael to take a hike at that
point—it would have saved me a world of hurt later. But Frank was too
nice, too conflict averse. And, he told me later, he didn't think he was
as creatively qualified as Michael. If he'd taken the top job, Eisner
would have walked, and then Frank would have had to go find someone else he liked who had a knack for story. It wasn't easy to find someone who could read a script as shrewdly as a spreadsheet: there were

only a handful besides Eisner, including David Geffen, Barry Diller, Terry Semel, Bob Daly, and Frank Price.

Over the next ten years, Michael turned Disney around and made it a real power, with crucial support from Frank and from his studio head, Jeffrey Katzenberg. CAA was perfectly positioned to profit from the relationship. But we never did much business with Disney—they just wouldn't pay market price.

MY TECHNIQUE AND CONFIDENCE HAD BECOME SUCH THAT I felt that if I could get in a room with a client, any client, I could sign him or her. My record was pretty good. James L. Brooks simply refused to leave ICM, though I busted my ass trying. I had to unsign Arnold Schwarzenegger, after signing him, because Sly Stallone felt threatened and blew up at Ron (Sly was one of the few who didn't buy our "No conflicts, no interest" theory). But Arnold came over later. And I couldn't land Mel Gibson because he wanted to pay just 5 percent in commissions. But that was about it.

Every actor, writer, or director believes he or she is responsible for his or her own success. All I did was sell that belief back to them. "Look, you're going to make it with or without us," I'd say. "But we can keep you at the top, because we see every project first, we develop for you, we represent every important studio executive—so we can match you with the perfect projects. And we take care of all your other personal needs so you can focus on your work. Going with us is just like taking out career insurance." A lot of agents preyed on people's anxiety and desperation, pitching themselves as a golden ticket. "You can't make it without me!" To me, that went against the grain of human nature.

If a potential client was reluctant, I'd say, "You should take all the time you need. No pressure." And by "no pressure," I meant, "No pressure until the next time I'm in touch, which may be in an hour." I tried to avoid coming across as a nudge, while making myself ubiquitous and inexorable. The smarter clients could see what I was doing, see how it worked, but it worked nonetheless because everyone wants to be wanted. And the realization that your would-be agent has a plan to handle whatever may be coming, and that he can execute it, is reassuring. I signed Kevin Costner, in 1989, in part by convincing him that he needed to take $3 million for directing and starring in his passion project, *Dances with Wolves*. He wanted to take just a million, to keep the costs down so it could get made. I told him he had to trust me, and that he'd understand why later. So he took the $3 million, and when the production ran out of money, as I knew it would—first-time directors on big projects always run out of money—he was able to draw on the extra salary to finish shooting. I'd gotten him the insurance he needed to finish his dream film.

Creating a zone of calm, in a chronically overexcited world, proved disarming. Whenever disputes arose with a studio, and I had to deal with an exec sputtering with outrage, I'd go even calmer and say, "I'm confused about something." Or, slightly more aggressively: "Could you educate me?" They're expecting you to ream them, and you've put them at ease by being neutral and mildly curious. Also, you've gotten them talking, and you're learning. It preserves your options.

Another move I developed, almost unconsciously, was ground shifting. If someone on the other side of the table very confidently asserted a number that was confidential or that was plausibly in dispute— the budget of a rival studio's competing film, for instance—I would instantly say "It's higher" or "It's lower," depending on which served our interests. That assertion would throw the other guy off balance, and suggest that I knew everything, when in truth I only knew some things. At the very least, it would give me a gauge of how solid their information was, and how confident they were. If they fired right back with "No, you're absolutely wrong," I'd just say, "That's not what I'm hearing from the highest levels," or something equally ominous, then change the topic.

I resented it when people called these techniques agent tricks. I viewed them as tactics for achieving a preconceived strategy. My whole affect was transactional: I was soft-spoken because I wanted people to have to work hard to hear me, to have to move closer. When I did explode, which was rare, it was almost always expedient. When an agent named Robb Rothman left us for Jim Berkus's agency, which later merged into UTA, I screamed at him, "I'm going to make your life a living hell!" It was the Hail Mary after I'd done everything I could to express how much we wanted him to stay. Then, and only then, did I pick up the club and threaten to drop him into a boiling lake of fire. You want the guy to reconsider. Do I regret screaming those sorts of threats, as I did whenever an agent left us? Yes and no. Yes, because it never worked and because it reinforced my image as a vindictive bastard. No, because it's who I had to be.

———————

MY RECURRING NIGHTMARE WAS A BIG PUBLIC EVENT where the name of a client or potential client might escape me. I took to having one or two assistants study the guilds' mug shots and shadow me, warning me sotto voce when they spotted a relevant face. Even then I feared I'd blow it. I had a huge zone of protection around me—five assistants—and it never felt like enough.

One assistant, such as Richard Lovett or David O'Connor, was being trained to become an agent; two handled incoming and outgoing calls; one was in charge of my schedule; and one just gave gifts. We instituted CAA's famous gifts office in the late seventies on the uncontroversial theory that people love free stuff. I had learned about gifting from my father, with his bottles of Seagram's. So one of my assistants kept track of all our clients' hobbies and charities. When an agent found out some new bit of relevant data—Tom Hanks is taking scuba lessons, or the like—it got passed to the gifts assistant via a buck slip, or interoffice memo. The next time the client had a birthday or a book coming out or a movie shooting, he'd get an outdoor watch or a nice piece of luggage or, say for Paul Newman and Tom Cruise on *The Color of Money*, an ornate pool cue. When Ron told me Sylvester Stallone admired my old Ferrari, I gave Sly the title. When *Laverne & Shirley* became a hit and I kept redoing Penny Marshall's deal, I told Paramount's Gary Nardino, "By the way, add a washer and dryer as a gift. From you to Penny."

We pioneered the start-date gift—the $500 "survival kit" food basket that would arrive in an actor's dressing room, on some remote set in Malta or New Zealand, the first day of shooting. We gave them to nonclients, too, working the theory that a nonclient is just a future client who hasn't realized it yet. A typical memo from my right arm, Susan Miller, covering a three-week period of birthday presents, noted that I had given (among many other gifts) "Dustin an E-Tak, Armyan Bernstein a CITY OF NETS book, Walter Yetnikoff AKG headphones, Robert De Niro a FUTURISMO book, large MATISSE book, and several CDS"—his father was a painter—"Robert Redford a Malcolm Morley print, Terry and Jane Semel some Abrams art books, Sean Connery AKG headphones, Michael Jackson a personalized robe & Hollywood Musicals book."

Except for start-date gifts, my rule was that important gifts shouldn't be disposable: no champagne, no muffin baskets. Instead, rare first editions from Heritage books, ancient Greek coins, paintings and prints, even the occasional car—sturdy, thoughtful presents that would last. If a client was paying us $500,000 a year in commissions, and we spent $5,000 on a gift for him or her, it didn't hurt us much and it made the client feel fabulous. Our gifts office spent more than $500,000 a year, and generated a ton of good will (though we did send one writer for *The Simpsons* the same Weber grill on three separate occasions). Every Christmas we gave Tiffany key rings or the like to the secretaries of our favorite executives, and we messengered over $500 to $1,000 to our favorite restaurant owners and maître d's, those who'd made us seem more important at the beginning than we actually were—Ronnie, Tommy, Julius, and Pearl at Chasen's; François and Anna at Harry's Bar; Tom at Yamamoto's; MaryLou and Monte at Scandia; Peter and Pam at Morton's; Nobu at Matsuhisa; Giorgio and Elena at Giorgio's; Jimmy and David at Jimmy's; Gigi at the Palm; and on and on.

I had two assistants handling calls because the calls never ceased.

I'd look at the phone logs every morning and afternoon and put dots next to each message in red ink. Five dots meant "call back right now"; four dots was "call within thirty minutes"; three was "call before next meal"; two was "call by end of day"; and one dot signaled "call before end of week." Even the most important clients wouldn't necessarily get a return call right away. When I signed Marty Scorsese, I told him, "I'm not going to spend an hour on the phone with you a day—then I can't be doing everything else I need to do to find out what's going on, and I'm worthless to you." So when Marty called me, if it wasn't a crisis, one of my assistants would say, "He's tied up, but he'll be back to you by the end of the day." Then Jay Moloney would call back for me, talk to Marty for an hour, and write up a buck slip explaining why Marty had called. The buck slips themselves would be ranked in order of importance—the rule was that if a buck slip contained a question, it had to be replied to by the end of the day—and I'd call whoever needed my attention most.

If we were trying to transition a client whom I'd signed to the agent who'd be handling him day to day, I'd keep having that younger guy call back for me, and usually by the time I got back to Al Pacino, say, he was fine with having his daily business handled by Rick Nicita. All the senior people passed down their top artists as soon as younger agents could handle them, by slow-rolling the return calls. Manipulative, yes, but the pass-down process took pressure off signers like Ron and Bill, allowed younger agents to get in the game, and spurred CAA's continuing growth. Warren Beatty once told me, "It's smart of you guys to give so much work and support to the young guys—it makes you look that much more important." He was right: it was self-serving for the agency's leaders, but also agency serving. Those impulses felt synonymous, at least at that point.

Still, though, every time I went to New York I'd have to sit down with Al and catch up. My goal was to design myself out of a job and have no clients at all, but about thirty-five clients would talk only to me about the important stuff, including Kubrick, Levinson, Hoffman, Newman, Redford, and all the *SNL* people. Hundreds of others thought of me as their agent even if I really wasn't. So I was working harder than ever. Agencies are built on the lie that your agent will give you his total attention—but there simply isn't anywhere near enough time in the day for that.

BACK TO THE FUTURE, THE BREAKOUT 1985 FILM FOR DI-rector Robert Zemeckis, was developed at Columbia. After Frank Price (in a rare misstep) put the script in turnaround, Universal picked it up and the film grossed $350 million worldwide. The franchise was so hot that Lew Wasserman and Sid Sheinberg decided to make *Back to the Future II* and *III* back to back on one long shoot.

The problem was Bob's back end, which fell short of our standard. He felt reluctant to ask for more because he was close to the producer, Steven Spielberg. Our Jack Rapke pushed on Bob's behalf but the studio refused to bend. Three days before principal photography, with the director still unsigned, Jack called Universal and said Bob wasn't comfortable starting work the next Monday.

Sid was on the line to Jack and me five minutes later: "You can't do this! You're putting the studio at risk for hundreds of millions of dollars! We'll sue!" A lawyer by training, Sid viewed litigation as a profit center. He was my next-door neighbor in Malibu, and he later sued me when the ocean overran my sandbags and came onto his property. (It was dismissed.) He sued Sony (and lost) for abetting piracy with their Betamax technology. He almost seemed to prefer depositions to scripts.

"Lew is here," Sid said. "I'm gonna put you guys on the speakerphone."

Though we'd all heard tales of Lew's operatic invective, he and I had yet to face off. On speaker, Lew delivered the most articulate tirade imaginable. He was very loud but very calm. He laid down his argument like a stonemason, chiseling each point into place. How *dare* I do this, he said. Zemeckis should be working and I should not be stopping him. The studio made a good-faith commitment to finance the movie, and we were putting them in an impossible position. Agents were undermining the business, wrecking deals we were supposed to facilitate. He paused for breath and I began to reply, but then he started all over again. From time to time Sid chimed in to say, "Mr. Zemeckis can't do this!" He mispronounced Ze-*meck*-is as Ze-meck-*ees*, and it took all the self-control Jack and I had not to laugh.

When Lew finally wound down, I said, "Lew, are you done?"

"I'm done." I had no idea if he knew that I'd modeled myself on him, but he'd done his act, and now I was going to do mine.

"Lew," I said, speaking as calmly as he had, but much more softly, "I take all your points. But Bob needs to get paid on the back end. If you can do it, we'll be delighted. If you can't, we'll be forced to keep postponing the start date. You know how much he wants to make these movies, but we can't let him walk on set without a fair deal."

Sid cried, "Mr. Zemeck*ees* owes us this, Mr. Zemeck*ees* owes us—"

"Sid," I interrupted, "I think we've said all there is to say. We're around all weekend; you know how to reach us. We're planning on Bob showing up on Monday, because we're assuming you guys will do the right thing and come back with a fair offer."

I hung up and called Steven Spielberg before Sid could wedge him: "Let this be their problem, not yours."

By evening Universal had made an offer consonant with what our other top directors were getting, between 5 and 10 percent of the adjusted gross (gross box-office receipts less the studio's standard deductions). Bob went to work on Monday, and *Back to the Future II* and *III* brought in a combined $575 million. Everybody made out very well. But from then on Lew had it in for me. A generation after he disrupted Hollywood with *Winchester 73*, CAA was changing the game again. The pendulum was swinging back to the talent and their agents, and there was nothing he could do about it. We were using his playbook against him, but he appreciated neither the homage nor the irony.

———————

UNDER THE STUDIO SYSTEM, BACK IN THE DAY, THE STUdios didn't just put talent on their payrolls. They saw to the daily care and feeding of their directors and actors and writers, providing name changes and fictitious backstories, such as the one that turned Theodosia Goodman, a tailor's daughter from Cincinnati, into the siren Theda Bara, born to a French artist and an Arab princess and "weaned on serpent's blood." The studios gave their stars legal help and media training and emergency babysitting and drugs to make them lose weight and be happy, or at least glassily functional. The studios covered up numerous affairs, provided illegal abortions, and even destroyed evidence at the scene of a murder or two, all so their clients could maintain their spotless reputations and keep working.

By the late seventies, studio contracts, and the studio system, had been a thing of the past for nearly a generation. And actors and directors had paid the price: public meltdowns, stalled careers, needless scandals, bankruptcies. We stepped into the breach by providing full-service management. Our rote functions, called on every half hour, were getting clients a copy of a film, theater tickets, or reservations at a hot restaurant. The next level of ask, which often rose to my desk, was someone who needed to get their children into a school, or needed an appointment with the best knee guy or a high-powered divorce lawyer. The highest level ask, which occurred strangely often, was for an audience with the pope. We couldn't swing that—wrong religion—but we always said we'd look into it.

If someone needed a personal trainer or a dog groomer or an impossible dinner reservation, our assistants were on the phone until it got done. Multiply that process by a thousand, and you get a reputation for taking care of *everything*. We gave the wedding party for Tom Cruise and Nicole Kidman, and counseled each of them during their divorce, and both stayed with the agency. We gave advice to both Rob Reiner and Penny Marshall during their divorce, and both stayed with the agency. We got Bette Midler's kid into a private school with four weeks' notice, and she stayed with the agency through enormous career ups and downs.

One of my best trainee assistants, David O'Connor, got a call one afternoon from a furious Micheline Connery. Her rental car had stalled in the middle of the San Fernando Valley, and David was surely to blame, as he'd brought her the vehicle that morning. After rushing to Micheline's aid, David discovered she was out of gas; she had driven all day and drained the tank. It had never occurred to Micheline that even a car provided by CAA might, eventually, need gas. David found a gas station. Problem solved.

Clients would often ask to be set up with other clients, but I had no interest in being the house pimp. One of the most excruciating requests came from a movie star who wanted me to set him up with a woman he'd spotted in our mailroom. I temporized, put him off, hoped he'd forget about it—but he kept hounding me. I finally said, "It would look like I was asking an employee to go out with a prized client. You can see why I can't do that, right?" He glumly assented.

I went to Rupert Murdoch's house for lunch once, and, always looking for an edge, asked who his internist was. When he said he didn't have one, I immediately made an appointment for him with the head of internal medicine at UCLA. He got great care and became a donor to the institute. Years later, in the early '90s, I had a problem when one of our top stars had been caught on video being chased by a disgruntled husband. It seems the star had slept with the guy's wife on one of his films. A Fox entertainment show was planning to run the video, and our client, who was also married, was very upset. I called Rupert and explained the situation and said, "I would be eternally grateful if this problem went away."

He said, "Michael, I cannot interfere with any of our shows or magazines—you better than anyone should understand that." He paused, then added, "But I will look into it." He called back the next day and said, "We have looked high and low for any such video in the Fox library, and we simply cannot find it." Then he hung up. I owed Rupert forever after that, and contributed to every charity and political candidate he asked me to.

The most urgent personal asks were medical. One day Dustin

Hoffman called me and said, "I'm sitting in an emergency room with Barry Levinson at Santa Monica Hospital. Barry's son had a bad fall and keeps blacking out."

I said, "I am sending you an ambulance right now to take him to UCLA to be looked at by Dr. Warwick Peacock, the leading child neurologist." We sent a mobile ER over to pick up Barry's son, and when it got to UCLA, Peacock and twelve of his residents were waiting at the door. I had reached him at home, where he told me he was recovering from a bad flu, and insisted he go in, saying, "You're the only guy I'd trust to lay eyes on him." As I kept Barry company all night, Peacock decided, at 3:00 a.m., not to operate on Barry's son's brain, which was a giant gamble. But the kid pulled through. And then Peacock collapsed and *he* went into the ER. When he got out, I sent him a giant TV set, which his wife told me he really wanted.

Barry was one of my closest friends, but I would have done that for any client. That sort of when-the-chips-are-down reliability, that total focus on others when it's life or death, reassures me that I can be a decent person. It reflects the best part of me to myself.

Yet treating my clients like family was hard on me and my actual family. I was up at 5:45 a.m., and fifteen minutes later I'd be riding the bike in my gym and making calls to Europe and skimming five newspapers, marking articles for my assistant to strip out and distribute to the firm. After forty minutes on the bike, I'd do thirty or forty minutes of martial arts, working to exhaustion. By 8:00 a.m., after showering and eating a fast breakfast, I'd be on the car phone en route to the office. After our morning meeting, I'd take meetings, have lunch, a drink with a colleague, and a working dinner, all in between "running calls," up to three hundred phone conversations a day—Spielberg to Kubrick to De Niro to Hoffman to Murray, each call as important as the rest. I had all these brilliant and talented children as clients, and I could never give them enough time and attention. And unlike with my actual children, I could never make a mistake, or they'd fire me.

After being a chameleon all day at work, it took me an hour or so to figure out who the fuck I was when I got home. And all the time the phone would keep ringing, which drove Judy crazy. She would want to discuss my day, to feel closer to me, but I was exhausted by my day and didn't want to talk about work in front of the kids; I wanted them to feel normal and safe. I tried to structure our lives so we could maximize our time together. Once I even flew in from the Allen Conference in Sun Valley, Idaho, to see Chris in his Little League all-star game, watched a few innings, then flew back. We bought a place in Malibu so the kids would join us at the beach, and later a place in Aspen so we could all go skiing together—so they would have no excuse to go elsewhere for vacation. They knew that missing a Thanksgiving would be sacrilegious.

When the kids got old enough, I'd bring them along to client dinners, to normalize our family as much as I could. You know, the standard family dinner with Paul Newman and Joanne Woodward. But after the kids went to sleep, I worked every night, skimming through a couple of the three or four VHS cassettes I'd brought home and chipping away at the stack of screenplays. Then I'd fall asleep to Johnny Carson at midnight.

For years I worried that the stoniness that agenting required of me would make our children hard, too. But my kids viewed my world less as something to aspire to than as something to lure me away from. They often noticed that though I was playing with them (when they were young) or asking them about their days (when they were older), my attention was elsewhere. "Could you come back to reality?" they'd say, or just "Earth to Dad!" I used the car as a place to return phone calls, viewing travel time as dead time. They, quite rightly, viewed it as family time, and they'd regularly disconnect me or grab the phone from my hand.

I found it impossible not to answer the call, even if only to say "I'll call you back"; a large chunk of my life was given over to calling someone back to tell him I'd talk to him later to schedule a time when we could really talk. But I worked at being around for my kids, if not always fully present, as much as a workaholic could be. And they knew I'd drop everything for them when it mattered.

A FEW YOUNGER AGENTS STOOD OUT. THEY BECAME KNOWN as the Young Turks: Richard Lovett, Kevin Huvane, Bryan Lourd, David O'Connor, and Jay Moloney. I mentored each of them, but I felt closest to Jay, who'd come to us as a summer intern in 1983. He was tall and handsome and gregarious and remarkably likable. He promised that he'd work harder than anyone else and make my life so much easier. And he proved to be the finest assistant I ever had and one of CAA's best agents. He had superior taste and instincts in complex situations; he was outstanding at follow-up and at putting clients at ease and making them feel everything was under control. Like all the great ones, Jay was a gifted manipulator. There was something about his transparent eagerness to have me warm to him that made me warm to him. When he told me he'd graduated from USC, I gave him $10,000 to buy some suits so he could work for us as an agent. It turned out he hadn't quite graduated from USC, but minor details like that didn't trouble him.

Jay had Ron's charm and my instinct for how to frame a situation; in a strange way, he was like our child. He went up to Meryl Streep at a party and said, "You should definitely be my client!" She laughed and said, "Why?" He grinned down at her: "Because it would be great for me!" He could get away with stuff like that. I moved him into the lives of Dustin Hoffman, Sean Connery, Marty Scorsese, Mike Nichols, and Bill Murray, and they all loved him. He took things off my plate, anticipated, made my life easier even as he expanded his own clout. He'd look at my schedule, see that I'd just had lunch with John Calley, and call him to say, "I hear the greatest things about you, John, and I know you just had lunch with my boss, Michael Ovitz. If there's anything I can do for you, it would be an honor. . . ." He talked himself into, and then out of, relationships with several CAA actresses, including Jennifer Grey and Gina Gershon.

Jay took up martial arts training, like me; he'd later buy a Lichtenstein, just like me (he had me help him with the transaction); and he spent so much time at our home that he felt like one of the family.

Knowing that I collected watches, he gave me a gold Chronoswiss with MSO LOVE AND GRATITUDE JM engraved on the side. It felt like the gift of a son to a father. Privately, I thought he would make a natural successor to Ron and me.

Yet once Jay grasped that his charm could extricate him from sticky situations, he got into more than his share of sticky situations. He was constantly using my name with clients, saying I'd said things that I hadn't, pushing, overreaching. Almost every day I heard something about him that annoyed me, momentarily, before I let it go, because I, too, was nothing if not an overreacher, and because manipulating people was a big part of the job. If he was agenting me, then it meant he could become a great agent. I held him to a lower standard than anyone else—and I dearly wish I hadn't.

AS CAA GREW, RON AND BILL AND I WERE THE UNQUEStioned rainmakers. We generated 90 percent of the agency's business. All of our agents sold the CAA creed: "You don't have one agent, you have five"—and, later, "ten," "fifty," "one hundred." But signing clients and steering the agency really came down to the three of us, and, often, to me. My evenings and Saturday mornings were swallowed by the demands of a growing service organization, from tax planning and pensions to training programs. Human resources and legal and accounting all reported to me. When it came time to buy a new Xerox machine, I chose the model—one-sided printing or two? Each time I walked through our front door, I felt a physical chill like the chill you felt in high school before a final exam. How much did we have to earn today to cover our costs and overhead? What if the business shifted and the money dried up? The feeling would recede, for a time, once I sat down at my desk and began to work, but I carried those fears to my last day there.

By 1985, I was running most aspects of our business and I was responsible for the lion's share of our income. Ron had a crew of reliable earners, including Michael Douglas, Whoopi Goldberg, Cher, and Sly

Stallone, but after him the other earners at the agency fell off dramatically, and I got tired of carrying so much of the load without due reward. With our packages generating millions, it didn't feel fair to me that Rowland was sharing in that when he wasn't keeping the pace that Bill, Ron, and I were. Marty had helped us enormously over the years, but the fact was that he wasn't signing new clients, and his mainstays, Blake Edwards and Julie Andrews and Bo Derek, were earning less and less. In 1986, we got Rowland and Marty to sell us their equity in return for a million dollars each and lifetime contracts paying $500,000 a year. After that, I owned 55 percent of CAA, with Ron and Bill splitting the balance, 22.5 percent each.

That same year I bought a Learjet 35A with Sydney Pollack for $750,000, with just 10 percent down. It was CAA's plane, and I used it so I could visit two widely separated sets in one day and still be back for work the next. Over the years, I kept upgrading the plane. One of Ron's complaints was that I didn't let him use it enough, and he was right. But the last thing I wanted was for CAA to become Warner Bros., which ran a wasteful fleet of five planes, and I knew that if anyone but Ron and me realized we had a plane, they'd all want to hop on it. So when I booked it for any of our other agents to fly to a set for an emergency, I always said that it was Sydney's plane, and that he was just letting us borrow it. The Young Turks were furious, later, when they found out about it. But I always felt it was none of their business.

RON AND I SPENT ALL OUR TIME TOGETHER. WE SHARED everything, from mundane work issues—should we fire this guy or can he learn on the job?—to the deepest secrets about our marriages and our kids. We finished each other's sentences. And increasingly, as I played different roles with different clients, becoming the man with a thousand faces, the font of power and granter of dreams, it was comforting to know that there was one guy, in the office just below mine, who liked me for who I really was, warts and all. I was convinced that, decades hence, we were both going to end up divorced but living in retirement side by side at the Motion Picture Home, still going through the old routines, like Walter Matthau and George Burns in *The Sunshine Boys*.

Ron and I vacationed together with our families, going to Venice, Lake Como, the Kahala Hilton in Hawaii. We had the same raw sense of humor—outside the Guggenheim in Venice, in 1987, we took a photo of ourselves with *The Angel of the City*, a Marino Marini sculpture of a man with a huge erection riding a horse. Knowing that the producer Ray Stark had the same sculpture, only in a version lacking the erection, we sent him a Tiffany box containing the photo, with the caption "Ray, we found your dick!" We then prevailed on the Guggenheim to help us cast a model of the penis, and presented it to Ray as a dinner gift.

We were also united in how we treated our enemies. We never forgot how William Morris had tried to put us out of business or how they had behaved toward Phil Weltman. (Indeed, we put up a plaque to Weltman in our offices, dedicating the agency to him.) So we punished the agency, taking first a number of their agents, then more than seventy of their clients in the first few years, mostly television writers, producers of daytime television, and character actors. As we grew, so did our appetites. After the death of Stan Kamen, WMA's top film agent, in 1986, we picked off Warren Beatty, Goldie Hawn, and Chevy Chase. Even as late as 1989, I dogged their client Kevin Costner hard to get him to come over. He was a big star, and I believed I could make him into Gary Cooper, but it certainly added to his allure that he was with WMA. People called it a war, but it was an unrelenting conquest: Morris didn't take from us.

Even minor misdeeds got punished severely. After Bob Shapiro at Warner Bros. stopped returning our agent Laurie Perlman's calls, Ron and I told everyone in a staff meeting, "No one call Bob back." After a week or two of this, Bob's wife, Sandy, phoned me in a panic and I explained, "We'll be happy to call Bob back when he calls Laurie." He immediately called her, apologized, and life went on.

A little while later, I grew incensed at the talent manager Bernie Brillstein, who had gotten a job running Lorimar without telling me he was angling for it. As we handled a number of clients together, I would have appreciated the heads up—and, more important, I wanted to look like I was involved in every executive hire in the business. So before Bernie next dropped in for a meeting, I told everyone that no one should speak to him. Ron backed me, but we both knew it was a radical step, because Bernie's daughter worked for us as an agent, and he and I had been close. Bernie came in and started chatting, pitching a few ideas—into dead silence. It was a very short, very uncomfortable meeting. Bernie called me afterward, humiliated, and said, "That was horrible!" He was right, but nonetheless I told our agents that Lorimar shouldn't get any CAA material while Bernie was there—and his tenure lasted less than two years. Wounded in my pride, I totally overreacted, I'm ashamed to say. (I should have done the opposite: sell Lorimar everything we had that we couldn't sell to anyone else.) Our relationship was never the same, and Bernie described it as a feud, though I can't say I gave it that much thought.

When Judy Hofflund and David Greenblatt left us to start Inter-Talent, in 1988, Ron got furious at them, particularly after he came to believe that Judy, his former assistant, was the source of an unflattering story about him that had appeared in *Variety*. They took Ari Emanuel from us, one of our greatest trainees, as well as a few smaller clients, and Ron decided to crush them. First he fired Tom Strickland because Tom had known about the impending defection and hadn't told us, and because he assumed Tom was going to InterTalent anyway (which he then did). Then Ron unloaded in a staff meeting—one of the few times he sounded like me—and told everyone to bad-mouth them all over town. We were breaking our own fourth commandment, but we no longer cared.

Our agents began calling studio and network execs, in the guise of being friends of the court, to subtly disparage InterTalent's lawyers, leaning on the execs to make lowball offers, saying InterTalent's business affairs guys wouldn't push back. Ron set up hit teams of five agents to call each of their clients, seeking to rattle, undermine, and poach.

Within four years, he put InterTalent out of business. For once, I had little to do with it—but I totally supported him. If you hurt us, we counterattacked with all our might and fury.

When an agent named Peter Grosslight, the head of the Triad Agency, tried to poach Eric Clapton from us by kissing up to Clapton's manager in 1987, I called Peter and set him straight. As I wrote later in a memo to Tom Ross, the head of our music group, Grosslight "stated that he is friends with the manager and that Clapton did not have a strong prior relationship with us and therefore it created an insecurity. I explained to him that I did not expect him to take advantage of any insecurity and for the matter it would not make sense for him to continue his 'friendship' with Clapton's manager." Knowing that we could destroy his agency if he didn't back off, Grosslight backed off.

Ron deployed these same moves—albeit with a friendlier, easier manner—but he never appeared quite as concerned with money and the aura of invincibility as I was. At night, after busting his ass till 9:00 p.m., Ron was going out with beautiful women like Ali MacGraw while I'd be having a working dinner with John Calley at Warner Bros., laying plans on the agency's behalf. Ron was the Warren Beatty of agents, able to cut a wide swath and never get called out, and I envied his lifestyle. For his part, Ron thought I was too uptight. He would have been a great talent agent at William Morris if I hadn't come into his life, but without me he'd never have reached the heights, as he often acknowledged. Ron used to introduce himself as my keeper, my agent—half in jest, but with a buried, wounded sense that he was born to be a number two. Of course, without him I never would have reached the heights, either. We rose in tandem and amplified each other. I counted on Ron's candor, and he periodically reined me in: "You're pushing our people too hard. Ease off on the gas a bit." He was always right.

It was hard for me to let up: by 1985 I was taking home more than a million dollars a year, and additional wealth and power seemed just around the corner. The fear of poverty had receded, but I was like an athlete who wanted to keep topping himself, setting new records. There's an apt scene in *Patton* where George C. Scott says, "I don't want to get any messages saying we are holding our position. We're not holding anything. . . . We're advancing constantly." That scene when Patton slaps the shell-shocked soldier to get him back onto the battlefield—I wouldn't have *slapped* him, but I would have talked him out of there somehow and back into the fight. Patton was a threatening motherfucker, and so was I.

Or so I'd become, anyway. Over the years I'd split off most of my feelings and emotions, the human part of me, and let Ron display them for both of us—just as he'd off-loaded his cunning, ambitious side and let me express that for him. As a result I got the credit as the agency's visionary, and he got to retain most of his soul and to serve as the caretaker of mine.

In the mideighties, I thought we should launch a "B" agency that would handle the leads in TV series: unprestigious actors who made a ton of money. We had already signed a few, such as Bert Convy and Donna Mills, and I worried that we were going to become like WMA, a volume "sell 'em, don't smell 'em" business. With a B agency, we need have no compunction about signing Robert Wagner and Stefanie Powers in *Hart to Hart*, Bill Shatner in *T. J. Hooker*, and John Forsythe in *Dynasty*. The B agency would feed the A agency talent if those actors became film stars—as Johnny Depp later would from TV's *21 Jump Street*. And if an Erik Estrada never made it to the big leagues, the B agency would still profit handsomely from *CHiPS*. Ron was strongly against the idea, feeling it would tarnish our brand, so I dropped it. He was right at the time—it would have tarnished us. And I was right in the long run; today, with television and film equally important, you'd just expand the A agency to handle everyone.

Every year I wrote up a one-year, three-year, and five-year plan for us. At year's end I'd destroy the old ones—I feared another agency getting wind of our plans—and write new ones. The one-year and three-year plans proved to be the most useful: often we accomplished the three-year plan in two. But Ron and Bill had no strategic instincts for that kind of thing. Ron was a purist who just wanted to represent more and better clients, and Bill didn't want the extra work of new challenges, though he always did the work, and superbly, once I'd cajoled him into it. By the nineties, I'd stopped showing them my plans because my unceasing ambitions just pissed them off. My thinking was that I'd go do what was best for us, and they'd be grateful later.

Right.

CHAPTER TEN

SHOWTIME

OTHER THAN TO PUBLICIZE THEIR FILMS, WE ADVISED OUR clients to keep their heads low and their mouths shut. In those days, Tom Cruise's profile as a Scientologist was minimal because we'd told him, "Keep your religion and your work separate, just like anybody else." I read *Dianetics*, by Scientology's founder, L. Ron Hubbard, to better understand what we were up against, and then I went to see David Miscavige, Hubbard's successor, and explained to him that we had a common interest: "We don't want to see Tom's name in the paper for anything but his career." It was a warning phrased as a tip. We also worked with Tom's publicist, Pat Kingsley—who was known as Dr. No because she refused almost every interview request—to clap a lid on the sort of tabloid gossip that would boil over once we were no longer in Tom's life. Steven Spielberg told me that on the set of their 2005 film, *War of the Worlds*, Tom went so far as to set up a Scientology booth to proselytize the cast and crew.

The agency adhered to the same button-your-lip posture. Outside Hollywood, CAA was almost entirely unknown, and that suited us fine. As a privately held partnership, why reveal our MO? Our agents were forbidden from taking reporters' calls. A memo I sent around in

1985 noted that "no one (repeat NO ONE) should grant an interview with a reporter in any media (i.e., television, radio, newspaper, magazine, etc.) without first advising me." If anyone advised me that they wanted to do an interview, I advised them not to. The only people preauthorized to speak to the press were me, Ron, and Ray Kurtzman—and we didn't talk, at least not on the record. As a co-owner, Bill Haber had the right to talk, but fortunately that wasn't his style.

Tom Johnson, the editor of the *Los Angeles Times*, was proud of his newspaper's card file, a compendium of everything written about L.A. for the past half century. When we met at his office one day, Tom said, "Let's see what we have on Michael Ovitz and CAA." He typed my name into their UNIVAC computer and, to his dismay, it spit out just a single listing: a photo of the CAA partners, with no text.

In December 1986, the *Wall Street Journal* blew our cover. A sharp-eyed reporter named Michael Cieply caught me working the room at Chasen's after a premiere. I used parties as a way to return about twenty-five phone calls, and Cieply watched me move among groups of execs like a bee pollinating flowers. His page-one story was headlined HOLLYWOOD STAR: AN AGENT DOMINATES FILM AND TV STUDIOS WITH PACKAGE DEALS. It began, "By some accounts, the most powerful individual in Hollywood is neither a star nor a studio chief. He is an agent, Michael S. Ovitz." Under my leadership, Cieply wrote, CAA had "emerged as the predominant broker of Hollywood talent and story material." Though I'd declined to cooperate with the *Journal*, I thought the story could help our business. But how would my partners feel about it? Throughout CAA's first decade, Ron and I had been perceived as equal partners and the company's coleaders. Ron told me, "The story will be good for us," and insisted the spotlight on me didn't bother him. But I'm sure it planted a seed of resentment.

Once journalists deduced that I was the quarterback, more coverage followed. I made *Fortune*'s roll of "Most fascinating business people" and *People*'s "Most intriguing" list, whatever that meant. And then, beginning in 1990 and for three years running, I topped *Premiere*'s "Power List" of the one hundred most powerful people in

Hollywood. The first time I saw the rankings, anxiety shot through me, head to toe. Mystique is ten times better than publicity; it's much better to be thought of as the great and powerful Oz than to be revealed as merely another schemer behind a curtain.

Whenever I walked into a room, execs began saying, "*There* he is, the most powerful man in Hollywood." I'd go, "Yeah, yeah, yeah," trying to get rid of it, and they'd go, "C'mon, you love it!" I really didn't because there was no way to make it work for me. I felt watched every moment. I felt I couldn't be too silly with my kids in public or too lively at a party.

CAA seeped into the public consciousness as a kind of jeweler's window for the stars: every time there was an awards show on television, tourists would drop by our building the next day, hoping to spot a celebrity or two. The day after the 1990 Academy Awards, an attractive woman in her thirties approached our reception desk. She was wearing a Chanel suit and Chanel shoes and carrying a Chanel shoulder bag, and she wore a gold Rolex. "Is Tom Cruise here?" she asked, politely. One of our three receptionists said, "No, I'm sorry." The woman said, "Is Madonna here?" Our security guard, Hank, who sat alongside the receptionists, began to pay closer attention.

The receptionist explained that Madonna wasn't there, either—and then, in response to the woman's further inquiries, that Paul Newman and Robert Redford also weren't around. The receptionist explained that the building wasn't an actors' home or clubhouse—it was just where their agents worked. The woman nodded and said, "Well, then, is Michael Ovitz in?"

"I'm sorry, he's not. Can I take a message?"

The woman shook her head and turned away. As she turned, she let her shoulder bag slip into her hand, and then turned back and swung the bag with all her might at Hank, clobbering him in the head. The bag held a brick, and Hank was knocked into the wall behind him. Somehow he was able to shake off the blow, vault the counter, and tackle her as she ran for the exit. Her screams reverberated through the building until the police arrived.

That kind of thing ramped up my already acute paranoia. Trying to modulate my image, to make it softer—Good Ol' Uncle Michael—I sought to cultivate the press. I began taking time to talk to reporters off the record, explaining what we were doing, ingratiating myself, offering myself as a background resource on the business. If a press release was going out at 5:00 p.m. with news, I'd let a trade reporter know at 3:00 p.m. But all the spinning and massaging didn't do much: my image was fixed, largely through my own maneuverings, as the Machiavellian master of the dark arts. For the first time it struck me how vulnerable I'd be if I ever lost my perch at CAA.

It wasn't supposed to turn out that way. I had never longed for the bright lights, the grinning photo ops with a coterie of stars. But I should have realized that celebrity follows power, just as celebrities do. When Judy and I bought a house on an Aspen ski run in 1986, we just wanted to keep our kids coming in for family vacations as they grew. Michael Eisner bought a house in Aspen at the same time, for the same reason—and then many of our artists began renting or buying there: Ivan Reitman, Chevy Chase, Michael Douglas, Kurt Russell, and Goldie Hawn. CAA Aspen was born. Before long we were hosting daily lunches for dozens of clients and their extended families, up to two hundred people at a time. We had visitors for fourteen straight days one Christmas, the house open to all from noon to 3:00 p.m., though many guests would stay till dinner. One afternoon the guests included our usual locals as well as Sean Connery, Michael Caine, Dustin Hoffman, Sylvester Stallone, and Barry Levinson, all huddled around Goldie Hawn and Kurt Russell as she recalled her days on *Laugh-In*, and he told a story about pouring elk urine over himself before going hunting.

Work always came into it, but the atmosphere was jollier in Aspen than in Los Angeles. Eisner and I shared a ski instructor, a charming young man named Patrick Hasburgh. As a lark, almost as a practical joke, we got him a job writing for Stephen Cannell on the TV show *The A-Team*. It was like, "Can we create a Hollywood player out of thin air?" Within a few years, Patrick had cocreated *Hardcastle and Mc-Cormick* and *21 Jump Street* with Cannell, and become one of the biggest TV producers around.

Make of that what you will.

––––––––––

FROM THE START OF CAA, ANY UNENCUMBERED CASH went into our building fund. Artists' careers are in constant flux, so it reassures them—as well as the buyers of their talents—if their agency projects solidity. Owning our own space would certify our permanence. That was my belief, anyway, and my partners rolled their eyes and went along.

By the mideighties we had $10 million in the bank. And after I saw I. M. Pei's John F. Kennedy Presidential Library and Museum in Boston and his East Building of the National Gallery of Art in D.C., I narrowed our list of architects to one. In 1985, just ten years after we'd started, I called Arne Glimcher, whose gallery the young Pei had designed years earlier, and asked a favor: "I have to get in to see I. M. Pei."

He said, "Sure, what about?"

"I want him to build the CAA headquarters." As Pei was then at work on the Louvre Pyramid and the Bank of China Tower in Hong Kong, I'm sure I sounded delusional.

"It's a bit small for him, but you never know," Arne said, diplomatically.

"Don't ask for a meeting; ask if he'll give me fifteen minutes. Make it just before lunch."

Arne set it up. When I entered Pei's office, on Madison Avenue, I laid my watch on his desk to acknowledge that I was on the clock. I.M. was the most sophisticated man I've ever met. He spoke Mandarin and French and better English than I did. Nearly seventy, he was polite, reserved, clearly skeptical. I knew that his sole Los Angeles work was an apartment building from 1965, which suggested that he wasn't a fan of our city.

I began by telling him about CAA, and then I said, "We're in L.A., and I know you don't want to be there, but I'd like to talk to you about our headquarters and why we need you."

I pitched my heart out. Fifteen minutes turned into thirty, then forty-five. I.M. said, "Why don't we get some lunch?"

Perfect.

At the restaurant he kept telling me why he couldn't do it. He had so many projects and so little time. The Bank of China building was eight hundred thousand square feet, and I wanted something a tenth that size. But I talked up our location at Wilshire and Little Santa Monica, the central business intersection of Beverly Hills. Then I told him I wanted a mural in our atrium.

He said, "How are you going to do that?"

And I said, "I want outdoor space indoors," an idea I'd appropriated from his National Gallery. It would be unoccupiable space, an extravagance that gave architects great freedom.

The lunch lasted three hours. At the end I said, "I can't do this without you. There is no second choice."

"What if I say no?"

"Then I guess I won't build the building," I said. At that moment, it was true.

He frowned. "You know, I can't do this."

"Okay, I hear you," I said. "No pressure."

After that, I asked to see him every time I was in New York, and we'd meet for twenty minutes or an hour at his office to talk about art and my building plans. At the end of one lunch, he said, "You know, I've been thinking about what you said about outdoor-indoor space." He pulled out a sheet of onionskin and set it on his desk. "I don't have the time to do it, but were you talking about this?" He drew a rectangle with a curved form on either side. As his pencil moved, he kept asking, "What do you think of this . . . and that . . . and this?"

I tried to contain my excitement as I studied his drawing. "I like this, and this," I said casually, pointing out details. "And I love that. This is exactly what we want."

"I still can't do it."

"I'm going to assume you can't do it, but let's start anyway. Let's do some drawings."

"I don't have time."

"Okay, we'll get somebody else to do them for your approval. But you have to do the first one." That was the drawing he'd started sketching in front of me. (The completed version now hangs in my library at home.)

The next step was to get I.M. to Los Angeles. I flew him out in March 1986 and arranged a first-class visit; my assistant Dan Adler hovered near him the entire time he was in L.A., making sure his feet never had to touch the ground. I hosted a dinner where I.M. was surrounded by people like Dustin Hoffman, Kevin Costner, Terry Semel, and Michael Eisner. I had Eisner approach him about doing a hotel for Disney World, which was then a popular pastime for high-profile architects. I.M. didn't warm to the idea, and I dropped it.

The next day I.M. asked to be left at our building site with a folding chair. With my assistant waiting in the car, he sat there in his Hong Kong suit. The lot was vacant except for the tiny Western Federal branch, shuttered years before. I.M. stayed for four hours, just looking and thinking. After his trip, he wrote me a letter laying out a schedule for the project, and it began with words that warmed my heart: "Dear Michael: You are without a doubt the most thoughtful man I know." All the attention to detail had paid off.

Three years later, the critic Paul Goldberger would write in the *New York Times*:

> The CAA building positively brims over with conservative good taste: in the context of Los Angeles, it is a Chanel suit among polyester jumpsuits, a BMW amid Hyundais, a Mont Blanc amid Bics. . . .
>
> Indeed, for all its small size this is one of I. M. Pei's best buildings. . . . CAA may be the most beautifully made modern building Los Angeles has ever seen.

The three-story building was criticized in the industry as being over the top, a cold monument to power, but to me it felt exactly right. I found the light amber façade and glass-and-aluminum curtain walls to be warm, almost cheerful, even as the stone walls and turrets underscored the fortress mentality I'd repeatedly discussed with I.M. Inside these battlements, you'd be protected. Outside, you were on your own. Us versus them.

The capstone was the atrium mural. We needed someone who could work on an outsized scale, and I.M. shared my enthusiasm for Roy Lichtenstein. Armed with a cardboard architectural model, I pitched the idea to Roy's dealer, the legendary Leo Castelli. Roy loved the building and revered I.M. We struck a deal.

Over the six months or so before Roy started on our commission, I was privileged to visit his studio on Washington Street in the West Village. I would sit for an hour over coffee and just watch him paint. For those precious minutes no one could reach me, and I would emerge reborn, my stress drained away. Long after the project was completed, I continued to make visits to Roy's studio a fixture of my trips to New York.

Finally I was summoned to view a scale model. When Roy pulled off the draping, I knew I was looking at a masterpiece. Roy had reimagined a painting that hung at the Museum of Modern Art, Oskar Schlemmer's *Bauhaus Stairway*, in reference to the open stairway in our building. "Any suggestions?" he asked. "Changes?" He had a wry sense of humor.

"No changes," I said.

The deal we made with Castelli called for Roy to paint the mural on-site. He and his wife, Dorothy, hung out with us for four weeks, most of which Roy spent perched on scaffolding. We were privileged to watch the twenty-six-foot-tall mural take form, to watch an extraordinary creative act, in the midst of making our phone calls and closing our deal points. It was a reminder of what we could aspire to.

The painting was nearly finished when we celebrated our new headquarters with a party in the atrium, a candle-lit dinner for four hundred clients, studio and network executives, and Roy and I.M. Noting that I.M. had never formally signed on for the job, I toasted him by saying, "Someday I hope you'll agree to do the building."

While CAA's executives were free to choose any furniture they wanted, we suggested a contemporary style. We offered two carpet colors, beige and beige-green, neutral hues to complement I.M.'s clean lines. Everybody fell into line except Bill Haber. He ordered a Technicolor Asian rug and a fake fireplace. His furniture was Louis XIV, richly carved and gilded, and his bathroom contained a bidet. It was a mild fuck-you to me, and a strong statement of who he was.

I GREW UP AN L.A. LAKERS FAN IN THE DAYS OF JERRY WEST. But the first time I saw the Lakers play live was in 1980, when a gangly rookie grabbed my attention. Earvin "Magic" Johnson moved his team down court in a style both fluid and forceful. He never lost his cool or took a shot when he could pass to an open teammate. He was 100 percent about winning. When I had the chance to buy season tickets on the floor of the Forum, next to Jack Nicholson, I jumped at it.

Four championships into Magic's glorious run, I took a call from Joe Smith, the CEO at Capitol Records. No one rooted harder for the Lakers than Joe, a season-ticket holder since the franchise had moved to L.A. from Minnesota. "I know you don't handle athletes," he said, "but you need to meet with Magic Johnson. He wants to talk about a business career."

"You're right," I said. "I don't handle athletes."

"Do it as a favor to me."

Reluctantly, I agreed to a meeting. There was little incentive to represent pro athletes in the late eighties. The average NBA salary was half a million dollars, and the league capped commissions at 4 percent. The Lakers had fifty-plus home games a year, counting playoffs, and their agents were expected to be at every one. Limited income + heavy servicing = bad deal.

Magic arrived on time and bent his six-foot-nine frame through the doorway. As he folded himself onto my couch, I said, "So what do you want?"

Magic said, "I want to learn about business and investments, so I don't end up in my forties with nothing."

"I love watching you play, and I applaud that you're thinking ahead—but we don't work with athletes," I said.

He called to ask for another meeting, thereby passing my first test: he was determined. This time we talked about his Lakers contract. After his historic rookie season, owner Jerry Buss had given him the richest contract extension in the history of sports: $1 million a year for twenty-five years. It was a fabulous deal—for Jerry Buss. With the prime interest rate hovering in the teens, the contract was steeply discounted the instant it was signed. I told Earvin he should be getting a minimum of $5 million a year for five years. I said the same to Buss, who agreed to go along—*if* I could finesse the NBA's salary cap, which constrained what teams spent.

I met David Stern, the league's commissioner, in his New York office to make my case. Stern yelled out, "Bring the books!" In walked Gary Bettman, the NBA's general counsel (who's now commissioner of the NHL). He carried the league's very thick, very carefully worded collective bargaining agreement. Bettman and Stern were cheerfully smug about my chances of breaking it. I needed to find another way. I went back to Jerry Buss and pointed out that personal service contracts in California were limited to seven years. He agreed to accelerate Earvin's payments and to sell him a piece of the team when his playing days were done.

My third meeting with Earvin was at Spago. When we stepped in, the diners gave him a standing ovation. Here was a celebrity, I saw, who was already his own brand. He just needed to make it pay off for him.

I found Earvin bright, sincere, and open. I gave him a *Wall Street Journal* and told him to read the front page every day. He glanced at it and said, "I have no idea what they're talking about. I don't understand the fundamentals." Just jump in, I said: "The only thing holding you back is overcoming the jock stereotype and sounding as savvy as I know you are." I bought him subscriptions to the *Journal*, *Forbes*, and *Fortune*, and quizzed him weekly, over the phone, about current business deals and trends. A naturally charismatic speaker, Earvin studied tapes of his TV interviews to become more polished.

Our first move was to pursue a Pepsi-Cola bottling franchise; we happened to know that Pepsi badly wanted more minority owners in its system. Craig Weatherup, Pepsi-Cola's president, was looking for someone to partner with magazine publisher Earl Graves to take over the Washington, D.C., franchise, and we put Earvin up for the slot. For the first time since high school, he had to interview for a job. We swamped him with research on the soft-drink industry. We sat him at our conference table for group interrogations on Pepsi history, revenue, earnings, and marketing. We critiqued his responses over and over until we knew he was ready.

Craig set the meeting at the 21 Club in New York, and Earvin was on edge as we went inside. But he started off warmly sociable before shifting into business mode, as we'd rehearsed, and the execs were truly impressed. When we made Earvin's deal with Earl Graves, it was Pepsi's largest minority-owned franchise in the United States.

I later introduced Earvin to Sony Pictures, and he bought into their theater division and developed Magic Johnson Theaters, focused on movie houses in African American neighborhoods. Magic Johnson Enterprises has since expanded into commercial real estate, private equity, restaurants, and a cable TV network catering to African Americans—and it's now worth more than a billion dollars. In 2012, Earvin and Guggenheim Partners purchased the Los Angeles Dodgers for $2.15 billion, the most ever paid for an American sports franchise.

We never took a penny in commissions. I guess I was paying Earvin back for all the pleasure he gave me at the Forum.

IT WASN'T ALL SUCCESS. ONE OF MY MORE DRAMATIC SLIP-ups was *Legal Eagles*, a 1986 Universal release. In collaboration with the director, Ivan Reitman, I envisioned it as a buddy picture for Dustin Hoffman and Bill Murray. Then Dustin became unavailable and Bill dropped out, and Ivan retooled it for Robert Redford and Debra Winger, as a starchy assistant district attorney and a balls-out young lawyer defending her client. After *An Officer and a Gentleman* and *Terms of Endearment*, Debra was white hot. She was sexy and warm and funny and seemed poised to become the Jennifer Lawrence of her day. I thought she'd make an ideal foil for Bob, who had long wanted to try a romantic comedy. Ivan made his comedies work, and he had a solid script from two CAA clients, Jim Cash and Jack Epps Jr., who had high-concept hits in the pipeline with *Top Gun* and *The Secret of My Success*.

I was wrong on every count. In preproduction it became clear that Bob disliked Ivan because Ivan was too commercial, that Ivan disliked Debra because she was a prima donna, and that she disliked Ivan right back. Bob and Debra had zero chemistry, and the script was all concept and no highs. When I went to Tom Mankiewicz, a top script doctor, for a rewrite, he called it a TV movie. My sinking feeling told me he was right, but it was too late to back out.

On set, every bad relationship got dramatically worse. As Debra's scenes with Bob flatlined, she took it out on me for getting her into this mess. One day Ivan called and said, "I think you better get out here."

Lightning was splitting the sky outside my window. "What's wrong?" I said.

"Your client is refusing to leave her trailer."

"Why?"

"She doesn't like her dialogue."

I sighed. "I'll be there." By the time I weaved through traffic to the Universal lot, it was absolutely pouring. "Okay, Ivan," I said. "Let's go talk to her."

He gave me a pained smile: "Too late." After sulking for two hours, Debra had walked from her trailer to the soundstage in the rain and said, "I'm ready to shoot." By then, of course, her hair and makeup were ruined and her costume soaked. It would have taken another

two hours to make her camera ready again, so Ivan just sent everyone home.

Though *Legal Eagles* recouped its costs, I kicked myself for ram-
ming it through. Debra savaged me in the press for treating her like "a
commodity" and then left CAA, the first and only star to defect in my
time there. Other stars got upset—Bette Midler road tested three of
our agents before settling in with Rick Nicita—but we kept them in
the fold. Even Debra returned to us a few years later. She was impetuous, but not so impetuous she didn't recognize our value. When we
"slapped her into something," as she put it, she said yes. And then she
cashed her checks.

SHORTLY AFTER WE MOVED TO OUR NEW BUILDING, MY AS-
sistant received a call from David Rockefeller's office, asking if they
could set a time for him to ring me. "It sounded real," she told me.

"Tell Bill I'll call him back." Both Bill Murray and Dustin Hoffman called my office a lot pretending to be some celebrity, often a dead
one. One day it might be a marble-mouthed Marlon Brando, the next
a probing, childhood-obsessed Sigmund Freud. Just in case, though, I
asked her to call David's office in New York to verify. Two hours later,
David Rockefeller, the famed East Coast philanthropist and power
broker who was chairman of the board of the Museum of Modern Art,
was indeed on the phone.

"I'd like to come out and talk to you about something," he said.

I told him I'd be delighted, but offered to see him in New York.

"No," he said, "I want to take a look at your building and see you
there. I'll come to you."

At that point, I wasn't easily overawed. But it seemed surreal to me
that David Rockefeller would make a special trip to visit a kid from the
Valley who hadn't seen his first real painting until he was eighteen.
When David walked into our building, it felt like George Washington
dropping by. And when he asked me to join MoMA's board, it was the
ultimate validation—one of the great honors of my life.

Watching how David worked taught me the efficacy of elegance and understatement, how to sell by not selling. When MoMA was launching a capital campaign, David took Judy and me to dinner, and during the three-and-a-half-hour meal never once mentioned a donation. He just talked about how great I was, how great Judy was, and how magnificent the museum was going to be. Somehow, by the end of the meal, we knew we had to give at least the minimum: $5 million.

Even after I joined other boards and prestigious institutions, such as the Council on Foreign Relations, I never quite felt that I belonged in that rarefied world. In 1993, David hosted a dinner for Akio Morita, the head of Sony, at Glorious Food on the Upper East Side. There were only thirteen people, and the guest list included Henry Kissinger; James Wolfensohn, the head of the World Bank; and Gustavo Cisneros, who basically owned Venezuela. They were all talking about countries and the global economy, and how to pull those levers, as casual as could be. I excused myself to go to the bathroom, and I called Judy from a pay phone. "I just needed a reality check," I said. "Why am I here at this dinner?"

Judy said, "You're there because you are in your industry what they are in theirs." I didn't entirely believe her, but it was a very sweet thing to say.

———

ONE MORNING IN 1987, RON CAME INTO MY OFFICE, SHUT the door, and said, "I've got a problem."

I said, "Shoot." We'd had a thousand conversations that started like that.

"I lost a lot of money in a poker game, and I can't pay up."

I was shocked, but I said, "Okay, we'll take care of it." I figured it was a hundred thousand dollars or so. "How much?"

"I'm not sure you'll be able to take care of it."

"How much is it?"

"Over five million."

As I strove to underreact, Ron told me he'd been going to Vegas several times a week. He'd make the flight after work, play deep into the night, and grab a few hours' sleep before flying back to L.A. in the morning and working his ass off as usual, never missing a meeting.

I was unable to process this. When Ron and I went to Vegas on business, I'd occasionally watch him play blackjack for half an hour and win or lose $500. There was no hint he gambled for astronomical stakes. *He must be a phenomenal poker player*, I thought. *He has no tells.*

Then again, he must be a shitty poker player because he'd just lost *five million dollars*. That was a substantial portion of his annual income. My immediate reaction was to feel worried for him, and want to help—but I swiftly suppressed that impulse because I'd read enough about compulsive behavior to be terrified. My partner, my best friend, the guy I was tied to for life, clearly had an unconscious need to throw away everything we'd worked for. (I would later learn that Lew Wasserman's only weakness was gambling—he, too, lost big in Las Vegas, and had to get bailed out by his mentor and close friend, Jules Stein.)

I told Bob Goldman, our chief financial officer, "Ron got himself in a jam, and we need to help him fix it. We've got to sew up the cut." We lent Ron a million dollars, and Bob canceled his credit cards. Ron swore it would never happen again. I don't know where he got the rest of the money, but he eventually paid our loan back. I put my concerns to rest, happy to sweep it all under the rug. And I never did tell him, "Hey, I'm worried about you. What's going on, and what can I do to help?"

For the next year and a half, Ron and I worked harder and more closely than ever. Then one morning, he closed my door, took a seat, and looked at me with a funereal expression. "You're not going to believe this," he said, "but . . ." Another poker game, an even bigger loss: $6.5 million.

I felt like he'd smashed me with a baseball bat. Who *was* this man?

Ron and Bill and I were joined at the hip. The three of us signed everything together, from loans and leases to contracts; if one of us tripped, we all fell down. And I had no way of knowing if Ron was telling the truth, even now. His debt could be several times what he'd admitted—and what else might he be hiding? What if he lost $25 million at the next game?

I was deeply, deeply shaken. Ever since Judy and I left the Valley, I'd been haunted by the fear that one day I'd have to go back. I'd done all I could to prevent that eventuality, locking every door and hatchway to our fortress—and, just as in a horror movie, I'd locked the problem in with me. *The phone call came from* inside *the house.*

I told Bob Goldman, "Ron's problem is back." He grimaced. "What can we do to protect the business?"

Bob said, "All we can do is try to control his spending—cancel his credit cards, put him on an allowance."

We budgeted Ron enough to sustain his standard of living and not penalize his children, but no more. This time he had to cover the debt on his own, which we hoped would deter him in the future. He borrowed the money from friends, which I found immediately reassuring—he'd put a Band-Aid on the wound—and also deeply troubling. He had a network with deep pockets and the skill set to take advantage of it, so why wouldn't he keep taking advantage of it?

Ron resented that I didn't give him any more money and that I put a limit on his credit cards. (What Bob and I didn't know was that in Vegas, Ron could easily get advances that vastly exceeded his card's supposed limit.) But he did not strain visibly against our leash. He said, "You guys are right, I screwed up, I'm going to fix this." I wish he'd fought with me about it so we could have gotten to the bottom of it. Instead Ron did what he did best. He handled me.

Despite my 360-degree paranoia, I hadn't seen any of this coming, which scared the crap out of me. I prided myself on reading people and forecasting from subtle clues. Is Tom Cruise great, or just a polite and attractive guy? Is Hal Ashby such a genius we should overlook his foibles, or is he too toxic? And here I hadn't been reading Ron right for ten years. That fact was so shocking to me that I instantly tried to forget it. I couldn't, though, and from then on I was constantly worried that Ron would take the agency down. Still, it never occurred to me to think through the logic of the way Ron introduced himself to people as my agent—to think about how much any agent keeps secret from his client. And it certainly never crossed my mind to worry that Ron would take *me* down.

CHAPTER ELEVEN

DINOSAURS AND FOOT SOLDIERS

BY THE LATE 1980S, WITH CAA ESTABLISHED AS THE CLEAR industry leader, interview requests flooded in. I hired a top New York media relations firm, Rubenstein Associates, to keep us *out* of the paper. But our aversion to talking to newspapers and magazines left us helpless to shape our public profile. We'd have been better served to soften our position—it might have diminished the impact of our only real scandal, which occurred in 1989.

It began when Joe Eszterhas, whose screenwriting credits included *Flashdance* and *Jagged Edge*, decided to get a new agent. Or rather, when he decided to go back to his old one. Eszterhas was a big, bearded, noisy self-promoter who'd gotten his start as a Cleveland newspaperman, moved on to *Rolling Stone*, then become a screenwriter after his first script got made as the Stallone film *F.I.S.T.* Joe had come to CAA after his original agent, Guy McElwaine, left ICM to take a studio job at Columbia.

Joe was a handful. What he styled as "colorful" was actually pure pain in the ass. But his energetic screenplays sold for $1.25 million, and served as the platform for lucrative packages. So we swallowed hard and reminded ourselves that it was a service business. After burning through two of our best agents in two years and bringing our tough-minded Rosalie Swedlin to tears, Joe was being handled by Rand Holston. Then Guy McElwaine was fired by Columbia and returned to ICM. Joe began telling everyone how much he loved Guy and how he felt honorbound to return to him. In September of 1989, he informed Rand that he wanted to leave. When Rand passed on the news, I winced and figured it was probably a lost cause. But I had to give it the old college try: I badly wanted to keep Joe as a client, and it was always a great tag line in pitch meetings: "No one ever leaves us." Debra Winger had left—but she'd come back. Hell, Joe himself had left us in 1982—but he, too, had come back. Yet he was now a bigger, noisier deal, and I worried that this time he wouldn't come back. My overriding fear was that if one big client left for good, it would embolden ten to follow, and then a hundred.

What happened after Joe walked into my office later that day became show business legend. Joe allegedly demanded to be released; I allegedly lost my temper and threatened him in the vilest terms; he allegedly left our offices in a rage. Two weeks later he shot off a heated letter with copies to his producer, his lawyer, and Guy McElwaine. He claimed I had threatened to sue him if he left CAA and tie him up in depositions so he couldn't work, and that I'd added, for good measure, "My foot soldiers who go up and down Wilshire Boulevard each day will blow your brains out" and "If you make me eat shit, I'm going to make you eat shit."

Joe's letter was leaked to the press. I put out a reply disputing his version of our meeting and inviting him to go back to Guy if that was what he wanted. Joe responded with a second letter that attacked me all over again.

For months the entertainment world buzzed. Joe's version of events sounded plausible to anyone who knew me, and my letter of reply, written by our lawyers—who were petrified that the Writers Guild would get involved and investigate us for restraint of trade—sounded weak and defensive. It's absolutely true that I didn't take losing agents or clients well, and that as a last resort I would threaten to scorch the earth, trying to make the wayward realize both how great a friend we were and how fearsome an enemy.

But Joe's account was total nonsense. Here's what happened: Joe sat on my sofa and confessed that he was happy at CAA. His problem was that he couldn't see how to stay with us without seeming disloyal to Guy. In jest, I said, "It's simple, Joe. Tell Guy I threatened to make your life difficult and you didn't need that kind of pressure. Tell him I said my foot soldiers will blow your brains out." We both laughed. Then I advised him to say publicly that CAA was holding him to his contract and commission obligations—which would give him an out, and, I thought, be good advertising that we played hardball.

He seemed relieved and pleased to have a plan. "Great," he said. Even as we shook hands, I had a hunch that our private understanding wouldn't stay private long, and that a wild man like Joe might leave us anyway. And so he did. I sensed—as I'm sure Joe did—that there was a lot going on beneath the surface of our meeting. Joe reminded me of the bullies in my elementary school, and I'm sure my disdain for toughs like him conveyed itself. He was neither dumb nor insensitive. Still, it never crossed my mind to anticipate that he'd claim my scripted "threat" was genuine and play the innocent victim. It was his word against mine, and Joe shouted louder. Think about it, though. What, even according to his version of events, was I actually going to do to him after he left? Break his typewriter?

When the controversy broke, Ron supported me both inside and outside the agency, but not wholeheartedly, and Bill wrote me a note saying that I should have just let Joe go. He was right: Joe was such a loose cannon we were better off without him. But I did wish, while I was being attacked on all sides, that Bill had stood with me. I also wished that I hadn't established a public persona that set me up so neatly to take the fall for Joe. I would have had a much happier life if I hadn't been so determined to appear all-knowing and invulnerable.

The fake controversy made Joe famous. Not long afterward, Guy got him a record $3 million for the screenplay for *Basic Instinct*. By bashing me and CAA and gaming the press, Joe had more than doubled his price. Four years later, with his career cooling, Joe approached one of our people to see if he could return to us.

I declined. Politely.

I BECAME A MICHAEL CRICHTON FAN WITH *THE ANDROM-eda Strain*, his first scientific thriller. Michael was a Harvard MD and Salk Institute research scientist. He'd been published in *Atlantic Monthly* and *Playboy* and the *New England Journal of Medicine*. He wrote with authority about subjects as far-flung as architecture, computers, and Jasper Johns. He could delve into any topic and make the reader feel like an expert within a dozen pages. He also wrote cinematically; his books unfolded as a series of pictures in your head. I called him out of the blue to say how much I liked *Coma*, a film he'd written and directed from the Robin Cook novel. A year later, in 1978, when I visited Sean Connery in England on the set of *The Great Train Robbery*, which Crichton had adapted from his own work, I met the author. He was six foot eight, shy, and such a polymath that I felt smarter after talking to him for just a few minutes. It was the beginning of what would later become a beautiful friendship.

My opening came the following year, when I made the deal for Bob Bookman, Michael's movie agent, to move from ICM to ABC Entertainment. Michael was talking to other agents, but he had yet to sign. He felt frustrated, he told me, because nobody believed he could drive a hit film. Most agents were bound by yesterday's thinking: audiences came out for movie stars. But Michael's novels sold on his name, and people flocked to his lectures. I told him he was a brand in the making, which was what he wanted to hear—and also true.

Signing Michael would eventually give us entrée to his powerful book agent, Lynn Nesbit, the head of ICM's literary department. Bob Bookman—who moved on from ABC to Columbia, giving us a friend there as a buyer, and then joined us at CAA in 1986—told me how angry Lynn was with her agency, ICM, after it had snubbed her for a partnership. Bob and I met Lynn for lunch in New York and then went to Mort Janklow with a proposal: Why didn't he and she partner up? Mort disliked ICM, so he was resistant, but we kept at it until he and Lynn joined forces in 1989. CAA's toughest rival in the lit arena was now our ally. Janklow & Nesbit remains one of the largest literary agencies in the world.

Though we began working with Michael with high hopes, his first two screenplays misfired. We planned to package a new Crichton novel with another director and keep Michael focused on his next big idea. But he slid into a depression. For two years in the late 1980s, he shut down completely. I called every day to try to get him up and moving, and I visited him often. When offers came in for him to direct or to rewrite a script, I had our agents say he was busy on an original.

A pillar of CAA's philosophy was that we told our clients the truth. That didn't mean we told everyone else the truth. I often had to offer more than I could deliver in order to be able to eventually deliver what I had offered. If the truth was bad for us, we had to change the reality, and then deliver it as what we'd said it was all along. In the meantime, well, you'd get creative. One of our best cover-up jobs was convincing the town, for two years, that Michael was hard at work when he was actually curled up in a ball. We didn't get caught on this kind of smokescreen because it hardly served the client we were protecting to throw us under the bus.

I never viewed this kind of misdirection as lying. Lying, to me, is a point-blank misstatement with no purpose in mind. I viewed what we did as positioning, molding, manipulating: taking fact sets and making them work for the result we wanted. That mind-set underpinned every single conversation we had with the buyers and they had with us, all day long. For instance, a studio exec calls me and says, "We want to replace Bob with Fred"—both are CAA clients—"for the next rewrite of the script."

"Not going to happen," I say. Because Bob is more expensive than Fred and I know Bob can get this done if the studio gives him a chance.

And the exec says, "Well, it is, because we already talked to Fred." He's trying to outflank me with a lie, and I know it's a lie because *I* already talked to Fred, and he'd told me that he didn't want to replace Bob (another lie).

And I say, "I already talked to Fred myself and he told me he doesn't want to replace Bob, who by the way is one of his closest friends"—a complete fib, but it makes the exec feel bad for getting between them and gives me some momentum. "Furthermore, Bob is already three quarters done with his next draft and it's terrific." Not even close to true, but at this point who can tell? And on it would go.

They were never lies to me. They were tools I needed to use to get shit done.

ONE DAY MICHAEL CALLED AND SAID, "I WANT TO TELL you about an idea I've been working on." I was elated to hear the vigor in his voice, and we made a date for lunch.

He arrived in his signature blue blazer, gray slacks, and penny loafers. As he folded into his seat, he said, "Three scientists get trapped in an amusement park where they're cloning dinosaurs. The clones overrun the fences, and everyone has to flee for their lives. Chaos ensues. What do you think?"

I said, "Wow!" Everyone I knew was nuts about dinosaurs, from my kids and their friends to my seventy-year-old father. Having quietly put in months of research as his depression began to lift, Michael said he could finish the manuscript in six months. I told him we'd all stand in line to see *Jurassic Park*, and we spent the rest of lunch plotting the book's afterlife as a film.

Research was the phase Michael enjoyed most. After putting off writing as long as possible, he went at it eighteen hours a day, seven days a week until he was done. He banged out *Jurassic Park* in a fury. It was like he'd been in hibernation, amassing energy for his signature work.

I read the rough draft in two sittings. "I think it's the best thing you've ever written," I told him. "And it's a gangbuster movie."

With Michael's assent, we did something unusual with his unpublished manuscript. We offered *Jurassic Park* exclusively to Steven Spielberg—who *still* hadn't signed with CAA. Steven was the one director Michael and I knew who possessed both the technique and the sense of wonder to pull the plot off. Playing favorites on this one would alienate a lot of our other filmmakers, but it was worth it. Bob Zemeckis, for instance, saw everything that came through CAA except for one or two projects. This was one of the one or two. When he and a half dozen other directors asked me about *Jurassic Park*, I told each of them, "Michael Crichton feels very strongly that only Steven can pull it off. If that doesn't work out, I will absolutely get you a meeting."

It was worth all the flak because this was how I could finally land Steven Spielberg as a CAA client.

To instill urgency, I asked Steven to read the book in one evening. He called at 6:00 the next morning and said, "I love this story. I'll do it." You couldn't get a top director to attach to an unfinanced project, much less to attach himself overnight, but *Jurassic Park* was the very rare exception. Kathleen Kennedy, Steven's partner and producer at Amblin Entertainment, followed his lead. With Michael helping to adapt his book as a screenplay, all the key elements were locked down. Casting would be secondary; the dinosaurs were the stars.

Given Steven's close ties to Universal's Sid Sheinberg, there was no screen rights auction. I called Sid and said, "I have good news and bad news. Which do you want first?"

"The good news?" he said, uncertainly.

"The good news is we have a Michael Crichton book about dinosaurs that will be published in six months. Steven has committed to direct it as his next film. Michael will write the screenplay with David Koepp. Kathy Kennedy says it can be done for sixty million, all in."

"That sounds fantastic! What's the bad news?"

I said, "The bad news is we own it and you don't."

Sid laughed nervously and said, "Well, how do we remedy that?"

I laid out the deal, a more radical version of what we had done on *Twins*—a fifty-fifty joint venture between the studio and Michael and Steven, who'd waive their above-the-line fees up front. Costs came off the top. Once the gross covered the budget, every subsequent dollar would be split down the middle. If the movie flopped, my clients wound up with nothing. But *Jurassic Park*'s story and talent made that a smart gamble.

As Universal was mired in a long dry spell and desperate for a blockbuster, Sid didn't come back to us asking for 70/30 or 60/40 or even 55/45. He came back with a *yes*. We'd moved from typo-ridden manuscript to fully financed studio commitment in less than a week. And Steven was finally a CAA client! We never actually had that conversation or filled out any paperwork; I just started representing him from that point on, taking it for granted.

The hardest part of *Jurassic Park* was fielding the calls from the other studios. The execs were furious—not with Michael Crichton, but with me. Eisner was a master at beating the crap out of me, trying to soften me up for next time, but it was a ritual they all engaged in. They'd say, "How could you do that to me after we did [Movie X that bombed] with you?" I'd say, "You're right, and we feel awful." And then I'd explain the particular circumstances: in this case, that "Michael wanted Spielberg, and Spielberg insisted on honoring his relationship with Universal." They'd call back after the movie had a test screening to repeat their complaints if it looked like a hit. If it tanked in testing, they didn't bother.

It was all theater.

STEVEN NEVER WATCHED HIS FILMS WITH AN AUDIENCE, never held a test screening. He was as sure of his instincts as he was sensitive to rejection, so what was the point? But I felt so confident about *Jurassic Park* that I coaxed him into joining us for the opening at the Avco Embassy. Judy and Kate and I dragged him into his back-row seat as the curtain rose. From the first jolting scene with the raptor in the box, the audience was *there*, riveted. After shielding his eyes with his hands through the first fifteen minutes, Steven began to relax. As the credits rolled, and we ran out of the theater amid wild applause, he was higher than I'd ever seen him.

Jurassic Park grossed nearly a billion dollars, minting money for Universal. And for once the deal was equally good for the artists who made the film.

WITH MICHAEL'S NAME BACK IN THE NEWS, WE CANVASSED our files for old material from him that could feel new. A young agent named Tony Krantz recalled a screenplay Michael had written in 1974 about a hospital emergency room, a setting derived from Michael's stint as a resident. "It's very avant-garde," Tony said, "and too small to be a movie." But not too small, he thought, for a dramatic TV series.

I called our old friend Tony Thomopoulos at Steven Spielberg's nascent television company, Amblin. (We helped Tony get that job after he was forced out at United Artists.) Then we brought in Warner Bros. to guarantee the financing and distribution and we pitched the idea to NBC, which bought a pilot.

Per Michael's and Steven's specifications, the pilot was made in an abandoned hospital in Los Angeles. It was fast paced and propulsive, all handheld cameras and people yelling over one another and blood everywhere. It felt fresh and strikingly authentic. But not to Don Ohlmeyer, NBC's West Coast chief. Don wore cashmere sweaters and no socks like a country club golfer, but he was a profane cowboy. He called me and said, "This is the biggest piece of crap I've ever seen. There's no way this shit is going on the air!" The audience research on the pilot— the equivalent of a test screening for a film—was also very negative. Don went on, combatively, "But I know you're going to try to force this on me."

I said, "I'm not going to argue with you on that." I hung up and called Les Moonves, a client of ours who ran Warner Bros., and then we each called Don's boss, Bob Wright, who ran NBC, to double-team him. We both stressed how groundbreaking and visceral the show was, and I told Bob: "Bottom line: Spielberg, Crichton, Warner Bros., and CAA." He wouldn't want any of those relationships to suffer a profound dip.

"What do you want?" Bob asked.

"Six more episodes," I said. The usual first order would have been six total, including the pilot, but I had such belief in the show I wanted viewers to have as many chances as possible to see it and love it. Bob agreed to pay for an additional six episodes filmed on a set built at Warner Bros. The cast was top-notch and the shows, overseen by a writer-producer named John Wells, were exquisitely crafted. I took a call from Ohlmeyer, expecting to hear some pleasure at how well it was turning out, and maybe even a backhanded apology.

"You guys really stuck it to me, didn't you?" he bellowed.

ER went on to win twenty-three Emmys over fifteen seasons, the longest run for a prime-time medical drama in history.

THOUGH MICHAEL HAD BEEN MARRIED FIVE TIMES, HE was by nature a loner. He was newly single when we met and he'd come solo to the weekly Ovitz "family" dinner parties for friends like Sean and Micheline Connery, Dustin and Lisa Hoffman, and Sydney and Claire Pollack. I remember one dinner that went until 1:30 in the morning, unheard of in L.A. Michael's flair for discussing the potential of computers or the various sources of Jasper Johns's inspiration made him the fulcrum around which conversations swung.

A number of years later I was introduced to Sherri Alexander at Toscana, the Italian restaurant in Brentwood, where she'd come with my good friend Teddy Forstmann, the private-equity billionaire. Teddy and I had met in the mideighties and I'd warmed to him, though a lot of people didn't. I ended up on five of his boards, and I served as his love-life consigliere, a busy role. He never married—

though he was famously involved with Princess Diana and Padma Lakshmi—because he could never find the right woman.

Of course, he wasn't the easiest guy. In the late nineties I put him together with Marcy Carsey and Tom Werner, the producers who'd made a bundle off shows like *The Cosby Show* and *Roseanne*, in a bid to buy the Family Channel, a network that aired a lot of old sitcoms. I prepped Teddy carefully, trying to get him to sand his rough edges, explaining that it was an entertainment deal and he had to play nice. He promised to be good. At the table, the first thing he said was, "Look, you're going to go bankrupt. So you can either sell to me now or come back to me in six months and get a lot less." No deal, unsurprisingly. Teddy was right about the channel's future—the owner did lose control of it—but that's not how you start a meeting. Still, he was wonderfully loyal: when he died, in 2011, his ex-barber, his ex-driver, an ex-cook, and five ex-girlfriends were still on his payroll.

At Toscana, Sherri Alexander and I chatted for two hours; she was a charming and vivacious conversationalist, though Teddy didn't seem to notice. As dinner concluded, Sherri rose to stand . . . and kept rising . . . and rising. How tall *was* this woman?

After confirming that she and Teddy were just friends, I called Michael and said, "I have finally found a woman you will actually enjoy and get along with—and she can look you in the eye." He laughed and took her number, but kept losing it or forgetting to call. At last I told him, "If you do not talk to her by tonight, I will not speak with you again." He did call, they went out—and instantly found the love they'd both sought all their lives. Tragically, they were together just four years before Michael's life was cut short by throat cancer.

Michael and I shared the same taste in art: Johns, Lichtenstein, Rauschenberg, and Claes Oldenburg. Michael considered Johns the definitive American painter. After I acquired my *White Flag*, he would sit in my living room, staring at the work by the hour and telling stories about Jasper. He never tired of that painting. Whenever I look at it today, I think of him.

In one of his essays, Michael wrote:

If you want to be happy, forget yourself. Forget all of it—how you look, how you feel, how your career is going. Just drop the whole subject of you. . . . People dedicated to something other than themselves—helping family and friends, or a political cause, or others less fortunate than they—are the happiest people in the world.

He was my wisest friend and the most steadfast; he was quiet when I succeeded but generous and comforting when I screwed up. As he liked to say, "There's always another race and another racetrack."

I miss him every fucking day.

CHAPTER TWELVE

WRIST LOCKS

AS A HIGH SCHOOL FRESHMAN, I DID GYMNASTICS AFTER school. I remember being stunned by the Sakamoto Brothers, respected local gymnasts who showed us martial-arts wrist locks. What awed me was their discipline. They had a *stillness* that set them apart from the kids I grew up around—or from me and my temper.

Inspired, I taught myself *budo*, the philosophy of martial arts and self-defense. I soon learned about the danger of a little knowledge. When I tried my beginner's judo moves on a bully named Scott Craig, he beat the crap out of me. After I lost, I thought, *I do not want to keep being terrorized by a bully who only lives a few blocks away.* So I congratulated Scott on beating the crap out of me, praising his power and technique. After that, whenever he came around the corner on his American Flyer bike, I'd wave and call out. A few weeks into my charm offensive, he became my friend and then my protector. It was a great lesson in how to make your enemies your friends.

At William Morris I began going to Ed Parker for Saturday classes in *Kenpo* karate. After we started CAA, I switched to a trainer in Santa Monica and to the more traditional *Shotokan* style. I finally focused on aikido, a blend of dance, chess, and combat in which you redirect your opponents' force against them. It felt a lot like being an agent, where you had to redirect a client's passion for doing something ruinous in a new and more productive direction.

My forty-five-minute morning workouts grew legendary after I began inviting people to my house on Saturday to watch; karate became part of my mystique. Richard Lovett, one of our young agents, treated me with noticeably more respect after he saw me toss my instructor around like a feather. Norman Lear couldn't get over what he'd seen, and started taking lessons. But he stopped, because it was hard: it required discipline, dedication, and hours and hours of time. Everyone stopped. I didn't stop.

One day Marty Baum told me, "I met the most amazing martial artist. I've never seen anything like what he does—you've got to meet him."

His name was Steven Seagal. After moving in his teens from California to Japan, he became the first foreigner to run an aikido dojo. He had 2,500 disciples, extraordinary for a *gaijin*, or outsider. He had returned to Los Angeles to help Sean Connery with a fight sequence for *Never Say Never Again*. I asked for a lesson, though I was a little concerned to hear that he'd broken Sean's wrist.

My new instructor rolled up our driveway in an ancient Rolls-Royce. It took fifteen seconds on the mat for me to see what Marty was talking about. Seagal was six foot four, strong, slim, and he moved like a gazelle. I hired him for three workouts a week at fifty dollars an hour.

A few weeks in, after we bowed to each other at the end of a session, Steven went to his backpack and pulled out a script he'd written. "Would you read this?" he asked. "I want to be an actor."

I said, "Steven, I know you want to be an actor, or you wouldn't be here teaching me. I'll read it over the weekend." I read the script on a Friday night, before our Saturday workout, and then I told him, "The script is fine"—which was overstating it—"but let me see what I can do more generally." As Chuck Norris had shown, a guy with the right physical attributes didn't need acting chops or a great script. In an action movie, all you need is a character and a mission and a blocked-out outline of the action. I loved action movies—they relaxed me—and I believed that a new action megastar would percolate up every decade: Eastwood, Schwarzenegger, Van Damme, and, later, Vin Diesel and Dwayne "The Rock" Johnson.

Warner Bros. had Eastwood, but he was shifting into less physically demanding roles. I called Terry Semel, Warner's president, and pitched a series of martial-arts films around a fresh face. "I'm going to send this guy over," I said, "and I want you to set up some mats and sandwiches and get your secretaries and assistants to come out at lunchtime for a demonstration." Then I told Steven I wanted him to bring his best apprentices and I wanted blood and shock.

He showed up with four black-belt protégés. He strode to the center of the mat, pricked his thumb with a butcher's knife, showed his audience the blood, and wiped it on his face. Then he shouted something in Japanese and all four guys ran at him full tilt with knives. Steven slipped aside and then picked them off one by one, sending each one flying, and flipping the last guy high into the air. There was blood all over the mat. Steven bowed and left without a word.

Terry was still jonesing on adrenaline when he called: "What the hell was *that*?"

"That," I said, "is your new action star." The studio budgeted $8 million for a nonunion production of *Above the Law* with a promising young director, Andy Davis. When I saw the rough cut, I thought, *This guy is going to be huge.* The opening scene was essentially the battle he'd choreographed for Terry Semel.

We previewed the movie by invitation in Burbank. Steven prowled the hallways of the theater, totally unrecognized. Bob Daly, the studio's CEO, came over and said, "Michael, you really screwed me on this one. I ran this movie last night, and it's terrible." He'd watched it by himself, and he was not a chopsocky aficionado, so he had no idea what he was talking about.

"Bob, I know martial-arts movies," I said. "This one's terrific."

"No, you screwed me."

"I'll tell you what," I said. "CAA will buy it back from you right now. I'll send you a cashier's check for eight million dollars tomorrow morning." I knew that Fox needed a spring replacement for a film they'd canceled. I could resell *Above the Law* with one phone call.

Bob said, "Deal!" and we shook hands.

That Burbank preview marked aikido's screen debut in America. As Steven hurled bad guys through plateglass windows, the audience response was electric. At the end, after our hero had dispatched a rogue CIA agent and a savage drug ring, there was a standing ovation. When the lights went up and people spotted Steven, they swarmed him.

I turned to Bob Daly and said, "Too bad you don't own the movie."

"Nonsense!" he replied.

While *Above the Law* did just okay at the box office, the videocassette went through the roof. Steven Seagal made a series of movies that together grossed nearly $300 million, and he was by far Warner Bros.' most profitable star in the early nineties. He got $150,000 for *Above the Law* and he was thrilled. We got him $3 million for *Hard to Kill*, and $40 million for the next three movies. Including the back end, CAA made at least $10 million off him. Though Steven was growing fleshier by the release, I thought he could go on for years.

But he wanted more. One day he told me, "I think I'm as good an actor as Hoffman, De Niro, all those guys."

I said, "Steven, I'm not sure about that, but what makes you special is that those guys can't do aikido."

"You don't understand," he said. "I want to direct my next movie and win an Academy Award. And I want you to help me."

It's true that we were often able to do nearly impossible things. In 1982, Prince came to see me in the office. He was wearing a one-piece gold lamé jumpsuit and huge wooden platform shoes that clip-clopped in our hallways like a cart horse, and he was accompanied by the largest bodyguard I have ever seen. After I persuaded Prince, not without difficulty, to leave his bodyguard outside, he told me that he wanted to make and star in a musical movie. I told him we could do it. But Bob Daly at Warner Bros.—whose label put out Prince's music—was completely resistant to the concept.

So I called his son, Bobby, to get him to talk to his father. I didn't know that Bobby was a Prince fan, as fortunately he turned out to be; if he hadn't been, I'd have said, "Let me send you over some albums and then we'll talk." Bobby spoke to his dad and convinced him that Prince was indeed the future, and *Purple Rain* ended up being huge. That's a move I still make, getting people's kids to tell their influential parents what's really going on. After you hit thirty-five, maybe even thirty, you no longer have any idea what's coming next, assuming you ever did. I only became convinced Madonna was a true superstar when my daughter, Kim, started dressing like her.

Yet CAA's reputation as miracle workers meant we were constantly being asked not merely to heal the sick but to raise the dead. After *The Wiz* hit big for our client Michael Jackson, we took a meeting at Michael's house, and Michael told us he wanted to be the star of an action movie. As he talked, his hat fell into the guacamole in front of him, and he picked it out and put it back on—unfortunately, with a blob of guacamole attached, which began to slide down the brim. Ron Meyer tapped my leg to draw my attention to it, and we all watched in horrified fascination as it slid lower and lower while Michael was pitching us hard on how he was America's next action hero. Then the blob fell off, and Ron totally lost it. I cracked up, too, despite my best efforts at self-control, and Michael stalked out.

I went and found him and explained for fifteen minutes that we hadn't been laughing at *him*, but at the incident. That we'd never laugh at him, as we had so much respect for him as a man and an artist. And so forth, over and over, more and more vehemently. Finally, Michael's face cleared. "Okay, Ovitz. Okay," he said. "But I want to play James Bond." I am proud to report that I didn't laugh, this time. I nodded empathetically, as if I were really thinking through the possibilities, and then I said, "You're thinly built, you're too sensitive, you won't be credible as a brutal block of stone. You'd be great at it, of course, but it'd be bad for *you*."

Steven Seagal's secret dream of playing a sensitive, tortured artist was, unfortunately, just as unlikely. Discerning my lack of enthusiasm, Steven left CAA. He went on to direct himself in *On Deadly Ground*, a total misfire. He had fallen prey to the dangerous, entirely human delusion that if you succeed in one arena you can do *anything*.

———

JUDY MADE IT CLEAR THAT, FOR HER, THREE KIDS WAS plenty. But I'd always wanted to have five or six kids. The idea of a large family milling around together, particularly on vacations, was deeply appealing (perhaps because when I was growing up we could never afford a real trip anywhere). So as the kids grew I began adding to our family ad hoc. When Chris's friend Jordan Harris graduated from Colgate and needed a place to live, I encouraged him to move in. Jordan lived on and off with us for years. He became my godson and our family's behind-the-scenes peacemaker—an incredibly upbeat, unflappable kid who always made sure everyone else was getting along.

In the late nineties, I met Rickson Gracie, the Brazilian jujitsu star, and became curious about his dynamic brand of martial arts. I was soon working out seven days a week with Rickson's protégé, Marco Albuquerque, a twenty-three-year-old kid from the favelas of Rio. Marco was five foot nine, with a twenty-inch neck and a scarred, shaved head. Despite his formidable appearance, he was remarkably sweet tempered, and he became like a son to Judy and me and like an older brother to our kids. He was always watching out for them. It gave me an extra sense of comfort knowing that he could really handle himself: on Saturdays, he was teaching FBI agents how to control white-collar criminals during an arrest. (He brought me in as a guest teacher on the topic of wrist locks.)

One night when Chris and his friend Jake Hoffman, Dusty's son, were in their early twenties, they were out at a club called Nacional. A big, tough-looking drunk got very aggressive when Jake accidentally bumped him. Jake apologized immediately, but the guy started to threaten him. Then, from nowhere, Marco was in the guy's face screaming at him in Portuguese. Terrified of this pitbull of a man, the guy said, "Sorry, brother, my mistake," and apologized to Jake. Marco, still spitting fire, told the guy to go apologize to Chris, who was on the other side of the bar. The guy was so shaken he made his way to Chris, tapped him on the shoulder, and said, "Hey man, I'm so sorry, please tell your buddy that I don't want any trouble!" I always felt more at peace knowing Marco was watching my kids.

Marco did everything for us: he laid a tile floor for Judy, trained Eric in jujitsu, and helped him move into his apartment. Loyal and considerate, he came on every vacation with us, just as Jordan did. As a side hustle, he often went to Rio to guide American tourists, but when he was in L.A. he slept at our house three nights a week, and stayed at the beach house in Malibu the other four. To advance his cause with women he liked to let on that the beach house was his. When we were all on vacation off Capri, he brought three Italian women to the boat and gave them a proprietary tour. "Mr. Albuquerque, is there anything I can get you?" I said, playing along. "We'd like a bottle of the best chardonnay on the boat," he said, grinning at me. "Immediately, please."

On Christmas Eve 2010, we got a call from Marco's cousin in Rio: Marco had been shot and killed by two hoods from his old favela. High on angel dust, they wanted his Range Rover and the stack of presents he was carrying for his friends.

It was an enormous shock; a crippling jolt of unfairness, and it left a giant hole in our family.

He was thirty-nine.

CAA CAME TO SUBSCRIBE TO *NEMAWASHI*, THE JAPANESE style of bottom-up consensus. We didn't hire anyone from outside until they'd met with and been approved by the whole department. The process made onboarding smooth, easing new talent into the company.

(It helped that we promoted two people for each one we imported.) No one questioned our calls because they'd already signed off on them.

It may seem like anceint history now, but in the eighties, America was fascinated by Japan. It was the little-understood, much-feared Asian force that China is today. The intrigue with the Japanese culture began with our 1980 miniseries *Shōgun*, only to grow warier as Japanese industries threatened the American semiconductor and computer companies. Their cultural values—homogenous, self-deprecating, hard for outsiders to read—made them seem formidable. Who knew what they'd buy or disrupt next? As former vice president Walter Mondale remarked about the future, "What are our kids supposed to do? Sweep up around the Japanese computers?"

Believing that Japan had to be reckoned with, I read everything I could about the country and its culture, from the works of Edwin Reischauer, our former ambassador, to Akio Morita's *Made in Japan*, the story of Sony's remarkable rise. In 1963, after cofounding the company and choosing its English-sounding name, Morita moved his family to New York City. He enrolled his children in American schools and absorbed how Americans thought. He watched the Beatles on *The Ed Sullivan Show*. Our culture made a lasting impression on him—and vice versa. Sony eventually became a top brand name in the United States. Morita was a chameleon CEO: an Asian in Asia, a European in Europe, an American in America. But I was the only person I knew with a copy of his book, and it served me well.

My entrée to doing business in Japan came through Walter Yetnikoff, the brash president of CBS Records, then the world's leading music company. We became friendly after I snagged him a producer's credit on *Ruthless People*, a dark comedy with Bette Midler and Danny DeVito, and we began officially representing him in 1985 in "an exclusive motion picture deal with Disney," as I wrote the staff. Walter wanted to be in movies; I wanted to understand his world. Walter's style was to shake everything upside down and inside out, but his artists swore by him. Underneath a New Age veneer, he was a tough customer. "I'm very spiritual," he once said. "I connect spiritually with my inner self, then I go out and I try to fuck people."

In 1986, when Larry Tisch took control of CBS, Walter declared war on "the Evil Dwarf," as he called his new boss. After signing superstars like Michael Jackson and Bruce Springsteen, Walter felt he'd earned the right to make Tisch miserable.

Through his work for CBS/Sony Records, a thriving joint venture in Japan, Walter had cultivated a relationship with Norio Ohga, the Sony president who made Morita's vision happen. Ohga had a soft spot for "the crazy American." It was the pre-Apple era, when Sony set the standard for anything that fit in your hand. They introduced the mini tape recorder and the transistor radio, and then came the Walkman, the analog iPod strapped to every jogger's belt. Sony now wanted a piece of the content that played on those devices, which was where their crazy American came in. Walter was eager for Sony to buy CBS Records.

I began hanging out with Walter and his pals, music manager Tommy Mottola and attorney Allen Grubman, at an industry tavern on Columbus Avenue. They were never boring. (I watched Walter rip Allen's shirt off at Black Rock, the CBS headquarters on West Fifty-second Street.) No one divulged much in Hollywood, but the music business was completely different. One day Walter was gabbing loudly about CBS Records being for sale, disclosing all sorts of privileged financial data. I said, "Hey, you don't want anyone to hear this."

"What do you mean?" he said. "I want everybody to know I'm trying to get rid of the Evil Dwarf!"

Not fifteen minutes later I was summoned to Tommy Mottola's limo to take a call on his car phone. It was Michael Eisner at Disney, bottom fishing. "I hear Walter's talking, and we want to bid," he said. (As usual, he bid too low.) That's when I saw the method to Walter's madness. He was driving CBS Records into a fire sale so he could control it under a new owner.

This music deal was the first time Ron and I diverged. I didn't have the patience to sit on the phone with Cher for an hour; he did. I did have the patience to sit with Walter Yetnikoff for five hours as he savaged Larry Tisch and plotted how to sell CBS Records. Ron thought it was all a loss of focus and a waste of time.

With no real platform—I wasn't representing CBS or Sony or even Michael Eisner—I put myself in the middle of the situation. I was a connector; it's what I did all day, and now I decided to try to connect the parties and learn what I was supposed to be doing as I went along. Through a mixture of confidence and silent observation, I kept my place at the table. No one ever said, as they would have been perfectly right to do, "What the fuck are you doing here?"

I set up a meeting between Walter and Larry Tisch. "This doesn't have to be antagonistic," I told Walter. "Larry's a smart businessman; he'll listen to you." Whatever you thought of Tisch's management skills, he'd taken a theater chain and some second-tier Catskills resorts and built them into the $70 billion Loews Corporation. I thought he had earned some respect.

Walter proceeded to do everything I'd told him not to do. He ridiculed his boss's ignorance of the music business, called him "the Evil Dwarf" to his face, and flatly declined to prepare a budget for the coming year. I called Larry later to apologize. "I'm used to it," he said wanly. If Walter had tried that on Steve Ross, Steve would have laughed in his face and had two security men usher him out. GE's Jack Welch would have vaulted the table and coldcocked him. But Tisch was another breed of cat, and because Walter had bullied him into believing that CBS Records would fall apart without Walter, he was open to Sony's proposals. Anything to get Walter out of his life.

Sony's investment banker, the Blackstone Group, was founded and run by Steve Schwarzman and Pete Peterson, the Sony director who had served as secretary of commerce under Richard Nixon. In Japan, a Washington résumé made you a minor deity, and Akio Morita revered Peterson's judgment. My job was advising Walter, who ignored me, so I mostly stayed in the shadows to watch and listen. After Larry Tisch approved the sale of CBS Records to Sony for $1.2 billion, Bill Paley, the company's chairman and founding father, had second thoughts about dismantling a large part of his legacy. When CBS's board rejected the deal, Morita stayed calm, and he ended up paying $2 billion, which many people thought was too much. But Morita was very shrewd. By assuming sole ownership of the record company, Sony gained hundreds of millions of dollars in Tokyo real estate, an item somehow overlooked by CBS's auditors.

After this first exposure to corporate mergers, I made a list of M&A specialists—the right lawyer, the best accountant, a top public relations firm—and met with them to learn their craft. As I absorbed the nuts and bolts of making a deal, it struck me that it wasn't that different from assembling a movie package: you had to put all the elements together first, get the buyer and seller in sync, then strike a price.

With talent agencies barred, through our contracts with the talent guilds, from owning more than 10 percent of a studio or production company, the next best thing for CAA would be to broker those assets. If we had direct access to the moguls who owned the media, and would-be buyers had to go through us to get to those moguls—well, that would be a great position to be in. It became the heart of our (meaning my) new five-year plan. Ultimately, I wanted to own a studio, but I figured that if we became deal advisers or even principals, it would put more distance between us and the other agencies, bring in larger fees—and keep me from getting bored.

———

WALTER HAD A STRONG RIVAL FOR NORIO OHGA'S AFFEC-tions in Mickey Schulhof, head of Sony's U.S. operations. A physics PhD who spoke several languages, Mickey was the anti-Yetnikoff, smooth and methodical. Ohga valued Mickey's work ethic and trusted him entirely. Ohga didn't trust Walter at all, but he valued the executive's skill and chutzpah and the good life that surrounded him. Ohga

made around $400,000 a year, absurdly low by U.S. executive stan-
dards, but he lived well beyond his means, putting up in New York at
a penthouse duplex filled with high-end art near the Russian Tea
Room. Mickey and Walter were the left and right sides of Ohga's brain.

In the spring of 1988, shortly after Sony closed on CBS Records,
Mickey called Walter to tell him the execs in Tokyo were interested in
buying a movie studio. Walter dreamed of becoming a mogul, and now
he saw his shot. "Go find a studio," he told me, "and I'll buy it."

Knowing that Walter liked to set plans in motion without autho-
rization, I said I could not solicit a seller until I knew we had a legitimate buyer. "Okay," he said, "I'll put you in a room with Morita."

"Why not have him come meet me in L.A.?" I said, pretty sure that
would end the conversation.

"When?"

I gave him five openings. Walter confirmed the second date, two
weeks out, and set the meeting for 10:30 a.m. at my home in Brentwood. Unconvinced, I brought home a stack of work to fill the missed
appointment. At 10:30 on the dot, my bell rang. Outside I found an
elegant man with a mane of wavy gray hair parted in the middle, and
Walter and Mickey in tow. Akio Morita had come straight off the
company jet from Japan, but his suit was wrinkle-free, his shirt pressed,
his tie knotted. He looked tan and fit, like someone who'd just worked
out and showered. Morita introduced himself in flawless English. We
moved to my screening room and talked for two hours.

Morita was an ebullient guy who spoke candidly about the VCR
wars, a humbling defeat for his company. Sony's Betamax, the superior
machine, had lost to the VHS consortium led by Matsushita. "I don't
want to get beat again," Morita told me. "If I had owned a movie studio,
Betamax would not have finished second." He was a believer in synergy,
or what he called "total entertainment," a mesh of hardware and content. With the acquisition of CBS Records (soon to become Sony Music
Entertainment), his company was the world's leading producer of music. Thanks to Trinitron, it was the number one maker of televisions.
Video—movies and TV shows—seemed the logical next step.

His biggest challenge was the internecine warfare among his divisions. Sony Japan, for example, refused to communicate with Mickey Schulhof's Sony America. Had Morita asked me, I'd have advised him to stick to hardware, or to at least buy Columbia in partnership with a TV network, so he'd have help as he familiarized himself with the terrain. Hollywood is notoriously difficult for outsiders to grasp. But agents weren't paid to judge CEO's plans. My choice was to help Morita or not.

In CAA's interests, I chose to help. As the top supplier of talent to the major studios, we had a big stake in keeping them afloat. They needed cash, and what better source in a downturn than Japan? If we succeeded, the seller—CAA—would be buying a buyer. We'd go where no agents had gone before.

THAT FALL I MADE THE FIRST OF MANY TRIPS TO SONY'S headquarters in Tokyo. While Morita and his deputies knew more about Hollywood than other Asian executives did, they needed an insider to handicap the studio field. I eliminated four of the seven majors. Disney, thriving under Eisner, was too expensive. Sony had no chance at Warner Bros. under Steve Ross, and Rupert Murdoch was untouchable at Fox. At Paramount the problem was Martin Davis, the chairman of the parent company, Gulf & Western. He was a notorious tire kicker who opened countless deals but rarely closed one.

That left three candidates. MGM/United Artists was in free fall, but how much would you have to overpay? Then there was Columbia, owned by Coca-Cola. Coke had recently netted a billion dollars by spinning the studio off and merging it with TriStar. For the right offer they might be persuaded to take the rest of their money off the table.

My first choice was Universal, whose sagging stock price made it vulnerable. With movies, television, and music, along with four hundred acres of prime real estate, the company seemed a good fit, and Sony would inherit strong management in Lew Wasserman and Sid Sheinberg. But as chairman and absolute ruler of MCA, Universal's parent company, Lew wasn't ready to go gently. When I called to sound him out, he spat back, "Universal's not for sale, and under no conditions would I sell to the Japanese. Don't even think about it."

My next stop was Kirk Kerkorian, who'd been chopping up MGM's assets since buying the debt-ridden studio back from Ted Turner two years earlier. Like Warren Buffett, Kirk was an unassuming billionaire. He answered his own phone and lived above a garage in a modest house on ten acres in Beverly Hills. After ushering me into his office, Kirk said, "I want a lot for the company. How would Sony pay for it?" Meaning, stock or cash?

I laid a credit card on the table and Kirk started laughing. "I'm guessing you don't want their stock," I said. "I think they'll pay cash. But I'd suggest you meet with Morita first and find out if you see eye to eye."

We resumed in my living room, with Morita the last to arrive. The two heavyweights sparred as I steered the talk to new Sony technologies, a topic of keen interest to Kirk. Morita was a salesman even when he was buying, and he'd come prepared. He set down a box that contained the latest Sony Watchman, their portable pocket television. Kirk stared at it throughout the meeting. At the end Morita said, "I'd like to show you what we'll be releasing." It was the first color Watchman, and Kirk would have killed for one—it was the beginning of the tech age, and it was really cool to have a gadget no one else did. Then Morita packed up his Watchman and left. *If you want one of these, you've got to make the deal.*

But Kirk's religion was maximum return. He set the studio's price well north of a billion dollars, plus residual rights to the MGM name for his hotels around the globe. Morita said, "It's too high."

Then I heard from Herb Allen of Allen & Company, Hollywood's investment house of choice, that Columbia might be for sale.

SEVEN YEARS EARLIER, AFTER THE PRODUCER RAY STARK introduced us, Herb Allen had invited me to his first annual Sun Valley Conference, which eventually became known as the summer camp for moguls. Each day we had formal case-study presentations from the principals of America's biggest companies, and over lunch afterward, I found myself musing about life with Rupert Murdoch and John Malone, the CEO of the cable TV provider Tele-Communications, Inc. I had an avid interest in the corporate side of the media business, and the corporate guys were curious about how I linked up with talent. I went back every year. The Sun Valley getaways did wonders for my networking, and my image.

Herb was accessible to everyone but the press and the social set. He rose before 5:00 a.m., had dinner at 6:00 p.m. sharp, and was in bed by 9:00. One time I was at his Wyoming ranch when a phone call made me half an hour late to the cookhouse. Three courses were lined up at my place setting. Herb looked at me and said, "When I say 6:00, I mean 6:00." He was smiling, but I took his point.

Herb was a model of integrity. After Sumner Redstone broke a promise and engaged another investment bank, he sent Allen & Company a token check for $1 million. I was in Herb's office when it arrived. He took out his scissors, cut the check into tiny pieces, and returned them to sender.

Herb was supremely loyal. He never forgot a birthday and gathered old college pals to dinners and on biking trips. After one friend got sent to Leavenworth for a white-collar crime, Herb visited him twice a year.

And he was a masterly businessman. Herb had shepherded Columbia to Coca-Cola in 1982, when he parlayed his shares into a seat on Coke's board and briefly served as its chairman. Having masterminded the TriStar merger, he was still Columbia's godfather. In 1987, near the end of David Puttnam's stormy reign as studio head, Herb called me to ask, "Do you know anything about a movie called *Me and Him*?"

I said I did.

Herb said, "I've got a problem." He'd just heard from a livid

Roberto Goizueta, Coca-Cola's CEO. "They ran it for the Coke staff and had to shut it off."

"Do you know what the movie's about?"

"No, Roberto was yelling too much in Spanish."

"Well, Herb," I said, "*Me and Him* will never get released."

"Why not?"

"Okay, opening scene: Griffin Dunne is waiting for a bus. There's a beautiful girl walking down the street. Cut to Griffin Dunne, and you hear a voice going, 'Wow, she's really cute, isn't she?' And Griffin shouts, 'Shut up!' A conversation follows, but you only see one person." I went on, drawing it out, enjoying myself, until Herb interjected "Good God!" He'd grasped the problem: Coca-Cola, the all-American company, owned a film about a man with a talking penis.

Then came *Ishtar*, starring Dustin Hoffman and Warren Beatty, a notorious flop, and Coke decided that it'd had its fill of glamorous Hollywood.

Though Columbia hadn't been our first choice for Sony, it was the only viable option. First, I had to get the two sides in a room. That wasn't easy because Walter Yetnikoff had a long-standing feud with Victor Kaufman, the straitlaced Columbia studio chief. I shuttled between them to remind them that fighting each other was contrary to what their bosses wanted. Kaufman finally agreed to see Mickey Schulhof for lunch. Talks began in earnest after Mickey met with Herb Allen.

Though we sat on opposite sides of the table, Herb and his associates mentored me throughout. Enrique Senior walked me through the art of valuation, Paul Gould was my deal-point tutor, and Herb himself schooled me on how to keep the process moving. He could herd the most difficult people without cracking his whip or indulging his own ego. And because I had the highest regard for Herb's probity, I never worried that he would try to put anything over on us.

Sony commissioned CAA to appraise Columbia's creative assets. The studio's library contained more than two hundred television titles, including soap operas and Merv Griffin game shows. The movie side featured hundreds of classic films as well as some of the fruits of CAA's stellar run (*Stripes*, *Ghostbusters*, *Gandhi*, and *Tootsie*, among others). Our assignment boiled down to an extremely amorphous question: What was an ongoing show or an old but classic movie worth?

To solve it, we leaned on the Harvard MBAs we'd hired away from the studios and Wall Street. One was a young man who'd flunked his prior two jobs but came so well recommended by my friend and associate Mike Menchel that I gave him a shot. I put Sandy Climan through a tough meeting in 1986 and asked if he'd start with a token salary and my small conference room for an office, and he didn't hesitate. His brilliance with numbers soon made him my trusted deputy, and he went on to run our ten-person corporate finance unit. (Years later he'd tell people that I tasked him with conveying veiled threats to executives, which was laughable: Sandy was a short, plump Orthodox Jew who wouldn't frighten a mouse. If I had a veiled threat to deliver, I did it myself.)

With half a dozen staff members, Sandy compiled hundreds of pages of manually typed spreadsheets on Columbia's library. It was painstaking, deeply researched work. There was no one-size-fits-all algorithm; we reviewed each film or TV show, line by line. What contracts were out on a given title and when did they expire? What was the current cash flow, and what did the future hold? The variables were complex. One big hit in syndication could drag six less popular movies along behind it. With *Tootsie* as a hook, for example, a local station could program a Dustin Hoffman weekend. The trickiest part was predicting revenues for the 150 movies in Columbia's pipeline. But we'd read all the scripts and knew which ones we'd be packaging with our top clients, so we could estimate the box office with some degree of accuracy.

Pete Peterson and Steve Schwarzman had a crackerjack team at Blackstone, and they addressed Columbia's valuation, including its real estate, from every possible angle. Collaborating with Pete and

Steve and Herb Allen beat going to Harvard Business School; they taught me how to be an investment banker. (That was one of Blackstone's first big deals; it's now worth about $40 billion.) Pete and Steve digested our data and produced three numbers for Columbia's total worth—high, intermediate, and low. In the end, the price would be what Morita chose to pay.

―――――――

WHEN OUR DEAL TEAM FIRST VISITED SONY'S HEADQUARTERS in Tokyo, I fell in love with Japan. Tokyo's strangeness—the signs filled with pictographs, the elevated freeways—energized me. Running through litter-free fish markets at 3:00 in the morning, in a country where no one had firearms, I felt completely safe. The trains came on time and the stations were pristine. When Michael Jackson finished performing at a sixty-thousand-seat stadium, the audience stayed quietly in their seats until a man in a yellow jacket dismissed them by sections. I love order, so this was basically my dream country.

One of our hosts asked, "Is there anything special you want to do?"

I said, "We want to learn about the country. We are your students. Teach us." We accepted every invitation—a tour of the Imperial Palace or a Shinto temple, a side trip to Kyoto. I saw my hotel room only to sleep. Give me a spare hour and I'd peel off to a sushi bar in the Ginza, bow to the chef, and point to what I wanted. Or I'd visit Shibuya, Tokyo's SoHo, where teens wore Rolling Stones T-shirts and the latest Nikes.

My enthusiasm for the culture seemed to make an impression, but still, our meetings at Sony resembled the scene in *Lost in Translation* when the ad director carries on for an eternity and then the translator tells Bill Murray, "More intensity." When Ohga went silent or seemed to doze off as the others talked among themselves, I could only guess at what we were missing.

Only gradually did Sony's execs let their hair down. It turned out they liked the same things we did—martial arts and electronics, sure, but also golf, tennis, and movies. My half-dozen visits to Tokyo taught me about patience. It took many months to gain the trust of the Japanese. They did not rush decisions. Courtesy trumped candor; yes usually meant no, and no often meant yes. More than once I ran into Americans back from Tokyo who exclaimed, "I had the best meeting ever and we're going to close!" I told them to get back to me in a year. A year later they'd ruefully call to report that their deal was still pending.

HERB ALLEN MET MICKEY SCHULHOF THAT FALL AT TETER-boro Airport in New Jersey to hammer out the price. Mickey and I had worked closely all along, and I hoped to help him reach a fair number. Frankly, I thought he'd get eaten alive without help. Herb was a killer negotiator, deft and impossible to read. One-on-one it was a mismatch. But Mickey had the title and the relationship with Ohga, and he chose to fly solo. He either thought Herb and I were too close or he wanted sole credit for fulfilling Morita's dream. Like Walter, he had ambitions to run the Sony entertainment empire.

Mickey opened with a share offer in the low twenties. Herb countered at thirty-five—a stretch because Columbia had been trading as low as twelve dollars and was slogging through its second straight down year at the box office. It was an auction of one; Coca-Cola would sell to Sony or to nobody. Mickey might have done better to back off for a bit.

Behind closed doors, Herb traded on a rumor of an eleventh-hour bid from Rupert Murdoch—it being perfectly acceptable in deal making to use information or perceived information to better your position. (If Herb had said Rupert had made a firm offer with a term sheet, that would have been improper. Just as it would have been wrong for him to manipulate a reporter to get a story about another offer published, then traded on that—as some bankers have been known to do.) I knew Rupert didn't need or want Columbia. His sole interest was in their library, and he wasn't going past fifteen dollars a share. But Herb got Mickey thinking, *What if Murdoch moves in fast?* Knowing how badly Morita wanted a studio, he couldn't come back empty-handed.

Without consulting anyone, Mickey placed a midnight call to Ohga. Then he called Herb at home with a bid of twenty-seven dollars a share, far higher than Blackstone's low-end projection. Herb was delighted to take that number to Coca-Cola's board, which was delighted to accept it. It came to a $5 billion price tag (including $1.6 billion in debt), the biggest Hollywood deal ever and the largest Japanese acquisition of any kind in the United States.

In July 1989, more than a year after they hired me, Sony's board approved the Columbia purchase with one condition: a new studio chief.

———

WHEN OUR TALKS BEGAN, WALTER YETNIKOFF HAD CASU-ally remarked that he wanted me to run Columbia after it was sold. Sony's leaders had a similar idea, though they held off on a formal offer until the deal was nearly closed. I asked Bob Greenhill, the head of Morgan Stanley, to represent me in contract talks. But that was a pose to protect my position in the deal. Part of me—the part that had begun to view CAA as a stepping-stone—did want to run everything eventually. But the agency was humming along on all cylinders then, and I loved the place. I couldn't see stepping out of our race car to partner with the Japanese. I didn't speak their language, and Sony's bureaucracy was like the House of Borgia. Even the most ingratiating American would end up needing a food taster.

In any case, I couldn't possibly work under Walter. Sure, there was no beating his relationship with Ohga, Morita's designated successor as Sony's CEO. But as the deal entered crunch time, Walter vanished. The next time I heard his voice was from a pay phone at Hazelden, the Minnesota rehab center. His setback didn't hurt his relationship with Ohga, but others at Sony were less forgiving: Walter's influence was on the wane. Much as I liked him, I'd be hitching my wagon to a star that could go supernova at any moment. (In his memoir, *Howling at the Moon*, Walter later wrote about his martial-arts fantasy to fight me to the death in Madison Square Garden. He was something of a crazy man, but that would have been a very uneven fight.)

To permit the Japanese to save face, I asked for 20 percent equity and control over Columbia's board, a deal no public company could accept. When Walter told me he had to look elsewhere, I gladly helped him make a short list of candidates. My first choice was Frank Price, who'd run Columbia. He came out of TV, where story was king, and knew how to read a screenplay and speak the artists' language (and he'd always been open to CAA's packages). My second was Frank Wells, Michael Eisner's number two, a superlative deal guy. But Price shared my wariness of Japanese ownership, and Wells declined to leave Disney.

At that point, Sony's inexperience began to show. Walter leaned toward Peter Guber and Jon Peters, the production team that was riding high after Tim Burton's *Batman*. (They also claimed credit where none was due for *Rain Man* and *The Color Purple*.) I thought they were wrong for Sony. While I had a soft spot for Jon, the onetime hairdresser from the Valley, he was too impetuous for the executive suite. And I doubted Peter really wanted the job; he'd done it before and he didn't need the money.

I expected Peter to charm Ohga and Mickey Schulhof, who were Hollywood rookies. But I was astounded when Sony paid $200 million to buy Guber and Peters out of their company and another half a billion to get them released from their commitment to Time Warner. Had Walter gone to Steve Ross with a modicum of respect, as Mickey and I begged him, Steve might have canceled the contract as a favor. But Walter was always spoiling for a fight, and Steve wiped the floor with him.

My final task on the deal was presiding over a session to sort out any regulatory issues. It took an hour to run through Coca-Cola's checklist: the Hart-Scott-Rodino Antitrust Improvements Act, SEC concerns, and so forth. Then I turned to Sony and asked about loose ends on their side. A company representative said, "Nothing, it's all done. The appropriate parties have blessed the deal." Akio Morita was a keystone member of his *keiretsu*, an interlocking business association under the aegis of the Japanese government. He made one or two phone calls and the red tape disappeared.

———

COLUMBIA STRUGGLED UNDER ITS NEW OWNERS. JON PE-ters was forced out in 1991, two years after the deal was signed and a year after Walter Yetnikoff was fired from Sony Music. Peter Guber resigned in 1994, around the time Sony took a $3.4 billion write-off on Columbia, one of the largest losses in the history of the entertainment business. Mickey Schulhof lasted a year longer, before Ohga's successor let him go. I was happy I'd passed on Walter's offer.

The Sony-Columbia deal came to symbolize the hazards of invest-ing in Hollywood. But Akio Morita cared less about short-term profits than long-term positioning. He made a mint from CBS Records, and a no-interest loan from the Japanese government softened Sony's losses on the studio. Though his hardware-software synergy proved a mirage, Sony found redemption for Betamax when its Blu-ray DVD format prevailed as the high-definition standard, in part on the strength of Sony's movie titles. And Columbia Pictures rebounded in the late 1990s under John Calley and Amy Pascal. While the studio has had its troubles of late, it remains one of the six majors.

For us, the deal was an unqualified success. Columbia was in dan-ger of failing and Coca-Cola was set on divesting. They might have sold the studio off in pieces and wreaked havoc for our clients. Our intervention with Sony kept our biggest buyer intact. The studio didn't buy any more projects from us afterward than usual, but our broker's role helped us in subtle ways as we negotiated with their execs. They knew that I could call their bosses in Tokyo and they couldn't.

We earned $10 million off the deal. Ron appreciated his share of the profits, but I could tell from hints he dropped that he wasn't crazy about having to keep CAA running smoothly when I was in Japan or

Judy and me at the Allen Conference with Sydney Pollack and Herb Allen II.

Judy and me with Robert and Mary Ellen Zemeckis
and Kate Capshaw and Steven Spielberg, celebrating nothing in particular.

Ron Meyer taking me out for ice cream during a working vacation in Cannes.

With my high school classmate Sally Field and her husband,
producer Alan Greisman, at one of a thousand fund-raisers.

Judy and me with a wide-eyed Tom Hanks
at the Academy's Governors Ball after *Rain Man* won four Oscars.

The New York Times Magazine

JULY 9, 1989 / SECTION 6

MICHAEL OVITZ

HOLLYWOOD'S MOST SECRET AGENT

BY L. J. DAVIS

0354973 27

CREDIT: MICHAEL JACOBS

Price $3.00   THE   July 12, 1999

NEW YORKER

"So what if he doesn't know Ovid. He knows Ovitz."

The *New Yorker*'s view

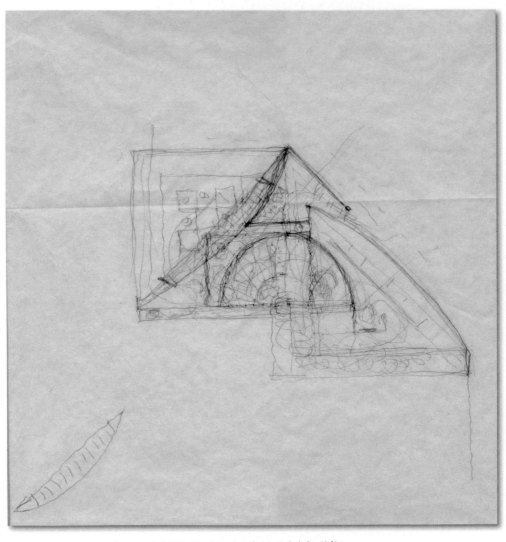

I. M. Pei's sketch of the CAA building,
drawn while he continued to insist that he didn't have time to take the project.

The CAA building, now an architectural landmark.

Dinner in the atrium of the new building to celebrate I. M. Pei.

Paul Newman beating me to the finish line at a slick track in Los Angeles.

To the Ovitz Family
with best wishes, and Thanks, *Bill Clinton*

The Ovitz family with President Bill Clinton at CAA's fund-raiser
for the Democratic National Committee.

With martial arts legend Rickson Gracie and Marco Alburquerque,
who would become practically a member of our family.

Tamara Mellon and me.

Eric and Kendall Ovitz's wedding.
LEFT TO RIGHT: Minty Mellon, Kim Ovitz, me, Tamara Mellon,
Kendal and Eric, Judy Ovitz, Ara Katz, Chris Ovitz.

Me at the groundbreaking for the one-million-square-foot UCLA hospital,
designed by I. M. Pei.

CAA staff in front of the Roy Lichtenstein in the Atrium.

A portrait by Annie Leibovitz of me in CAA's theater, in a rare moment of solitude.

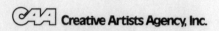 **Creative Artists Agency, Inc.**

INTER-OFFICE MEMORANDUM

DATE: 10/20/82

TO: MB, AG, TL, MFM, MJM, RM, RN, TN, LP, CAP, JRAP, TS, RS, FS, PW, RK, TS

FROM: MICHAEL OVITZ

RE: STAFF MEETING

Sorry to inform you all that I am back and looking forward to seeing everyone promptly at 8:50AM L.A. time tomorrow.

engrossed in spreadsheets. Excited by my new relationship with Akio Morita, and with Japan, I didn't realize that I was jeopardizing a relationship that was much more important.

The Sony experience taught me how much I liked the suspense of the acquisition game, the stakes and strategies, dealing with leaders who supervised empires. I set my sights on building CAA into the McKinsey of the entertainment industry, the indispensable adviser. I couldn't wait to broker a big transaction of my own.

It didn't take long.

CHAPTER THIRTEEN

BRINK'S TRUCK

AS THE SONY DEAL WAS WRAPPING, SANDY CLIMAN RANKED the most likely Japanese bidders for the next studio. First on his list was Matsushita, the giant electronics firm that owned JVC and Panasonic (which is now the parent company's name). They had almost no footprint in the United States—and $12 billion in cash.

In Japan, Matsushita was nicknamed *maneshita*, or "copycat." Instead of innovating, they mimicked competitors at a lower price point. Their low-risk strategy had been extremely profitable, but recently it had faltered. Sony was killing them with Trinitron and the Walkman and its new camcorders. After Akio Morita shocked everyone by buying Columbia, Sony owned a big chunk of the material that went into Panasonic video recorders. Companies are like people: when threatened, they get paranoid. What would Morita do next? What if Sony formatted Columbia's movies to play only on Sony machines? What if other studios followed suit?

The best defense, Matsushita decided, was a studio of its own. *Maneshita*-style, they reached out to the same people who'd helped Sony. Two weeks after the Columbia deal closed, I got a call from a JVC salaryman named Henry Ishii. He was the company's L.A. scribe, the operative who reported local goings-on to the home office in

Osaka. I had my secretary tell Ishii I was unavailable. Hierarchy was all-important in Japan; when two firms engaged, the top executives sat facing each other while their subordinates fanned out in descending rank. Seeming too eager would have lowered me in Matsushita's eyes. Ishii called for three weeks before I agreed to receive him in my office. Would I be willing, he asked, to receive a visit from his superior, Seiichiro Niwa, a senior managing director?

Certainly, I said. Niwa was a West-leaning executive who'd partnered with Larry Gordon, the ex-president of 20th Century Fox, in a new movie production company. When he arrived in my office, we bowed from the waist and exchanged business cards with two hands and a slight nod of the head. I presented my gift of a Baccarat crystal ball embossed with stars, a token of Hollywood and our world-famous clientele.

Niwa and I spoke only in the most general way. My guest said it was his view that Matsushita's future lay in software, in content, but that he was more inclined that way than some others at the company. The next day he sent me a book of sayings of Konosuke Matsushita, the company founder who'd died that spring at ninety-four. Then he asked if I would come to Osaka to meet with senior Matsushita management.

I said, "Who would that be?"

"Masahiko Hirata."

Good, I thought. At the top of the company sat the chairman, Masaharu Matsushita, the son-in-law of the founder, who'd adopted his wife's family name. He was a figurehead, like Queen Elizabeth. Next came the president, Akio Tanii, who governed by *nemawashi*, bottom-up consensus, in lockstep with his executive committee. While Hirata ranked third as the executive vice president and CFO, he ran the company day to day. He could drive a deal until Tanii blessed it pro forma. He was the one I needed to see.

I exacted one concession: that Hirata meet me first for three days in Honolulu, midway between Matsushita and CAA.

I found a Japanese bookstore in Rockefeller Center and bought a dozen volumes by the departed chairman. (He wrote forty-four.) I spent hours in electronics stores eyeballing Matsushita's product lines. After acquiring the company's hefty wholesale catalog, I homed in on video and audio equipment. Soon I could tell you to the last pixel how Panasonic's best big-screen TV stacked up against Sony's.

CAA's team and Matsushita's would meet at the Kahala Hilton, where my family vacationed twice a year. No one from L.A. would think twice if they saw me there. My travel team consisted of my inner circle: Sandy Climan, Ray Kurtzman, and Bob Goldman.

When we arrived at the Kahala just after Thanksgiving, Sandy asked his Matsushita counterpart about their preference for attire. The exec responded that "it is very considerate of you to suggest no ties"— which we hadn't suggested. The Japanese didn't want to wear ties in Hawaii any more than we did. In a nod to formality, we wore jackets into the room and quickly doffed them.

The death of Matsushita's founder enabled its next generation of executives, men in their sixties, to strike a new path. But working with Sony had taught me how slowly deals moved in Japan, and how they didn't move at all until you established relationships. As I told my colleagues over breakfast, "We are not here to discuss business. We're going to be in a social staring contest, and we cannot blink. You will want to gag at some of the stuff I'm going to talk about. Hold it in."

Hirata was about five foot three, reserved but with a healthy sense of humor. For two hours we discussed golf, our children, Japanese art, stereo equipment, my Japanese bronze flower vase collection, baseball, and my love of everything Japanese. Then we had lunch and contemplated the glories of chocolate chip cookies. I passed out a sampling Judy had baked for the occasion. We resumed in the afternoon to ponder the novels of James Clavell and the films of Akira Kurosawa. We considered how *Seven Samurai* inspired *The Magnificent Seven*. We talked about *Shotokan*, or Japanese-style karate.

It was much the same that afternoon and the following two days. At dinner, which we took turns hosting, everyone changed into blue suits and ties. We toasted with scotch, sake, beer, and wine, and conversed about friendships and women. We avoided all reference as to why we were there. It was oblique, maddening, hilarious, tortuous, and absolutely necessary. It was on-the-job training in the Japanese way.

On the last night we staged a meal to remember, beginning with heaping trays of shellfish on ice. Knowing the Japanese love of steak, I asked the hotel to find the finest chateaubriand in Honolulu and carve it tableside. It was a very Jewish meal, with every course in excess; our new friends seemed overwhelmed. During the final round of toasts, I took stock. Judging by the other side's bland faces, I concluded, glumly, that this visit had been a mere sniff around.

Then Hirata turned to me and said, "You know, we are interested in learning what it would take to acquire a motion picture studio. We would like to know what you would charge to help us."

I had had my answer planned for weeks. "We'll charge you nothing," I said, "unless the job we do makes you happy. If you're not happy, we'd like only our expenses—no fees."

Hirata said, "And if we're happy?"

"If you're happy?" I looked him in the eye. "We'd like you to hire a Brink's truck loaded with gold and send it to our office."

Hirata beamed and bowed till his head nearly scraped his dessert plate. Then we shook hands. I told him how glad we were to be working together. Then we all bowed and left.

As we drove to the airport, it occurred to me I was out on the longest limb of my life. If the deal fizzled and we didn't get paid, I'd get pilloried—with my partners at the head of the line. I'd be the Wizard of Oz after the curtain rose and the mic died.

But I was never one to dwell on the downside. CAA had gotten where it was by blazing new trails. Besides, we knew where Matsushita could start shopping.

———

WHEN WE FOUNDED CAA, LEW WASSERMAN'S MCA/UNIVERSAL was a power in film and dominant in television. Then the inconceivable happened—the last mogul got old. As the cost of making movies soared in the 1980s, in large part due to us, Universal hunkered down. Despite the runaway success of George Lucas's *Star Wars*, the studio passed on *Raiders of the Lost Ark* when Tom Pollock, Lucas's lawyer, demanded a fifty-fifty split. Paramount scooped it up on those terms and made a killing. Lew and Sid Sheinberg chose to ride out the bubble and pass on deals they deemed inflated. But the bubble lasted fifteen years. After Warner merged with Time Inc. and Sony bought Columbia, MCA began to look outmoded.

Their weakness was most glaring in TV. As Rupert Murdoch formed a fourth network at Fox and gobbled up Metromedia, Lew pulled back, at the last minute, from a merger with RCA/NBC—a terrible mistake. With RCA throwing off cash, Lew could have ruled MCA till his death. He had been the first to see TV's potential, but now he missed out on pay television and HBO. His company had everything it needed to ride those waves: expertise, cash flow, mounds of collateral, zero debt. He owned or controlled 19 percent of MCA's stock, and no one on his board dared cross him. Yet Universal, the fabled octopus, had crawled under a rock.

As MCA's share price swooned and sharks such as Steve Wynn circled, taking big stock positions, Lew stayed defiant. In 1984, at age seventy-one, he said, "I do not intend to sell, I do not intend to retire, and I do not intend to die." Six years later, all three of those events seemed increasingly plausible. If the share price dipped below thirty dollars, MCA's real estate value would exceed its market cap. A raider could sell the company for parts and haul off the studio's library—three thousand films and more than thirty thousand TV shows—for free.

By this point, with MGM/United Artists on life support, major studios were beginning to look like an endangered species—a terrifying development for agents because sellers had no leverage without multiple buyers. We were helping Matsushita to acquire a studio, but also helping the entertainment business to stay afloat. I felt like Louis Brandeis, who, after he spoke on behalf of competing interests in the

United Shoe Machine Trust matter, was asked whom he actually represented. "I represent the situation," he replied.

Less nobly, I was delighted by the prospect of jousting with Lew again. I knew we wouldn't end as friends—but then, we hadn't started as friends. I stood for everything he deplored in the new Hollywood, from the ever-rising cost of production to artists' demands to call their own shots. One of us would win this battle, and one of us would lose.

AFTER THE COLUMBIA DEAL AND MITSUBISHI'S ACQUISI-tion of Rockefeller Center, U.S. congressmen railed against the sale of the nation's cultural assets, and a *Newsweek* cover pictured Columbia's Torch Lady logo draped in a Japanese flag. I thought the backlash ridiculous. Foreign firms were doing us a favor by underwriting cash-strapped American businesses and protecting American jobs. They weren't pillaging—they were financing. As Senator Bill Bradley said of the Sony deal, "They can't pick up the studio and take it to Tokyo."

Matsushita was thinner skinned than Sony, so secrecy was even more imperative to them. They knew they were copycats, but they felt that if enough time passed before this deal broke, it wouldn't look as if they were brazenly emulating Sony. "If this gets out early," Hirata told me, "we'll deny it and be done with it." Our memos were handwritten and shredded after they'd been read. The only people who knew my whereabouts were my wife, my assistants, Ron Meyer, and Bill Haber. In Japan, for reasons I never discovered, Matsushita asked that I use the code name Mr. Nelson.

For our first visit to Matsushita in Osaka, in early 1990, we brought more expensive gifts than we had to Hawaii—a big-headed driver for a golf enthusiast, a Rauschenberg Statue of Liberty print for Hirata. To throw any reporters off the scent, we chartered a plane to San Francisco and flew commercial from there. We landed at 5:00 p.m. local time and were greeted by eight executives and four small Toyota limousines, one for each of us. The drivers wore white gloves and the limos were immaculate, with doilies on the seats and headrests.

Osaka was a sprawl of low-slung villages and clumps of high-rises, like L.A. but with even worse traffic. Cars crawled on the elevated two-lane freeways that snaked around and above the buildings. By the time we reached our hotel and showered and changed, it was 1:00 a.m. in Los Angeles and the dinner hour in Japan. Our hosts had bought out a large wood-beamed restaurant for the ten of us. We sat at a low *seiza* table with one geisha per diner for service and the subsequent ritual dance. Endless sake toasts took place before we could return to the hotel and fall into bed.

I rose at 3:30 a.m. to roll through my normal calls at the normal time, patching through my office to make it appear I was in L.A. At 9:00 sharp we were delivered to Matsushita's campus. The administration building looked like a citadel (or a penitentiary), with high walls and guards in shiny silver helmets. When a senior executive approached, the guards snapped to and saluted.

Inside it felt more like a factory, all dim lights and generic wood paneling. There was a flurry of introductions and then a series of meetings with every department head, on a strict fifteen-minute schedule. At an elaborate lunch we met Akio Tanii, the CEO. He was half a foot taller than Hirata, pleasant but aloof. Also present was Tsuzao Murase, a truculent senior executive who jockeyed with Hirata for Tanii's favor. He immediately hit me with a trick question, my first brush with Matsushita's barbed-wire politics: "Why do you think we need to do this deal?"

"You don't *need* to do the deal," I said, "but it's a great insurance policy. If Sony controls content, it could control the VHS market"—which Matsushita was making a killing in. From the closed expressions around the room, it was hard to tell if I'd said the politic thing or not. In Osaka we had no Akio Morita to squash disagreement, and no Norio Ohga to ram things through. Sony was beginning to seem like a model of transparency.

In the afternoon we met with finance, sales, marketing, and research. At 5:30, closing time, Hirata took me aside and said, "I want to show you something." Leaving his translator behind, he led me up to the executive floor. We passed down a long corridor to a locked door, which opened into a room the size of a walk-in closet. Hirata pointed to the stacked, plastic-bound volumes on the floor. I picked up one from Morgan Stanley, a signed letter from the head of its investment-banking division clipped to its cover. There were dozens more like it, multiple copies of proposal books from the top investment banks in New York, London, Paris, and Frankfurt.

The letters asked for the privilege of guiding Matsushita through the wilds of the movie business. They listed their services, each one with a fee. They charged for everything but continental breakfast. Hirata's smile grew wider as I leafed through them, and I understood: CAA was the only one to forgo a fee letter. In all our dealings in Japan we never had a written contract. Our attitude was, *We know you will do the honorable thing.* For an old-fashioned businessman like Hirata, that gesture was definitive. Despite his limited English and my nonexistent Japanese, we were going to trust each other.

———————

ON THE NEXT TRIP, WE BEGAN TEACHING OUR SEMINAR ON Hollywood. My associates at my side, I stood all day to present at a pair of whiteboards and six-foot screens. Hirata asked us to assume they knew nothing, which was close to the truth. We began with an in-depth history of the American film industry, from the old studio system to the present. We did the same for television. After answering questions, we ended with a factory visit. That was my favorite time, hanging out with the engineers. I had never seen a workplace so neatly organized. Workers wore company jumpsuits, a different color for each plant. Painted lines pointed the way along the spotless shop floor, with upbeat slogans posted every few yards. We spoke through translators all day, and by dinner they were flagging. I proposed alternating to give them a break—another show of good faith, since we'd have to rely on Matsushita's man when ours was off.

Though the Japanese were familiar with our top-grossing movies, the mechanics of how Hollywood worked—the packaging and distribution networks; the syndication deals—were an utter mystery to them. Once I flew New York to Los Angeles to Osaka, a long haul, and they took me straight from the plane to the city's best tempura bar. A round of beers, and another, then three shots of sake. I was nursing my first beer, straining to keep awake, when a board member named Keiya Toyonaga said, "Michael, could you explain creativity to us?" I groaned on the inside and blurted out God knows what. I still haven't figured out a stock answer to that one.

We plodded on. MCA's stock kept falling, and the danger grew that a raider would make a hostile bid that would scare the Japanese off, but it took until spring before Matsushita was ready to contemplate going ahead. For months we'd kept a single slide on-screen for them to look at, a grid with the seven studios down the side and a range of business lines across the top: movies, television, music, theme parks, animation, real estate, retail, publishing. The boxes bore an X wherever a studio was active. Only Disney had more X's than MCA.

That visual spoke loudly. Universal's film and TV libraries were second to none, worth at least $2 billion by themselves. The studio had a state-of-the-art production facility and strong potential for growth in video games and merchandising. I traced Lew Wasserman's history back to the 1930s, when he agented radio and nightclub acts. I spoke of his links to the Democratic Party and organized labor, how he ran Universal with an iron fist—and what he might achieve with a strong partner behind him. The man I described was, by design, the American version of Konosuke Matsushita.

More months went by, more trips, more symposiums. The same people asked the same questions, writing down our replies to see if our answers changed. Hirata and the higher-ups seemed to be leaning toward the deal. But I knew they'd rather be late to the party than crash while speeding to get there.

THE REAL CULTURE GAP WASN'T EAST VERSUS WEST; IT WAS hardware versus software. If you're the industry leader in videotape recorders, you design a dozen different boxes, but the pieces inside are the same. Your engineers tell you how long each part will last before breaking down. It's all hard numbers.

A movie idea, on the other hand, has no intrinsic worth. Give the same concept to ten directors and you'll get ten different films. Film artists don't make a garment from a bolt of cloth—they create the cloth. The finished product's value is subjective, your taste against mine.

It took a long time to get that point across in Osaka.

Our work on MCA mirrored what we'd done with Columbia. We sized up every film and TV show in the Universal library, from *E.T.* to *Miami Vice*—what it was worth then, what it might net in syndication or on the cable and video rental markets. Then we looked at everything in development: movies, TV, recorded music. What artists did Universal have under contract? What masters did they own?

Allen & Company plugged our data into their models for cash flow projections. I wanted Herb around for his candor: he didn't hesitate to say, "That's the dumbest thing I've ever heard." Knowing that my banker had my back greatly reduced my anxiety about the deal. Together with Allen & Company, we estimated MCA's worth at between sixty and seventy dollars a share. (We excluded WOR, an MCA-owned TV station in New York that might fetch another five dollars a share.)

That summer we selected our consultants, accountants, and publicists. They had to be smart and drama-free. We brought in Simpson Thacher & Bartlett, the one New York white-shoe law firm with no conflicts in the deal. I had learned from the strife between Mickey and Walter at Sony: though I'd lean on our people for strategy and execution, there would be only one channel between Matsushita and MCA. If this deal broke down, it was on me.

TO GET ANYWHERE WITH LEW WASSERMAN, WE HAD TO bring Sid Sheinberg onboard. I liked dealing with Sid because he was competent and candid. It couldn't have been easy running MCA under a man whose name was synonymous with the company. Lew had only one child, a daughter, and Sid was his surrogate son. But well into his seventies, when most execs were content with the chairman's seat, Lew kept his title as CEO instead of bequeathing it to Sid. Some businessmen—Sumner Redstone at Viacom was another—equate their companies with their lives. If they stayed in charge, fending off all successors, they would never die.

A few weeks before we formally pitched MCA, I dropped by Sid's house for an informal chat. Matsushita would be a blessing, I told him, because nothing would change. He and Lew could continue to run their domain with minimal interference. Best of all, Sid would remain Lew's heir apparent without an inside rival. "You'll be selling the company," I said, "but it's almost like an interim financing deal." I suggested that if MCA survived the current downturn under Matsushita, and rebounded, they could buy the company back from the Japanese. This was surely optimistic, but it gave Sid a pleasant frame to view the deal through—particularly as the increasingly likely alternative was MCA being taken over and carved up, with him and Lew dumped to the curb.

Sid was receptive, though he wanted to know more than I could divulge. Word got out a few days later that Lew was scrambling to revive a stock-for-stock deal with Paramount. I knew he'd rather merge with Americans, given a choice. But the talks blew apart when Paramount CEO Martin Davis, another control freak, refused to take Sid onboard as co-CEO.

IN AUGUST, AFTER OSAKA FINALLY APPROVED THE NEXT step, I made a formal pitch to Felix Rohatyn, the financier and MCA board member. It was an easy conversation with one of the people I'd cultivated ten years earlier. Felix was quiet, studied, and ferociously intelligent. While he was devoted to Lew, I could count on his pragmatism.

As Saddam Hussein had just invaded Kuwait, roiling the markets and dropping MCA's share price into the thirties, Felix cautioned me, "You can't be thinking in terms of where the stock's trading right now." I liked the fact that he was selling me. The issue wasn't *whether* MCA was for sale, he seemed to be saying, but for how much.

Over Labor Day weekend I phoned Lew to confirm my client's interest. He gruffly said he'd listen to any legitimate offer but that he wasn't looking to sell. We met at his home and I spelled out the deal's advantages. Matsushita's inexperience in entertainment worked in his favor—they needed him. They were ready to sign him to a new five-year contract at an annual salary of $3 million.

Lew didn't seem eager. But he didn't say no.

THERE IS LESS WIGGLE ROOM IN SETTING THE SALE PRICE of a conglomerate—even one with lots of hard-to-price assets—than you might think. Financial data, including cash flow and earnings and the historic trading range, points to a "right" number. For MCA it was somewhere in the sixties. As the stock was trading in the thirties, our deal had a strong tailwind.

Though Lew's target price of one hundred dollars a share was a pipedream, Matsushita knew its offer had to be appetizing enough to MCA's shareholders that it would oblige Lew to keep talking. On September 19, Hirata authorized me to say they were "contemplating" a price between seventy-five and ninety dollars a share. As a preliminary engagement number, it was on the button. The top end was close enough to Lew's fantasy to not offend him. The bottom, less five dollars for WOR, hit the high end of the range Herb and I thought was right.

I called the offer in to Felix Rohatyn. "I'll take this to Lew," he said.

TEN MONTHS AFTER MEETING HENRY ISHII, I FOUND MY-self tiptoeing through a minefield. I cringed when Matsushita endorsed an Arab-led boycott of Israel—Lew was a leading fund-raiser for Jewish causes. Meanwhile, a stubby Italian financier named Giancarlo Parretti was poised to buy MGM. Not counting MCA, three of the seven majors would be foreign owned. Xenophobia in the U.S. media spiked. But my main concern was a leak. Once news of a potential merger breaks, arbitrageurs goose the stock price. I had nightmares of raving shareholders, fractured alliances, panicked Japanese, and me shouldering all the blame.

On the morning of September 25, I met with Hirata in Osaka to time our next move. A salaryman entered and handed him a fax. Hirata blanched and passed it to me. The *Wall Street Journal* had just published a story that Matsushita was exploring an acquisition of MCA "for $80 to $90 a share."

"The cat's out of the bag," I said. "We need to ramp up the process before it falls apart." Hirata was noncommittal. MCA shares surged 57 percent, to fifty-four dollars; Wall Street was betting a deal was imminent. As I mediated between the two noncommittal sides that day, I felt much less confident.

Who leaked the story? David Geffen, who earlier that year had become MCA's biggest individual stockholder when the conglomerate bought his record company, might have used the *Journal* to boost his share price and increase pressure for the deal to happen. Murase, who was capable of doing anything to undermine Hirata, might have used the *Journal* for the opposite reason: to kill the deal. Herb Allen wanted to get the deal going—and he was friendly with Laura Landro, who'd written the story.

A lot of people thought the culprit was me. Later, in the *New Yorker*, Connie Bruck would write: "The widely held view among many people involved in the deal is that the person engineering the leak was Michael Ovitz." According to her sources, I had to force Matsushita's hand before Lew and Sid withdrew. Totally wrong—I'd been working overtime to keep things under wraps. I was convinced that public scrutiny never helped any private negotiations.

A statement from Hirata cooled things down: "Discussions with MCA are proceeding in an orderly fashion and there are no new

developments to announce. Any reports to the contrary are errone-
ous." As it turned out, the *Journal*'s story did galvanize Matsushita and
move the deal along—it made it feel real. But with each side blaming
the other for the leak, the prospective marriage was off to a rocky start.

THE PACE PICKED UP. I TRAVELED TO OSAKA ONCE A WEEK,
often for as little as twenty-four hours. (I made fourteen trips in all.) I
was on the phone daily with Hirata, Sid, Herb, and Felix Rohatyn. I
also touched base with Bob Strauss, an MCA board member who was
close both to Herb and to Matsushita board member Keiya Toyonaga.
Bob Strauss had a golden résumé: chairman of the Democratic National Committee, U.S. trade representative, Middle East peace broker, ambassador to the Soviet Union. MCA and Matsushita had
waived any conflicts to let Bob in as "a counselor to the transaction."
A good old boy out of Lockhart, Texas, Bob was the ultimate back
channel because he cared only about the deal. And another go-between
was just what we needed, as I was doing all I could to keep the principals apart. I didn't want Lew and Hirata to discover just how little they
had in common.

The Japanese were cowed by Lew's reputation and happy to bargain
indirectly, but Lew, egged on by Felix, wanted face-to-face talks so he
could size up the buyer. For a while I used Herb and Bob Strauss to
vouch for Matsushita's sincerity: they'd listened in on this call, they'd
read that fax. But by October, Lew could be put off no longer. I arranged a get-together at his home.

I warned the Japanese going in about Sid's mercurial personality
and admonished Sid that our guests were unaccustomed to raised
voices. To my relief, the meeting proved to be all small talk. Sid walked
Hirata around Lew's house, pointing out the Degas and the Matisse.
Lew remarked, "You buy the company, you get the paintings, too—
they're MCA property." It was a bizarre moment. Most people in Lew's
position would have saved that nuance for the closing, then asked
for—and surely received—the paintings as a gift.

Hirata seemed more impressed by the koi pond in Lew's backyard.

Two weeks later, as Lew mulled Matsushita's engagement number, we sprang another leak. The Nikkei wire service reported that MCA was demanding up to ninety-five dollars a share. According to an unnamed Matsushita official, the Japanese wanted "a cooling-off period" until mid-November. *Murase*, I thought. It all reminded me of *Shōgun*, warlords at each other's throats. If Hirata lost an internal showdown before we closed, we were dead. MCA stock fell 18 percent that day and Lew was boiling. "You better get this straightened out," he growled at me. His shares were so depressed that a raid seemed inevitable if our deal didn't take.

ON NOVEMBER 13, HIRATA AND TOYONAGA LED THEIR DELegation into New York. The MCA contingent touched down in Lew's private jet. At the kickoff dinner where both sides broke bread, Sid Sheinberg rattled on and on about how costly melons were in Japan. I felt even better that I'd kept him under wraps.

The next morning I went to Hirata's hotel for the magic number. If the offer was in the fifties, I feared Lew would walk. After our good mornings, Hirata made a brief, expressionless statement. I swiveled to the translator. "We will make an offer," he said, "of sixty dollars a share."

I pushed for more: "This will close much faster if we go in at sixty-five dollars and hold our ground." Early on, I'd warned Hirata that in dealmaking I represented both sides—which is how deals get done—and that I'd squeeze him if necessary. I was squeezing now.

Hirata shook his head. "We would like to offer sixty dollars," the translator said. I pushed no further. Every offer had some give to it, and any deal could close if the bid-ask spread was within 10 percent. Lew would be hard-pressed to reject sixty-six dollars a share, nearly double the stock's price before the *Journal* leak. Throw in five dollars for WOR, and we were close to the floor Herb and I had submitted two months earlier. A sixty-dollar bid was a savvy calibration, the lowest figure that would safely keep things moving.

Formal talks began later that morning at Trump Tower, where Sid co-owned an apartment with Steven Spielberg. As I led people through the agenda, the atmosphere was quiet but tense. We made short work of the agreed-upon points. Lew and Sid got five-year deals; if Lew couldn't finish his term as CEO, Sid stepped in.

Finally, I addressed the price. First I noted that external conditions—war in the Middle East and the rising price of oil—had hurt MCA's value since Matsushita's initial overture. When I delivered the number, Lew professed outrage and accused us of misleading him. It was mostly an act.

Then my real work began. I spent three days bouncing among the two Midtown Manhattan law firms (Simpson Thacher for Matsushita and Wachtell, Lipton for MCA), Hirata's suite at the Regency, and Felix Rohatyn's base at Lazard Frères. Usually I walked, though limos were waiting if I needed to huddle with Herb or Sandy Climan. The first day crawled. Lew refused to consider sixty dollars and Matsushita wasn't budging. Herb urged me to keep people talking, which was easier said than done. At five o'clock Bob Strauss called and said, "We've got to get this deal moving, so I'm going to hold a board meeting."

"What are you talking about?"

"Come to the Regency and see for yourself!"

I went over to Bob's parlor suite, which had the longest bar I've ever seen. Hirata and his associates were crowded around it and on their way to getting soused. "Let's get social!" Bob said. We talked and drank, and talked and drank some more. No real business got done, but it kept everyone talking.

The next morning, two days before Thanksgiving, Hirata gave me a new number: sixty-four dollars a share. I thought it was close and took it to Trump Tower for Felix and Sid and Lew's attorney, Marty Lipton. They said it was still too low and the deal wasn't going to happen. I tried to stay calm. The great unknown was the inside of Lew's head. I didn't dare press him for a counter because it might be so high the gap would be unbridgeable. Lew had demonstrated that he would kill a deal, even one he desperately needed, if pushed too hard.

What was fair payment for his life's work? "He's playing hardball," said Felix, who kept me apprised of Lew's mood. "I think we're at an impasse." When Felix told me he was leaving that night for his week-end place in Southampton, I understood. He needed to make it look like the deal was toast. If Lew saw everyone leaving, he might cave.

On Wednesday, arbitrageurs bid MCA stock up to $68.50, based on a projected purchase price of $85 a share. The number had no more meaning than a *Farmers' Almanac* weather forecast, but I feared Lew might use it as a basis for his ask. I went back to Hirata, knowing I had to tread carefully. If I pushed him too high, I might put him in Dutch with Tanii. I also knew he had a "shadow" adviser, the banking firm of Nomura Wasserstein, which likely was counseling him to slow-play his hand. With no other bidders, it was reasonable advice. But Nomura Wasserstein didn't know Lew Wasserman. My gut told me sixty-four dollars wasn't quite enough.

I said to Hirata, "I think we need to go higher. What about sweeping it up to sixty-six?" He said he'd think about it but made no promises.

Late that afternoon I left for Los Angeles. I wasn't going to sit in New York through Thanksgiving, a big day in the Ovitz household, while Lew and Hirata had a stare down. Herb Allen took off for Long Island. Marty Lipton went home as well, which really made it seem like we were done.

But the Japanese didn't leave, a good sign. And Lew remained at the Sherry-Netherland. That was his tell that he wanted to close, and Bob Strauss read it like Amarillo Slim. He stayed to keep Lew company, just in case.

I had barely made it home when Herb Allen checked in with an update: Lew was at the 21 Club with Bob. Bob called afterward and said, "I don't think this deal is dead. I think we can get it done for another two dollars." Lew had hinted as much on their car ride home from dinner. I woke up Hirata. When he got back to me with a trans-lator, I said, "It sounds like we can do this for sixty-six dollars a share."

"I'll have to think about it."

"Don't take too long," I said. "You're really close."

I spent most of Thanksgiving on the phone in my home office. After hours of back and forth with Herb, Felix, Bob, and Hirata's translator, Matsushita upped its offer to sixty-six dollars. I broke the news to Sid, and the two sides met that afternoon at Wachtell, Lipton. Lew and Hirata shook hands. It was killing me not to be there, but we had a tentative agreement.

What drove Lew to say yes? You could not use the word *panic* and Lew Wasserman in the same breath, but I think he saw the deal dissolving and understood what that would mean. For perhaps the first time in his career, Lew felt cornered. He'd spurned so many suitors no one was left but Matsushita—or the lurking raiders.

The Japanese were better than the pirates. He had no way to manipulate Hirata because all contact was through me. He saw that he had one move left and he made it.

For their part, the Japanese weren't going to leave New York without MCA in their pocket. As the uncontested buyer of a highly pressured seller, they held all the cards. They were prepared to bargain forever.

But, in truth, the sale price was about right. The Japanese went a little further than they'd planned and Lew took a little less than he wanted. Buyer and seller remorse is a fact of life. Objectively, both sides won. A studio was rescued from the vultures, and the Japanese had strong potential as partners. Lew had more money than he could spend and a long-term contract. The deal worked for everyone—or it should have.

Champagne glasses in hand, more than a hundred people convened in Simpson Thacher's conference room Monday morning. I stood behind Lew and Hirata as they sat with the documents. Strong emotion washed over me; it was the largest and most demanding deal of my career. At $6.5 billion, it broke Sony's record for a Japanese acquisition in the United States. I had convinced the last mogul to sell out before he went under, to a company he'd met with only twice. I had proved myself in M&A. I had won.

Hirata made good on the Brink's truck. He gave me a colossal check to distribute as I saw fit: $135 million. After paying the bankers and all the consultants, I was left with $60 million for CAA (worth $110 million today). It changed everything for us. First, it put more money in our partners' pockets—ten million for Ron; ten million for Bill, one to three million each for the guys who'd worked on it; and the rest for me. Second, it enabled us to hire more people without depleting our reserves. Third, it allowed us to keep paying our agents well-above-market rates and to ensure they didn't leave. And fourth, it signaled that our company had stepped up in class. In Hollywood, where people didn't know Goldman Sachs from Saks Fifth Avenue, everyone was dumbstruck that a talent agency could earn that kind of fee, let alone arrange and execute a deal of that magnitude.

Of course, my elevated profile pissed off my partners. And I began to feel that I was a hamster on a wheel. Part of me felt I was running on the wrong wheel, that I should be going into business for myself—and part of me believed I wasn't really a hamster, but a cheetah, the fastest animal in the field. Even as everyone from Ted Ashley to Ron to my wife was telling me to slow down, I wanted to speed up.

———

A FEW DAYS AFTER THE SIGNING, I WENT TO THE MCA COM-missary to offer Lew my take on Matsushita. "You're in a really good position," I told him. "You've got a five-year cushion with a company that wants nothing better than to make Sony and Columbia an afterthought." All he and Sid needed to do was communicate each day in writing with Matsushita's scribe, a man named Uede, to keep Osaka calm and in the loop. "They love to be told things ahead of time," I said. "Don't call them and expect a snap decision. If you want to do a deal, make sure they understand what they're buying before you ask them to sign the check." I offered to guide Lew through the transition. "They're paying me to consult for another two years," I said. "Let me earn my money. I've built a relationship with these people and they trust me. Let me help you."

Lew listened, but I could tell he had no interest. When I did business overseas, I took my cue from Akio Morita. I tuned to the local environment as soon as I stepped off the plane. But Lew was an American from the old school. He expected the world to adapt to him.

And he never forgave me for saving him on someone else's terms. After the deal closed, I brought Tanii and Hirata and Toyonaga to the Universal lot to take formal possession of MCA. I pulled up to the front gate by Lankershim Boulevard, parked my car, and escorted my guests to the walkway, where Lew and Sid were waiting. I made the reintroductions. Without a word, Lew and Sid turned their backs on me and walked the Japanese into the studio. I kept my face impassive, but I was hurt and upset, as Lew surely intended.

I never spoke to Lew Wasserman again.

CHAPTER FOURTEEN

PICASSO

MUCH OF THE ENTERTAINMENT BUSINESS REVOLVED around ego and fear. People contorted themselves not to contradict a star, even when the star was obviously wrong. Someone had to be Dad, and it fell to me: *No, you can't back out of that handshake deal. No, you can't talk to the studio like that. No, you can't go a week over budget.*

One morning in 1992, I heard from my client Sherry Lansing, the Paramount studio chief. She was very concerned about *Indecent Proposal*, a CAA package with Bob Redford, Demi Moore, and Woody Harrelson. "The dailies aren't good," Sherry said. "Bob's close-ups look awful." As Bob was playing a virile executive who gets a younger woman into bed (albeit by paying for it), this was bad news. At Sherry's request, I went to Paramount and screened the dailies. Sure enough, Bob had bags under his eyes.

I stopped by Bob's trailer and said, "Is there something I should know about?"

"Everything is fine."

"Everything doesn't look fine. You look tired in the dailies and the studio is petrified to say so. What's wrong?"

Bob glared at me and said, "We're done." Meaning: you're fired.

Back in the office, I was steeling myself to tell the staff we'd just lost one of our biggest stars when Bob called and asked me to come back. I stepped into his trailer and waited. "I haven't been sleeping well," he said softly.

"Happens to me all the time," I said. Without prying for details, I said we'd have the movie suspended on the studio's insurance and get him a long weekend. After he had some rest, I said, "We'll reshoot all this stuff and get it right. Sherry is completely behind you."

I was speaking with no authority, but Sherry understood actors. When I told her Bob needed a break, she shut the set down. Bob went to his place in Malibu and got squared away with a few sleeping pills. He returned the following Monday rested and strong. He didn't look young, but at least he didn't look old. The movie grossed close to $300 million.

————————

MORE THAN A DECADE AFTER WE'D SIGNED HIM, I STILL had to spar with Sydney Pollack on every project. When Paramount bought rights to *The Firm*, John Grisham's breakout legal thriller, they attached Tom Cruise to star. We went to Sydney to direct, and he said no, as usual: "Loved the book, hated the ending." In Grisham's novel, the protagonist, Mitch McDeere, goes on the lam after skimming $10 million from his crooked Memphis law firm. Sydney found this unsatisfying.

I said, "Why don't you talk to Grisham about changing the ending for the movie?"

"That's an idea," Sydney said, "but no author in the world would do it." He would not make the call. I arranged for him to speak with Grisham's agent, and a surprised Sydney phoned me to report, "Grisham's fine with a new ending."

"That's great!"

"But I still don't know if I want to do it," he said.

"Syd, this is *The Firm* with Tom Cruise. You've got to do it." I pushed and pushed until Sydney agreed to consider it. He devised an ending he liked better, with Mitch McDeere honest to the end. He met

Tom and sat with the writers. And then he vacillated. Sydney was always deeply worried about selling out. He wanted the adulation of mass success, but he hated looking mercenary.

At wit's end, I phoned our client Stanley Jaffe, the president of Paramount. "Let's try something with Sydney," I said. "I want you to congratulate him on taking *The Firm*. Go on about how delighted the studio is, and how it's going to be a hit, and how you'll back it to the hilt. Don't let him get a word in edgewise, then thank him and hang up."

Then I called Tom Cruise and said, "I want you to call Sydney and tell him how thrilled you are to be working with him and how great it's going to be. Lay it on heavy, then hang up."

Our staff was on a retreat in Ojai, ninety minutes up the coast from Los Angeles. I told Mike Marcus, Rosalie Swedlin, and Paula Wagner, who handled Sydney and Tom, not to answer if the phone rang in their rooms.

Stanley reached Sydney first, and then Tom came through on his other line before he could respond to Stanley. When Tom abruptly signed off, Sydney shouted to his assistant, "Get Ovitz on the phone! Get him on the phone *now*!"

Donna tried me and reported, "He's on a retreat."

"Get Mike Marcus or Rosalie Swedlin!"

"They're at the retreat, too."

"Get Paula Wagner!"

"Same retreat."

I waited five hours to call back. "How are you, Syd?"

"You son of a *bitch*!" he screamed. "How could you tell them I'm committed? I'm *not* committed. This is crazy, I'm not doing that movie!"

"I have no idea what you're talking about, Syd. I'd suggest you call Stanley Jaffe and Tom Cruise if you don't want to do the movie."

"You call them!"

"I'm not going to call them. I think you should do the movie."

"Son of a *bitch*!"

Sydney had the most relaxed shoot ever in Memphis—great food, friendly people. He and Tom became close. *The Firm* was a giant hit.

And it would be the same tortuous process the next time around.

WHEN DISNEY WAS MAKING *ALADDIN*, ROBIN WILLIAMS was slotted to do three days of voice-over work as the Genie. But his ad-libbing was so wildly funny and prolific that Michael Eisner tossed the script aside and rebuilt the movie around Robin—without revising his compensation. Afterward, Robin asked me to come by his apartment in New York to discuss the issue. He began telling me about it in character, as the Genie. He was a troubled but lovable man, and he'd often take refuge in the voice of some character or other. I said, "Talk to me as *you*, Robin," and he finally did, very quietly. We spoke for two hours, and I told him I'd fix it.

I called Eisner, who tried the usual "Your client had a contract, and he got paid." I told him Robin didn't want any more money, but that he deserved a significant gesture of recognition for what he'd done for Disney—the movie would gross more than half a billion dollars. Michael finally agreed to give Robin a showpiece painting, such as a Picasso. I went and found a suitable Picasso at the Pace Gallery, and told Disney to send Arne Glimcher a check for $4 million. I knew that, expensive as the painting was, it was worth much more. At that point Eisner declared that the painting would remain a Disney property, but that he'd lend it to Robin. I got mad and said, "If I didn't have a client as nice as Robin, I'd demand fifteen million dollars." Robin got his Picasso.

At Eisner's surprise fortieth birthday party—and it was a genuine surprise because I threw it on his forty-first birthday—the producer Larry Gordon gave a toast to Eisner that, in passing, noted that I was always telling the studios how to run their business. The truth is I had learned, over the years, that creative people were much better at taking candid criticism than businesspeople. A Bob Towne would thank me for my notes on his scripts, but execs got intimidated and thought I was telling them I could run their businesses better than they could. I wasn't telling them that, exactly, but there were certainly times that I *thought* that.

My self-confidence alarmed Eisner in some fundamental way; he was surprisingly threatened by potential competitors. His wife, Jane, and I repeatedly tried to turn him around on his longtime deputy, Jeffrey Katzenberg, whom he was always accusing of imaginary crimes and planning to fire. There were real crimes to accuse Jeffrey of—he was dull to the point of robotic—but Michael's main problem with him was that Katzenberg was capable and insanely hardworking, and therefore Michael's obvious successor.

Part of me loved Michael Eisner like a brother—he could be so charming and funny—and part of me thought he was even more paranoid and manipulative than I was. I watched him eviscerate numerous people over the years, but I always thought there were three people in Michael's inner circle he'd never hurt: his childhood friend John Angelo, Larry Gordon, and me.

When Michael had quadruple-bypass surgery, in 1994, I was at his side in the hospital round the clock, driven to try to fix him up. He was in terrible shape, depressed, shaky, and slow. One day, to galvanize him and get his mind back on business, I mentioned a big idea I'd had for a way to break the studio-network-cable stranglehold on content distribution. The phone companies had plugs in everybody's walls—why not use them to bring content to the home? I told Michael I'd gone to Ivan Seidenberg, the NYNEX president, who had an eye for next-gen technology. Together we envisioned an interactive service that would combine telephony, TV, and the internet, all through existing phone wires. We'd have an array of news and sports and entertainment, with original programming by CAA clients. We had signed up not only NYNEX but also Bell Atlantic and PacTel and brought in CBS's Howard Stringer as our CEO and Sandy Grushow from Fox to assist him, planning to rapidly establish a national footprint. It was a huge deal—CAA would get $50 million across the next five years, and own a quarter of the enterprise—and we believed we were going to completely disrupt the nascent cable industry. (As it turned out, Tele-TV was a great idea that was too far ahead of the technology: the cable "triple play" was five years off, and Verizon Fios more than a decade away.)

After I left his hospital room, Michael immediately called Ivan Seidenberg to try to get him to leave me for a similar deal with Disney. When he struck out with Ivan, he called his deputies and had them sign up Americast and GTE to compete with us. Furious, I confronted him, but he danced away from what he'd done, as usual, and he was so sick I didn't have the heart to press him.

MGM WAS IN REAL DISARRAY. AT A CAA MOVIE-DEPARTMENT meeting in the late eighties, one of our agents announced that he'd gotten an offer for Sean Connery for *The Russia House*, a spy picture based on the John le Carré novel. Another agent piped up: "Um, I have an offer for Michael Douglas for the same role." Two MGM executives had gotten their signals crossed, the kind of screw-up that could prompt a star to shop for a new agency. We told both actors what had happened and got lucky—Michael passed after reading the script and Sean took the part.

As MGM's debt mounted, Kirk Kerkorian sold it to Ted Turner. Ted ran into financing problems and sold most of it back to Kirk, who threw it on the market once again. By then the studio was releasing fewer than ten films a year. In November 1990, Kerkorian sold MGM at a nice profit to a mystery man. Neither Hollywood nor Wall Street knew much about Giancarlo Parretti, who'd financed his $1.3 billion offer through Crédit Lyonnais, the largest bank in France. Parretti bought an $8 million house in Beverly Hills and made all the parties and premieres. I gave him a wide berth, instinctively distrusting the kinds of guys I called pop-ups—outsiders who popped up in our business looking for fun, glamour, or unrealistic profits.

Over lunch one day Sean Connery remarked, "Damnedest thing about this guy Parretti. I met him when he was a maître d' at the Savoy

Hotel in London. I can't quite figure out where he came up with a billion dollars." There may have been less to Parretti's fortune—and his home's stunning art—than met the eye. After he gave Terry Semel a lovely small Picasso, Terry was ecstatic. Then he had it appraised and discovered it was a forgery. (Picassos in Hollywood are worth either much more or much less than you think.) MGM's savior lost $500 million in two years before defaulting on his loan. In 1992, after prosecutors on two continents brought charges of securities fraud, Crédit Lyonnais foreclosed, and the end for MGM loomed.

I saw an opportunity for CAA to replace MGM as the seventh major. Four out of five CAA packages turned a strong profit at the box office, and we'd been de facto executive producers for years. Why not take the next step and furnish the financing, too? My model was based in part on First Artists, a company put together in 1969 by Freddie Fields that featured Dustin Hoffman, Barbra Streisand, Steve McQueen, Paul Newman, and Sidney Poitier, each of whom agreed to produce three films. They had hits like *A Star Is Born* and *Uptown Saturday Night*, but the consortium slowly fell apart because Fields made the criminal mistake of not requiring the founders to make their big films for First Artists. Streisand did a dud called *Up the Sandbox* for First Artists the same year she made the hit *What's Up, Doc?* for Warner Bros. I was also inspired by The Directors Company, which my old mentor Tony Fantozzi had put together at William Morris, a group founded around Peter Bogdanovich, Francis Ford Coppola, and William Friedkin. (It had a hit with *Paper Moon*, a critical success with *The Conversation*, and then it, too, slowly fell apart.)

I wanted to assemble a group of our top directors, people like Spielberg, Zemeckis, Levinson, Scorsese, Pollack, Oliver Stone, and Ron Howard. The directors would pledge 75 percent of their projects to the cause. They'd get their normal deal, but 10 percent of their fees would go into a reserve fund to hedge against failure. After running the idea by five of the directors—all of whom said they were really interested— I asked Frank Rothman, the former MGM chairman and top litigator, to look into the jugular question: Could an agency produce movies?

Under our guild agreements, CAA could own up to 10 percent of a production or distribution company, but I had in mind a more intricate deal, where a studio would be bought by a consortium but controlled by CAA. We'd partner with a bank, a private equity fund, and the pool of our top filmmakers.

Frank's white paper doused my enthusiasm. He concluded that CAA would probably get sued, and that we'd have to take on—and take down—at least two of the three guilds. Though they were less than full-fledged labor unions and eminently breakable, we had close relationships with those people. The heads of the Directors Guild and Writers Guild were CAA clients, and Bill Haber and I had helped settle the writers' strike in 1988. The members counted on us in their skirmishes with the studios and networks. I reluctantly concluded that going to war with our clients was an unwinnable battle, even if we won.

IN MARCH 1993, I FLEW TO NEW YORK TO MEET FRANÇOIS Gille, the multilingual managing director of Crédit Lyonnais, which now reluctantly owned MGM. After a leisurely conversation about the south of France and our mutual love of the region's cuisine, we turned to the studio. Gille had met with eight leading investment banks. All offered the same advice: to deal with its $3.2 billion in troubled entertainment assets, the bank should break up MGM, lay off its 2,400 employees, and sell what assets were left, mainly the lion logo and sister studio United Artists's 1,100-title film library. (MGM's library already belonged to Ted Turner, and Lorimar already owned the famous studio lot.) On paper, that course seemed prudent, as the studio was burning through a million bucks a day. Total liquidation could shave the bank's losses to $900 million.

I said, "I have a different point of view. I think you should put another $150 million into MGM so it can start distributing movies again."

"And why would that be best?"

"Because your bank wants to open branches in New York and do more business in America. It would be terrible public relations to fire more than a thousand Americans and plow the MGM name underground for good."

After letting that point sink in, I said, "I believe I can get you most of your money back, if not all of it." CAA could jump-start the studio with a few movie packages, which would buy the French time to revive UA's tent-pole franchises: Rocky, the Pink Panther, James Bond. New production would boost the older titles' value. When Crédit Lyonnais eventually sold MGM, as required by the feds, it would get a much better price.

Gille said, "No one else agrees with you."

I stayed impassive, but my heart leaped. In any multiplayer contest, you want to be the outlier. I told Gille, "Everyone you've met with is in the business of selling assets. But I'm in the business of building assets, and I think you are, too."

"You've given me a lot to think about," he said.

A DAY OR TWO LATER, GILLE CALLED TO SAY THAT HE TOOK my points about his bank's image. (MGM was cherished in France, where people adored *Gone with the Wind* and *The Wizard of Oz*.) The bigger risk, Gille agreed, was to sack all those people and settle for forty cents on the dollar. The bank wanted to enlist CAA as its sole consultant.

On the heels of our work with Columbia and Universal, our work with Crédit Lyonnais would give CAA an inside track with half the buyers in town. Yet reactions from our colleagues seemed very positive. I took calls from a dozen outside agents who were eager to see MGM saved and United Artists revived. Even rival studios felt protective of the house of Marcus Loew and Louis B. Mayer.

Then came the backlash. In a story with ICM's fingerprints all over it, the *New York Times*'s Bernie Weinraub raised a potential conflict. How could CAA consult with a studio's owner while putting clients up for jobs in that studio's movies? ICM's chairman, Jeff Berg, publicly demanded that we divulge the details of our deal with Crédit

Lyonnais, calling it an "unholy alliance." He even went to the U.S. Department of Justice to ask for an antitrust investigation (which never happened).

I understood why Jeff took his shot. ICM had ruled the business in the late seventies and early eighties, but now they were a distant second. We had signed Michael Mann, one of Jeff's most important clients, and taken Meryl Streep, Glenn Close, and Mike Nichols from Sam Cohn. ICM still had Mel Gibson, Arnold Schwarzenegger, Julia Roberts, Richard Gere, and Eddie Murphy, but that was about it. All save Murphy were represented by Ed Limato—who was one of the people who'd called to thank me for MGM. He knew our plan meant more work for his clients.

Berg's next play was to front for the billionaire Bill Koch, who was toying with buying a movie studio. Believing that a premature offer could force the French to sell too low, we gave our seventy movie agents their marching orders: "Tell everyone you meet this week, and on every call you make, that the Koch story is nonsense and that Crédit Lyonnais is not selling MGM." In the days before the internet, a unified body like CAA could shape what Hollywood was thinking. Koch helped us out with a bungled public reference to "French Lyonnais" and a press release on "Metro-*Golden*-Mayer." He shelved his bid within the month.

The entertainment press called Jeff Berg Hollywood's second-biggest agent, but he couldn't have cracked CAA's top five. Ron Meyer had a far stronger client list. So did Bill Haber, Jack Rapke, Paula Wagner, Lee Gabler, and Rick Nicita, the cohead of our movie department. Not long before I met with François Gille, Rick told me that Jeff had asked to see him about the ICM president's job. I advised Rick to take the meeting, if only to find out what ICM had in the fire. "Just listen," I told him. "Pretend you're a client. Let him pitch you." Jeff sold Rick hard, saying he intended to go on a hiring spree—the standard bullshit when you're trying to poach a top agent. He said he wanted Rick so badly that he'd pay him more than he made himself, around $1 million a year. It had to be deflating when Rick said, "I'd have to take a huge pay cut." He was making more than three times Jeff's offer.

Of course, Jeff had a fair point about our work on MGM: CAA was, by design, a confluence of conflicts. Whenever CAA packaged a movie or a TV show, we represented a producer (who wanted the tightest possible budget) as well as the artists (who deserved the market rate). A week after we paved the way for Les Moonves to go to CBS, we were pitching our clients' pilots to him. The conflicts were all out in the open, known, factored in. That's how Hollywood worked. But I assured the guilds we'd keep hands off MGM's creative management and off any privileged information. (It made no difference to us what non-CAA clients were making, in any case—we were the ones setting the market.) The controversy ended there.

IN 1991, WHEN PARAMOUNT FIRED FRANK MANCUSO FROM the top job and stonewalled on the $20 million plus it owed him (depending on how you did the accounting), we had returned one of his many favors. I went to Martin Davis at Gulf & Western, Paramount's parent company, and reminded him that Frank was well liked in the community, and *especially so at our agency*. Marty paid Frank $15 million.

Frank was available, highly capable, and well disposed to us. My original plan was to bring in Frank under MGM's current chairman, Alan Ladd Jr., to get United Artists up and running. Then François Gille called: "We've removed Laddie," he said. "How do you want to restructure?"

By the next day we'd assembled an alternate hierarchy: "Let's bring Frank in as chairman," I told François. I'd found someone else for United Artists: John Calley, the former Warner production head. Twelve years earlier, John had called it quits at fifty and moved to his thirty-five-room house on Fishers Island in Long Island Sound. When we'd met up recently in New York at Mike Nichols's office, he'd told me, "I know your time is valuable, so let me lay it out for you. I'm sleeping twelve hours a day. I've read every book that's out there. If I stay retired, I'm going to die. I want to go back to work."

I instantly thought of the sad retirement of Ted Ashley, John's old boss, and I said, "Let me see what I can do."

Frank was sixty and John was sixty-two. They knew how to rapidly restock the studio's pipelines. We completed the team with CAA's Michael Marcus as MGM president under Frank. Mike was a first-rate film agent and packager, as good as anyone available, and I didn't care what our critics might think.

Crédit Lyonnais went beyond my proposal to more than double MGM's credit line and remove a mass of debt from the studio's balance sheet. It was money well spent. By 1994, the studio was out of danger. Two years later, Kirk Kerkorian paid Crédit Lyonnais $1.3 billion to once again become the studio's owner—more than double MGM's breakup price.

Frank Mancuso thrived at MGM until he retired in 1999. John Calley used United Artists as a springboard to a valedictory run as chairman of Sony Pictures, where he had hits such as *Jerry Maguire* and *Men in Black*. In 2005, a partnership headed by Sony bought MGM in a deal worth $5 billion. To this day the studio provides jobs for working actors, writers, and directors.

Six months or so after Crédit Lyonnais engaged us, we tallied MGM's movies in development. One agency had far and away the most clients working there, three times as many as CAA.

It was ICM.

CHAPTER FIFTEEN

ALWAYS COCA-COLA

I MET COCA-COLA'S TOP EXECUTIVES AT THE ALLEN & COM-pany conference shortly before they acquired Columbia Pictures in 1982. Don Keough, a gregarious man who'd been at Coke since 1950, was the ideal number two for Roberto Goizueta, a suave, shrewd chemical engineer. While Don shared Roberto's sweeping vision, he also sweated the details. (On a trip we shared to Texas, he found a pay phone to report an out-of-place Coke sign in the airport.) They functioned like co-CEOs, expanding a massive Fortune 50 company built on sugar and water. And they were fun to be around.

Coke had owned the studio for about five minutes when Don came to the boisterous premiere for *Gandhi*, a CAA package on its way to eight Oscars. Don threw his arm around me and said, "My God, the movie business is fun—and it's so easy!" Uh-huh.

Two years later, with *Ghostbusters* in postproduction at Columbia, we urged Don to put the movie's logo on Coke cans for the release. But he and his team in Atlanta were extraordinarily protective of their brand. Only after *Ghostbusters* became a hit did Coke begin using its logo, too late for much benefit to either party. We did get them a free ad, though. Years before product placement came into vogue,

Ivan Reitman took my advice and put a Coke in Sigourney Weaver's haunted refrigerator. It never hurt to ingratiate a director with the people who paid the bills.

At the Allen retreat in 1990, a year after Coke sold Columbia to Sony, I stopped by Herb's condo and found him on his back porch having coffee with Roberto and Don. The talk was of Pepsi's New Generation ad campaign, which had Roberto worried. I was sitting there quietly, sipping my Diet Coke, when Don asked me, "What would you do?"

"I've never thought about it," I said. "But as someone who watches a lot of television, I think you guys are getting clobbered in the image market."

It wasn't an offhand remark. Market consulting struck me as a natural next step for CAA, as we already had an extraordinarily accurate bead on mass culture. We received concrete feedback—ratings, grosses, album sales—on a daily basis, and we knew well ahead of the crowd not only what the buyers were looking for, but what Steven Spielberg and Norman Lear and Michael Crichton were doing next. Yet as much as I liked the Coke guys and their product, I hadn't considered working with them—until they sold Columbia and removed any possible conflict.

Not long after the Allen retreat, Don called and said, "We want to fly you out to talk about the company." Two days after that, he met me in the lobby of their twin tower headquarters in Atlanta and walked me into Roberto's office, where it was always 65 degrees. At 9:00 a.m. sharp they poured a round of Coke Classic into paper cups, and for the next three hours we discussed how Coke could stave off Pepsi.

Coke's nemesis was Phil Dusenberry, the chairman of BBDO. Phil had reshaped the cola wars in the 1960s when he helped conceive the "Pepsi Generation," advertising's first lifestyle campaign, and reshaped them again in the 1980s with his "The Choice of a New Generation" TV ads. His spots with Ray Charles saying, "You've got the right one, baby!" were memorable and effective. By casting Pepsi as the drink of the young, Phil cast Coke as the drink of the olds.

Coke still ruled the international market, but its North American margins were slipping, and Pepsi was catching up in supermarkets. "Five years from now," Roberto told me, "I think we could get beat." Coke's advertising had stalled. Its latest slogan, "Can't Beat the Real Thing," didn't move people.

Like Roberto, I knew it was a lot easier for a brand to lose prestige than to regain it. When I was a kid, my father drove a Chevy but yearned for a Cadillac. By the time I bought him one, Cadillac had been eclipsed by Mercedes and BMW, never to regain its luster.

But it wouldn't do for me to come on with a hard sell. I mirrored Roberto and Don's behavior, which was foreign to Hollywood—courtly, Southern, restrained. *Don't hype me, don't sell me, just tell me.* When I confided my plan to expand CAA into marketing, Roberto said, "What do you need from us to get started?"

I said that first I needed time to think about my approach. Detecting Herb Allen's hand behind the meeting, I flew straight to New York before he left the office for his 6:00 dinner. "Look," he said, "you've got something and they need something, and they're asking, 'Does it fit?' My suggestion is, Figure that out, and fast."

I called Don: "Here's what we propose. We'll bring a group of our executives for an all-day meeting with your division heads. We want to know their issues on the ground, what they think of their competition, what they like about your ads and what they don't. We want to hear it all."

We put together a team of in-house experts in movies, television, music, and books and we combed every Coca-Cola print ad and commercial since McCann Erickson got the account in 1955. Two weeks later we met in Atlanta with ten division heads, and then we broke into small groups for no-holds-barred discussion. The meetings lasted twelve hours, the best one-day education I ever had.

Weary but exhilarated, I returned to L.A. and told my partners we were moving ahead. Haber was all for it, but Ron didn't say much. I knew he was already imagining our artists calling him to complain: *What the hell are these guys doing? They should be working for me.* It was a legitimate concern. And there was this, too: by venturing into an arena where we had zero experience, we could be setting ourselves up for a big, fat, public failure.

But I thought Ron was missing the bigger picture. My epiphany came a few days later in Brentwood, after I put the kids to bed. I was in my home office, checking *TV Guide* to see what was on, and it hit me: *The same Coke commercials aired on all of these shows*. Traditional ad agencies cooked up seven or eight spots per client per year, and each one played morning till night: "One sight, one sound, one sell." But the TV audience was now as fragmented as the rest of American society. *Seinfeld* or *Letterman* aficionados weren't the same people who followed daytime soaps or the NBA playoffs. Friday-night sitcoms skewed younger than *Saturday Night Live* and much younger than ABC's *Sunday Night Movie*. Why not trade the shotgun for a rifle—why not customize ads for each group? My first big idea for Coke was to make different spots for *60 Minutes* and *The Simpsons*.

Our challenge was to restore Coke's cachet with young people, but first we needed to get and hold their attention. Infrared TV remotes had invaded the American household. Viewers clicked to a new channel when ads came on, or went to the kitchen or the bathroom. My kids ran off to another room to play. So Coke's commercials had to tell stories the way movies did, only much faster. They needed to *entertain*. Advertising wasn't subatomic physics. Make commercials fun to watch and viewers would embrace them. From there I worked back inductively. Ad campaigns had three essential components: raw ideas, creative types to develop them, and technicians to produce the finished spots. The first two were CAA's stock in trade and the third could be hired by the job. While outsourcing was frowned upon by ad execs (who raked in extra revenue by keeping everything in-house), film studios often outsourced their trailers. Why couldn't Coke do the same?

Ads were expensive because Madison Avenue bankrolled its own commercial houses and then marked up each fee by as much as 18 percent. CAA could undercut them by going straight to the talent. Our directors worked on big, draining movie projects. Many of them would jump at the chance to make a miniature film with total freedom for a six-figure paycheck.

I grabbed a legal tablet and jotted down our manifesto:

Holiday relay race.
More commercials.
Demographically stimulated.
No "one sight, one sound."
New music, new graphics.
Hire creative people.

The next morning I called Don and Roberto and said I had something, "and you're either going to love it or hate it. My guess is you'll love it, but it's high risk, high reward." Inoculation, pure and simple. Then I flew to Atlanta and, in Roberto's icebox of an office, made my pitch for CAA to produce two dozen Coke commercials for what McCann charged for seven or eight. My thinking was to roll out a few spots at a time, each set tied to a season or holiday. "Think of it as a relay race," I said. The summer was about heat, the beach, refreshment. In September, a back-to-school feel. Then family gatherings for Thanksgiving; snow and holidays up to Christmas; hope and resolutions for New Year's; love and companionship at Valentine's Day; family themes again for Easter.

Second, each spot would be tailored to a demographic niche on the networks' schedules.

Third, we'd blend people from movies and advertising to create a new kind of commercial, a mini movie.

Fourth, Coke would pay CAA a consultancy fee of a million dollars a month, plus expenses and outsourcing costs, but we wouldn't charge supervisory markups on other people's work. If we got the account, they'd pay us a fair price for the ads we did.

Fifth, we'd set our own ground rules. That meant no market research, because we trusted our taste more than we trusted focus groups. (Nontraditional agencies like Chiat/Day, which downplayed research as they devised daring campaigns like *1984* for Apple, were rising fast.) Once the commercials were finished, Coke could say yes or no—but they couldn't ask for changes. And we expected Roberto and Don to attend our presentation along with Doug Ivester, who was next in line for Don's job. I liked dealing with executives who could say yes; every intervening layer added another potential no. "I don't want your research guys interpreting our spots for you," I said.

Roberto said, "How many CAA people would you be using?"

I said, "Five or six, tops." Which must have sounded like science fiction, because McCann Erickson had more than three hundred staffers on Coca-Cola.

"Michael," Don said, "I think we're ready to shake some trees around here." He sounded sincere, but I knew it wouldn't be that simple. Hiring CAA would destabilize Coke's long relationship with McCann and its parent company, the Interpublic Group, and, like everyone at Coke, Don had close relationships at McCann. He was particularly close to his drinking buddy John Bergin, the McCann vice chairman who'd come up with Coca-Cola's last strong slogan, "Coke Is It!," in 1982.

Around Labor Day, Coke hired Peter Sealey and made him its first global marketing director. A former marketing chief at Columbia Pictures, Peter was a pro who knew that his job depended on a fresh approach to the company's $600 million annual ad spend. He was our champion from day one. But despite Peter's efforts, and my weekly calls to nudge things along, Don and Roberto waffled for more than a year.

THEN, IN THE FALL OF 1991, IN A STATEMENT THE PRESS called "the September surprise," Coke disclosed that it had hired CAA as "worldwide media and communications consultants." As Peter told the *New York Times*, "American culture broadly defined . . . has become the culture worldwide. We are in a global village and CAA represents the single greatest source in understanding that culture." I flew to Atlanta for Roberto's benediction—which was disappointingly vague. "We need a new direction in our advertising," he told me, "and I'm glad we're discussing what that might be." At big companies, nobody wants to own a new idea before it's clear whether or not it's a stroke of genius.

After someone complained to the Screen Actors Guild about our apparent conflict as agents and producers, we told the *New York Times* on background that CAA "would not be directly involved in producing commercials." The issue with SAG was moot because we'd never planned to use our clients in front of the camera. In those days, any big actor doing commercials was presumed to be washed up. Expectations have since relaxed considerably, but at the time putting Sean Connery or Jessica Lange into a Coke ad would have been like pimping them on the street.

Coke's announcement made us comfortable enough to hire a creative director. We chose Shelly Hochron, a studio marketing exec whom we'd seen do a great job with *Stand by Me*, even though it had no stars, and with *Reds*, even though Warren Beatty refused to do publicity. As an outsider to advertising, she hadn't internalized rules from the Don Draper era. And Peter Sealey, her old boss at Columbia, regarded her like a daughter.

To keep the peace for the time being, Peter announced a tripartite alliance: Coke would define the mission, CAA would generate the ideas, and McCann Erickson would produce the commercials. It was baloney and Peter knew it: we weren't going forward without total creative control. McCann later leaked a story to *Adweek* that we had broken the pact and were "actively recruiting writers, directors and producers to create the Coke ads independently." True, except there was no broken agreement: Peter preapproved everything we did.

McCann wasn't giving up its best account without a fight. They poached Gordon Bowen from Ogilvy & Mather and told him to put us in our place. But Gordon got buried in the firm's infighting. When he asked if he and John Bergin could work out of our Beverly Hills office a few days a week, I hesitated, leery of roosters in the hen house.

Bill Haber said, "Invite them in."

"Why take the chance?"

"Their company will never let it happen."

So I invited them in, even prepared a nice-sized office for them—and Bill's hunch turned out to be dead-on. John Dooner, McCann's president, vetoed Gordon's request, fearing we'd steal their secret sauce.

It never crossed his mind that they might learn anything from us.

IN 1992, AS DON KEOUGH NEARED RETIREMENT, PHIL Dusenberry turned the screw by backing Ray Charles with the Uh-Huh Girls, a sensation in their own right. Pepsi sales in supermarkets drew within two percentage points of Coke.

Patience, as I've noted, is not one of my virtues. I told Herb Allen, intending that he pass it along, that "we really want to do this campaign. But if Coke can't commit, we'll try our hand with someone else." Within days I heard from Don. Were we up for a shootout with McCann Erickson? A shootout was two or more agencies doing pitched battle in the same room. I didn't like the sound of it. While I was game for a fair fight against McCann, I worried this was a face-saving put-up job, and that politics would cost us the account.

I said, "Don, this is an elective for us—you came to me. Now you want us to compete for what I thought we already had."

"Look," he said, "it's different at a public company. You guys are in the driver's seat, but there are some twists and turns along the road. Come here in October and show us your stuff."

Stifling my frustration, I told him we'd be there.

To support Shelly, we hired the former number two creative guy at Chiat/Day, Len Fink, as her partner. Len had a deft feel for both urban and middle America. We met several times to assuage his doubts about our long-term plans, and then we offered him a 50 percent raise. (We later tripled both his and Shelly's salaries into seven figures.) Bill Haber jumped into the project with both feet. We added a mailroom trainee named Jonathan Schreter and sent him to an art bookstore with $3,000. The five of us convened in our creative room to rip out hundreds of pictures—from Monet and Magritte to Lichtenstein and Thomas Hart Benton—and tack them up for inspiration.

Within a few weeks we had three hundred raw concepts. Half made it to the storyboard stage, where Len and Shelly drew each scene in sequence. Eventually we narrowed it to the twenty-four spots we'd present to Coke. Though at times we felt puny compared to McCann, we had some advantages, too—no bureaucracy to zap our riskier ideas, no protocols to smother us.

We didn't want safe ads. We wanted great ads.

———

THREE MONTHS BEFORE THE SHOOTOUT, WE RECONNOI- tered with the enemy in Georgia to watch McCann submit slogans. Gordon Bowen suggested "A Spark of Life," which Don and Peter had previously rejected. Astoundingly, John Bergin trashed the idea and proposed "Always Coca-Cola" instead. McCann's top creative people were knifing each other in public!

When I saw that Don liked "Always," I said, "That's great, let's use it."

Don said, "You really think it's great?"

"It's fantastic." We bent over backward to seem friendly toward McCann. (We had to keep Interpublic onboard to implement Coke's global media buys.) I was agnostic about "Always" as long as we governed everything else. We cared only about the visuals' entertainment value—the slogan was an add-on.

I called Quincy Jones and asked him for the best unknown songwriter he knew. He gave me a twofer, the team of Jon Nettlesbey and Terry Coffey. They composed a two-bar theme and mixed it with a range of beats: country and western, middle of the road, urban, Latin, classical. To score points with Don, we ended each spot with our "Always Coca-Cola" theme song.

The October shootout was our title fight. McCann owned the legacy relationship, so we couldn't just beat them on points—we had to knock them out. I bought Armani suits for Shelly and Len, who'd be presenting. We packed white shirts and bright ties for a uniform look, like Hoffman and Cruise taking on the casinos in *Rain Man*. The day before the event, breaking CAA's no-daytime-fly rule, I scheduled a noon departure on Coke's Gulfstream IV. When we boarded in Van Nuys, Peter Sealey was on the plane to greet us. He so wanted us to win that he spent the flight prepping our team about Coke's internal politics.

We checked into the Atlanta Ritz-Carlton and were chauffeured to Coca-Cola for a dress rehearsal. Rather than practice word for word, I sailed through my remarks with lots of *yada yada yada* so as not to get stale. Shelly and Len checked the setup for their graphics and skimmed through bits of the commercials. We left for dinner at the hotel and were in bed by 10:00. The next morning Haber and I went to the gym. The five of us met for breakfast and a final run-through before changing into our freshly pressed suits. We looked and felt unbeatable.

We arrived fifteen minutes early. Up front were two tables for the combatants and a third for the Coke executives, with several rows of seats in back. Haber and I sat at CAA's table with Shelly and Len standing to our right. Roberto, Don, Peter, and Doug Ivester took their stations. Eleven a.m. came and went with no sign of McCann. Ten minutes later, two dozen disheveled ad people filed in. Next to our lean, mean team, they were corporate bloat personified: a mistake. After flying commercial out of JFK at 7:00 that morning, they were hungry, tired, wrinkled, and generally out of sorts. Not springing for a night's lodging in Atlanta: another mistake.

Peter Sealey asked who wanted to start. Before I could jump in, John Bergin said, "Let's do a coin toss." They won, and I was dying because I desperately wanted to go first. Then Bergin opted to go second, the by-the-book move to make the last impression: a final mistake.

We opened with a single slide, a calendar strip with Coke bottle images to mark the major holidays. I explained our relay race concept and stressed that our spots were designed to entertain. While I played to the Coke executives and referred to them by name, I occasionally turned to bore my gaze into McCann's rank and file, the dazed and disoriented group at the rear. No harm in trying to intimidate them.

In closing, I said, "Pretend you're sitting in front of your television set. You've had a rough day at work or with the kids. Your mind's floating. You're watching TV for the reason we all watch it—for passive entertainment. There's nothing you need to do but sit there and have fun. Enjoy."

Shelly and Len took it from there. Using their props (living-color storyboards, "rip-o-matic" videos, animation shuffle books), they acted out the commercials like a rapid-fire play. Some came with sound effects; one had Len panting like a dog on all fours. Others were introduced with an A-list name attached: "Dick Donner, the director of *Superman* and *Lethal Weapon*, will be doing this commercial." It was a blizzard of ideas pitched Hollywood-style, with motion and emotion. Each spot closed with our tape player cuing an "Always Coca-Cola" beat.

I was prepared to jump in if needed, but their delivery was flawless. Don and Roberto were laughing at each joke and swaying to the "Always" theme. When the Latin beat came on, Roberto looked ready to glide across the floor. (He ordered two hundred copies of the tape for friends and relatives in Florida and Havana.) At McCann's table, Bergin passed a note to the guy beside him. I caught the scrawled message: *We're screwed.*

We saved our best for last: vividly drawn polar bears swigging Cokes as they watched the aurora borealis as if they were at a drive-in movie. When we needed a mascot for the Christmas season, it was Shelly who'd said, "What's warmer or furrier or friendlier than a polar bear?" In real life, these animals are stone-cold killers. But curled up on a snow field, taking in the northern lights, they seemed positively lovable. Inspired by the bright primary colors in *Bauhaus Stairway*, the Roy Lichtenstein in CAA's atrium, our polar bear vignettes became an animation landmark.

By the time Bill Haber gave a crisp summation, our momentum

was an avalanche. I had the last word. Looking squarely at Roberto and Don, I said, "Give us six months and we'll give Pepsi a run for their money. We can take them out. What do you have to lose?" I sat down. John Bergin later told *BusinessWeek* that my presentation "was so charming that I almost started applauding."

Two young McCann creatives shuffled forward like death-row convicts, dead men walking. They made their first pitch, a stiff recitation off handheld notes. They began a second one—and then they crumbled. They broke off in the middle and sat down. Bergin said, "We're done." And they all filed out.

We had literally driven them from the field. The world's marquee ad account belonged to CAA.

COKE BOUGHT EVERY ONE OF OUR TWENTY-FOUR IDEAS. We asked Rob Reiner to direct a spot for the daytime serial set. He tracked a couple's romance from childhood to their fiftieth anniversary, with a Coke and two straws punctuating each time jump. For the soundtrack we wanted the Beatles song "When I'm Sixty-four," a real nostalgia trigger for baby boomers like me. We used CAA's clout to get the president of EMI to sell us the rights, albeit at a record price.

Other directors did little films for prime time, including a Tuscany shoot by Joshua Brand and John Falsey, the creators of *Northern Exposure* and *St. Elsewhere*. A Shelly Hochron special, it featured a sexy, sweaty glassblower crafting a Coke-shaped bottle while a sultry young woman watches through a doorway, clearly turned on. The sensuality and lack of dialogue were perfect for Europe. By making commercials that could travel overseas, we saved Coke millions in production costs.

The polar bear animation was outsourced to Rhythm & Hues, an L.A. visual effects studio that did wondrous things. (They went on to win Academy Awards for *Babe* and *The Golden Compass*.) We bounced their first drawings back, demanding more realism: Blacker eyes! Wetter noses! Furrier fur! Not a single execution went late or over budget.

And, contrary to Ron Meyer's fears, our clients loved the whole thing: two thirds of the commercials were shot by our directors.

"Timeline" was devised by Len Fink on an Apple IIe computer: "*In 1886, Coca-Cola was invented in Atlanta, Georgia, ushering in the modern period of peace, harmony, tranquility, fire and rocks.*" It was cool and funny and dirt cheap, conceived to run on *Saturday Night Live*. We billed Coke $35,500, exactly what it had cost us. They sent us $355,000. When we called the guy who cut their checks, he said, "It was Friday, we were closing, and we were sure you'd made a mistake." No Coke commercial in memory, he said, had cost less than seven figures.

IN FEBRUARY 1993, DAYS BEFORE OUR FIRST SPOTS HIT THE air, I asked Roberto to debut all twenty-four for the media in New York. Doubtful at first, he decided to trust in my enthusiasm. To avoid stealing our client's thunder, I skipped the event. While I felt great about our work, I didn't expect Coca-Cola to entirely share my confidence. I was stunned when I heard that Roberto ran the premiere himself.

The reporters were wowed. They watched lush stop-motion animation based on Thomas Hart Benton's *Heartland*, with farmers plowing golden wheat fields to a score out of Aaron Copland. They saw a Dick Donner spaceship comedy with a big payoff. (To catch an alien impostor, the captain quizzes his crew about the world's most popular soft drink.) We had a takeoff on Rene Magritte's surrealist *Golconda* with Coke bottles dropping from the sky, and a haunting urban night scene out of Edward Hopper. From the erotic glassblower to an all-percussion spot with the Blue Man Group, our ads were wildly eclectic. But the final image for each commercial—backed by the "Always" jingle—was Coke's "button," a red bottle cap with the century-old trademark in white cursive. Peter Sealey told us the polar bears clinched it, and the press conference became a love fest. Journalists like to be entertained, too.

The *New York Times* called our campaign "as extraordinary for who created and produced it as for its unexpected freshness, breadth and playfulness. . . . Almost all [the commercials] are infused with a cleverness, an assertiveness and an edgy, yet fun-filled feeling absent from Coca-Cola advertising since the 'new' Coke fiasco in 1985." *Time* wrote: "To the ad industry's dismay, nearly all the new commercials introduced last week were produced by CAA. Even worse, they are terrific." A few weeks later, Phil Dusenberry walked up to me at a New York cocktail party and said, "I don't know where you came from, but my hat's off to you. We've had to reassess everything we're doing."

Shortly after our first spots aired, Roberto Goizueta paid a visit to CAA. He strolled through the office passing out custom Hermès ties with a polar bear print: a victory lap.

Peter Sealey sent me a check for $10 million for the ads. Not bad, but I returned the check with a Post-it Note attached: "Pete. Let's discuss this." We did, and then I called Don and Robert. I was friendly but unrelenting, and Pete finally sent me a new check for $31 million. They thought it was too much. I still think it was too little. I should have insisted on a royalty for the polar bears, which they've used ever since.

IN THE SECOND QUARTER OF 1994, COKE LOGGED A 6 PER-cent gain in U.S. case sales and a 12 percent increase in profits. By then our second campaign was airing, and even *Advertising Age* tipped its hat: "The new pool of 30 spots is the best Coke advertising, and maybe the best soft-drink advertising, in decades."

CAA had demonstrated that no one had a monopoly on good ideas. We paved a two-way street between Hollywood and Madison Avenue; in years to come, commercial directors like Michael Bay and David Fincher would migrate easily to feature films, and all sorts of people—design studios, digital shops, integrated marketing firms—would grab pieces of the advertising pie. Many borrowed the ingredients we pioneered with Coke, from a seasonal relay race to demographic tailoring to dialogue-free commercials for worldwide use. It wasn't long before commercials, most notably for the Super Bowl, were *expected* to entertain.

In the months that followed, we were offered the accounts of Burger King and of GM's Oldsmobile and Buick lines. We didn't think we could do much with Burger King, and I told General Motors we'd only be interested if we could do *all* of their advertising, not just their two shakiest brands. I put it more politely than that, of course. We were also offered Kodak—but we knew, from our work with Sony, that digital photography was just around the corner, and that Kodak was basically doomed.

The overarching issue, and the reason I slow walked a lot of these inquiries, was that I had a plan with Teddy Forstmann to buy J. Walter Thompson, the huge multinational ad agency. That was my exit strategy. We'd give the Young Turks day-to-day responsibility for CAA, Ron would be its CEO, and I'd run the conglomerate, building it out to acquire other media properties.

I'd floated the idea with the guilds, telling them we were interested in an ad agency, and their reaction was violent: *You can't produce ads.* We thought that getting our clients ad work would help strengthen the guilds, but they didn't see it that way. Once again, being an agent had put me at the intersection of exciting possibilities—and prevented me from pursuing them. In retrospect, I should have just gone ahead with the J. Walter Thompson plan as a minority shareholder. CAA would take 49 percent, Teddy 51 percent, and I'd ease into the majority ownership later. It's exactly the move Ari Emanuel and Patrick Whitesell made recently at William Morris Endeavor; they're now producing ads. Of course, times have changed; the guilds, now eager to have work for their clients, didn't fight WME.

At the turn of the twenty-first century, *Advertising Age* celebrated the top hundred people in the modern history of the field. A number of my heroes made the list: Leo Burnett, Dan Wieden and David Kennedy, Jay Chiat, Phil Dusenberry. Number eighty-seven was a surprise:

Michael Ovitz. . . . In September 1991, he rocked the advertising world by signing Coca-Cola. . . . That partnership set off bicoastal shockwaves and embarrassed longtime Coca-Cola agency Mc-Cann Erickson, especially after the soft-drink giant began airing CAA's commercials featuring high-tech, animated polar bears and a catchy "Always" jingle. Such a la carte options still affect agency-client relationships.

We came into advertising—and went out of it—with a bang.

CHAPTER SIXTEEN

I'M NOT AFRAID OF YOU

IN THE EARLY 1990S, THE SLUMPING U.S. ECONOMY CREATED a slew of buying opportunities. With Matsushita sitting on mounds of cash, MCA could have bought a network, cable companies, a gaming company, and film libraries and made itself the industry leader. Instead it did nothing; Lew Wasserman and Sid Sheinberg flatly snubbed the Japanese. "You need to reach out to them," I kept telling Sid. "Take them out for drinks, go to a restaurant and try their favorite foods. Go to Osaka and learn about their culture. Their arms are open. They only need to understand what you want to do." Lew hosted one dinner in five years, and he and Sid treated the scribes like invisible men. The Americans took the money (Lew cleared $352 million in preferred stock from the deal; Sid, $92 million), but kept running MCA like they owned the place. Matsushita's $6 billion bought it only contempt.

Finally, Lew moved to buy Virgin Records, which would have jumped MCA to the top of the music business. I warned Sid that his owners might be put off by Virgin's name, and that he needed to help them understand what a British anchor could do for them in Europe. Sid never bothered to explain their thinking and Matsushita scuttled the deal.

It was the beginning of the end.

MY FATHER USED TO TELL ME STORIES ABOUT THE SEA-
gram Company's patriarch, Samuel Bronfman, the Canadian boot-
legger who built a billion-dollar dynasty. He was a seat-of-the-pants
entrepreneur, like the old studio chiefs. I could tell how much my dad
respected him.

In 1985, my father turned sixty-five. I'd moved my parents to a
house near us in Brentwood, but my father had no outside interests, no
hobbies; without work, he'd fade away. Edgar Bronfman Jr., Sam's
grandson, was the company's CEO. I made an appointment to see Edgar, whom I'd never met, in the Seagram Building on Park Avenue.
After the usual pleasantries, I said, "I'd like to ask a favor, and I'll
owe you."

"What's the favor?"

"My father, David Ovitz, has worked for you for forty-five years,
and he's about to be forced to retire. I'd like you to keep him on. I'll
reimburse you whatever you're paying him, including taxes, so it won't
cost you anything. I just want to be sure he doesn't lose his job."

Edgar said, "I know your father's been with us since Chicago."
He'd clearly prepped for the meeting, which I took as a sign of respect.
"He's a wonderful guy, and everyone likes him. I'll keep him on, and
you don't have to pay me anything." My dad worked for Seagram
until he was nearly eighty, and never knew why an exception had
been made.

Edgar, the third-generation Bronfman, wanted to recast the family
legacy. Seagram's capital was tied up in DuPont, the high-dividend
chemical giant that brought in two thirds of the company's earnings.
It was safe and secure, but Edgar wanted action. He began calling me
during the breaks in DuPont board meetings, saying, "Get me out of
here!" By 1992 he was asking me how he could buy an entertainment
company. I met with his father, Edgar Bronfman Sr., the Seagram
chairman who'd once had his own fling with show business (in the late
1960s, he briefly owned a controlling interest in MGM). And then I

gave a presentation to Seagram's board in which I said their best option was Time Warner, the conglomerate run by Steve Ross.

With the exception of a theme park, Time Warner checked every box on my grid. It owned a leading cable operation, the top music company (Warner Bros. Records), and more than a hundred magazine titles, including *Time*, *Fortune*, and *Sports Illustrated*. But Steve's advanced prostate cancer made the company's future precarious, as his second in command, Jerry Levin, was an unknown quantity. In M&A, instability is red meat. I connected Edgar to Herb Allen, who said, "Time Warner is the one." Edgar heard the same from Felix Rohatyn and John Weinberg, the ex–Goldman Sachs senior partner on the Bronfmans' board.

Edgar believed he had his father's blessing, but he wasn't sure about his risk-averse uncle, Charles Bronfman. When I met with Seagram's directors, it was Charles who'd asked the sharpest questions. But I thought he'd defer to his older brother when the time came.

We had agreed that any move should be tabled while Steve Ross was alive. I had another thought—why not go to Steve and work something out? Today's friendly investment could be tomorrow's power play. That September I reached Steve at his beach home in East Hampton. "I want to come see you," I said. "I've got an idea that might help."

"Come on out," he said. "I'll send the chopper for you."

I cleared my visit with Steve's doctor and nurse and called his wife, Courtney, to coordinate. The helicopter met me in Midtown Manhattan and landed forty minutes later at East Hampton Airport. When Steve came to his door, it was hard not to gasp: the strapping guy with thick white hair was a gaunt shell. It broke my heart to see him.

We went into the den, where Steve whipped out his omnipresent legal pad. The nurse granted me thirty minutes, so I got to the point: "Steve, I'm here because Seagram is willing to put six billion cash into your company, right now, to be used at your discretion. They want two board seats. They'll sign a standstill for three years, so they won't be moving in to take it over."

Steve came alive. He scribbled notes on his pad and threw out ideas about what he might do with the money—pay down debt, take on more debt, buy, sell. He was as sharp as ever. My thirty minutes stretched to three hours. The nurse came in and said, "Mr. Ross, I'm sorry, but we cannot allow this to go on. You need to come with me right now." After another ten minutes, she physically pulled Steve from the room. On his way out he told me to meet with his deal guy, Ed Aboodi.

"Sure," I said. "But I have the feeling Jerry Levin will view this as a threat."

"I'm still running the company," Steve said. "And this is what *I* want to do."

Ed Aboodi had no formal title. He was the emperor's trusted counselor, which made him formidable: as he wasn't subject to the usual chain of command, it was hard to leverage him. When I met Ed at the Palace Hotel, I could sense that I had no traction. I inferred that he had already aligned himself with Levin, who knew that Steve was terminal.

When I met with Levin not long after, my fears were confirmed. Some people were fooled by Jerry's turtlenecks and meek demeanor, but he was a bare-knuckled infighter who had risen to COO by out-maneuvering his competitors. When I told Jerry what the Bronfmans were thinking, I hit a wall. "We'll take the money," he said, "but no board seats."

I said, "You know, Jerry, the Bronfmans want to be in this business. They love your company and you're pushing them into a difficult position." My hint of a hostile play didn't perturb him. Steve no longer had the juice to lock things down. Our deal was dead.

With Herb's and Felix's approval, Edgar and I went to Seagram's board with our backup plan to slowly amass Time Warner stock using Allen & Company as the purchasing agent. The plan went into effect after Steve Ross died that December. By May 1993, Seagram owned more than 5 percent of the company. Eight months later it owned more than 11 percent. Herb Allen was skillfully amassing stock without attracting undue attention. The idea was to plateau at 15 percent before suddenly jumping to 20 percent. At that point Edgar could swing Time Warner's board and change top management at his pleasure.

But before Seagram could get there, Levin pushed his board to adopt a poison pill: any buyer moving past 15 percent would trigger a flood of newly issued shares, diluting the buyer's stake. Seagram had so much cash we could easily have bought the necessary extra shares and gotten the poison pill revoked, but Edgar, somewhat inexplicably, pulled the plug on the plan. (Much later, we learned that the Desmarais family—sometime business partners with the Bronfmans—also owned 5 percent of Time Warner, so perhaps Edgar was concerned about an SEC investigation.) He wanted to move on to an easier target with a more motivated seller. So we began looking at MCA.

IN NOVEMBER OF 1993, TEN MONTHS AFTER HE WAS INAUgurated, Bill Clinton called and asked me to host a fund-raiser for the Democratic National Committee, which was running out of money. Clinton himself would be the star attraction. Though I'd raised money for Senator Bill Bradley, one of his primary opponents, I'd been impressed by Clinton since I'd seen him speak at a lunch at the Beverly Hills Hotel a couple of years earlier, and I had raised money for him in the general election. We didn't know each other well, but the leaders of the DNC were very familiar with me, and Clinton knew that CAA was a conduit to a heavily Democratic industry.

I told the president, "Sure, I'd be happy to." Taking a deep breath, I added, "But I have a couple of conditions." We both laughed, recognizing that I was living up to my reputation. "One, I want to see the speech beforehand, to make sure you don't unintentionally say something that will get you into hot water out here. And two, I'd like you to consider announcing some sort of major legislative initiative. It's show business; your audience will want something theatrical."

He agreed, amiably—and then he told me the fund-raiser had to happen in three weeks. I laughed, stunned. Then, after we hung up, I started calling around like crazy to set it up. Ron and Bill weren't happy about the idea of hosting Clinton, because they didn't want to ask clients and buyers to an event they'd have to pay $1,000 to $5,000 to attend (the larger sum got you entrée to an intimate cocktail party with the president beforehand, in our conference room). I knew that they were probably right—it would be a quasi-extortionate ask—but I thought we should do it for the greater glory of CAA. So I went ahead.

Three weeks later, CAA's atrium was filled with more than four hundred people, including many of our leading clients as well as the town's top studio and network executives. More than fifty reporters were also present. As I stood at the podium to introduce President Clinton, I felt a real sense of consequence.

As politics depends on favors, too, I asked Clinton for a favor shortly thereafter. I was part of a small group raising $850 million for a new UCLA hospital. (On the committee with me, awkwardly enough—though we never spoke directly—was Lew Wasserman, who raised $125 million on the condition that the complex be named after Ronald Reagan.) I raised $350 million on my own, and then, after the '93 Northridge earthquake in Los Angeles, we applied for FEMA money. I called Clinton for assistance; he put Vice President Al Gore on the case, and FEMA gave us $400 million. Then I got I. M. Pei to design the hospital—which was actually easier than persuading the medical school's architecture committee to consider Pei. No one on the committee, astonishingly, had even *heard* of Pei. Maybe CAA's building wasn't quite as famous, even locally, as I'd thought.

Meanwhile, the agency was firing on all cylinders. In 1993 we signed a deal with Nike to develop and promote sporting events together, the result of my barraging the company's founder and chairman, Phil Knight, with schemes and suggestions for six months. In July, Phil and I had pitched the NCAA on our biggest idea: a seven-game playoff system (quarterfinals, semifinals, and a final) for college football teams, leading to a title game between the best two: a college Super Bowl. We projected that by building TV specials around the games, and showing the title game worldwide, the tournament would net the NCAA more than $100 million a season. But the organization sat on our idea for a year and finally rejected it. They eventually adopted a simplified version of our plan in 2014, the College Football Playoff that now crowns a national champion. As was often the case, I was a little too early.

———————

CAA HAD SO MUCH MONEY COMING IN THAT WE COULD pay someone like Jack Rapke, a great agent but hardly a household name, $4 million a year to handle a number of our top directors. The Young Turks were all making more than a million dollars a year. We were expanding in every direction. When I stood in our building, overlooking the atrium, and heard the phones ringing all around me—when I felt our turbines humming on every floor—I felt proud.

And yet our seams were beginning to fray. Ron and Bill were making well over $12 million a year—and in some years, many millions more from our M&A work—which papered over a lot of problems. But Ron still wanted Bill out. I kept telling Ron, "Look, I hear you, but I don't feel that strongly. If you want to do it, you should do it." Ron seemed as cheerful as ever, but my stonewalling on this point would eventually drive him, oddly enough, toward Bill Haber. In later years, they'd become very close friends, united, at least in part, by their growing distrust of me.

And I was growing annoyed that I was in the office every Saturday morning, working out tax deals and fretting about our overhead and not seeing my kids. The ceaseless work was taking its toll. Because I couldn't afford to be human all day long—because I had to seem interested and attentive and farseeing and wise with everyone—it made me less human over time. I became insensitive, impatient, someone to be avoided if at all possible. Colleagues transferred their childhood issues onto me: I was everyone's distant father or bad mother. One weekend our agent Tony Krantz, whose mother was the novelist Judith Krantz, called me from an EST seminar in Monterey, clearly at the prompting of the staff after a session exploring his demons. "I just called to say I'm not afraid of you," he said, his voice shaking. "That's great, Tony," I said. "I'm glad you feel that way, and that you have the ability to say it." I tried to be encouraging, but I'm sure that my customarily even tone had the opposite effect. Neither of us referred to that call again, but it informed every conversation we had after that. *I'm not afraid of you.*

When Frank Wells, Eisner's beloved right-hand man, died in a helicopter crash in 1994, the memorial service, held at a soundstage at Warner Bros., was packed with more than a thousand devastated mourners. I tried to cheer up Frank's widow, Luanne, by saying, "If I died tomorrow, there'd be twenty-five thousand people here to make sure I was dead." She laughed, which was my intent.

But it was true.

————

EARLY IN 1993, A SCANDAL AT MATSUSHITA FORCED THE resignations of Akio Tanii and Masahiko Hirata. The board replaced Tanii with Yoichi Morishita, a hardware man who'd never been to Los Angeles and had no interest in MCA. Lew and Sid didn't know it, but they'd lost their strongest allies.

Jurassic Park aside, Universal's movie division was struggling. *Waterworld*, the postapocalyptic epic being shot off Hawaii, was way over budget with no end in sight. The film's director and star was our client Kevin Costner, and though I'd never understood Kevin's passion to make the film, I flew to the Big Island with Sid Sheinberg and studio chief Tom Pollock to provide what moral support I could. We took a speedboat to the artificial atoll they'd built near Kawaihae Harbor. I wore jeans and a T-shirt because I knew what I was in for. Sid had on jeans and a button-down shirt. Tom came in dress slacks and a blue blazer, like some gentleman yachtsman.

A catamaran brought us to the atoll. To get onto the land we had to crawl across an expanse of netting as the ocean heaved beneath, drenching us. Tom froze midway across, turned green, and gave up his breakfast. We sent him back. Later the swells forced Kevin to stop shooting for two hours—an all-too-standard delay. There wasn't much we could do to help, other than voice hollow encouragement. Based on half a century of Kawaihae's climate patterns, Kevin's technical people had forecast flat seas through the shoot. But as soon as they arrived the weather turned capricious. The thousand-ton set kept bobbing in the wind, a big problem for matching shots in the edit room, and one storm washed the entire setup onshore. A stunt man commuting to work on a Jet Ski ran out of gas and was fifty miles out to sea by the time the Coast Guard picked him up.

Movies made on water have a grim history, and *Waterworld* would add its sad chapter. It grossed $88 million domestic but cost twice that much to make. Recently some critics have called the film an overlooked classic. Nobody was overlooking it at Matsushita, believe me.

As Japanese real estate crashed, Matsushita battened down. In June 1994, Morishita vetoed a Universal theme park to compete with Tokyo Disneyland. Three months later Lew and Sid flew to Osaka with an even more ambitious plan, a joint venture with ITT to buy CBS. It felt like do-or-die for Universal, the only major studio that lacked a cable or network distribution arm. I urged Sid to prepare his owners beforehand, again to no effect. For two hours he and Lew cooled their heels in an outer office, and then they got shot down. Morishita was merely dodging a confrontation, business as usual in Japan, but Sid took offense and wrote a scathing letter to Chairman Masaharu Matsushita. For a while I stayed current with the drama through Keiya Toyonaga. But after Matsushita officially killed the CBS deal that fall and Sid blasted them in the *New York Times*, the curtain came down. For weeks the Japanese spoke to no one.

In November they made their move. Matsushita didn't call me; because they'd asked me to keep an eye on MCA for them, they worried that I'd be sympathetic to those I'd kept watch on—even though Lew and Sid had frozen me out. Their call went to Herb Allen, who, displaying his characteristic class and loyalty, immediately said that he wouldn't work on a sale of MCA without me. The next week I joined Herb and a dozen top executives in Osaka. The execs posed their question carefully: *If* they wanted to sell MCA, what was it worth and who might buy? I was to say nothing to Lew, whom they venerated and feared, or to Sid, whom they despised. I couldn't talk in any case because of my nondisclosure pact with Seagram.

On my next trip I disclosed my ties to Edgar and outlined what Seagram was after. (Herb and I worked for both sides throughout the transaction. *No conflict, no interest.*) For form's sake I named five other potential suitors, including Polygram and TCI. I had a private interest in Seagram winning out: Edgar had made it clear that I was a contender to run MCA, and I was definitely interested. MCA had great bones: it was a forties-style studio that had a huge lot, a great library, and the best TV department in town. And running the studio had been my dream ever since I gave those tours there as a kid.

Trying to realize your childhood dream can be perilous. I started a snowball rolling downhill when I began talking to Edgar, and it would trigger an avalanche.

The Matsushita executives asked: "Of all the companies you've shown us, who can actually close, and close quickly?" They hoped to complete the deal within ninety days, the bare minimum to get past the regulators. Their goal was merely to make back what they'd paid for MCA, or close to it, to avoid a savaging in the Japanese media. I told them what I'd told Steve Ross: "Seagram can cut a check for the full amount. They're the only ones who don't need to line up a bank."

It rarely snows in Osaka, but that day it never stopped, and I had a weird, uneasy feeling. I flew out to attend Sid Sheinberg's surprise sixtieth birthday party that evening in L.A., leaving my associates. Six hours later, the Great Hanshin earthquake struck near the city of Kobe, less than twenty miles from where we were staying. Six thousand people were killed.

Spago Beverly Hills was filled with clients and rivals by the time I arrived. Sid and I did a lot of business and I felt traitorous giving him a warm greeting. Once Matsushita sold MCA, he'd be done, and I knew he'd be irate that I hadn't tipped him off. Yet my hands were tied. If Sid went to Lew and set off World War III, I'd get sued for breaking my nondisclosure agreements. And the deal would be made anyway, with or without me. Later on, Sid would indeed complain that I fucked him over by not giving him a heads up. Our houses were adjacent in

Malibu, and he simply stopped speaking to me—it was as if I no longer existed.

In truth, though, I felt worse for Lew. Even though he'd never had any use for me, he was one of the industry's all-time greats. I'd modeled my business life on his example, and it was only when I started doing things he hadn't dreamed of that I began to feel I was truly a success. Yet his private life scared me to death, because he had no hobbies, no social life, nothing except a close relationship with his grandson, Casey. Lew's whole being was devoted to MCA and Democratic politics, and without MCA he would no longer be a player. What would he do without his only reasons for being?

The question tickled a deep anxiety. For years, I'd viewed CAA as a launching pad for larger opportunities, convinced that I could leave at any time. But what if I was more like Lew than I thought?

———————

MY TEAM UPDATED OUR SURVEY OF MCA'S FILM AND TV libraries, what they had in the pipeline, the music business, the theme park. Allen & Company looked at the real estate and created the statistical models. The work went much faster this time, as we already had the template.

Two weeks after my return from Japan, a junior Matsushita executive—in deference to *nemawashi*—phoned Steven Banner, Edgar's chief financial officer, to sound out Seagram's interest in acquiring MCA. Banner confirmed Seagram's interest and reported the call to Edgar and to me. Talks within Seagram intensified. Charles Bronfman opposed the deal, and Edgar senior was lukewarm at best. But he couldn't bring himself to say no to his son.

Rupert Murdoch was sniffing around any available asset as usual, and Michael Eisner wanted MCA's library for Disney. But Matsushita wasn't out to bleed the last buck from a sale. They wanted a clean exit and agreed to grant Seagram an exclusive bidding window. By March 1995, when Edgar scheduled a trip to Osaka, it was Seagram's deal to lose.

I briefed Edgar on the basics: *Don't cross your legs and don't show the soles of your feet; it's disrespectful. Here is how you hand them a business card. Never take your jacket off in a meeting without asking everyone else if they want to take off their jackets, too. Never ask about the other person's health—that's strictly private.* I described each senior executive's personality, hobbies, and children. Edgar went to Japan ready and able. Unlike Lew and Sid, he was at home in any setting. I'd watched him handle himself in Sun Valley and New York and knew he'd be fine at Matsushita. In the first MCA sale, I did all I could to keep the two sides apart; in the second one, I pushed them together. The sooner Edgar and Yoichi Morishita established a relationship, the sooner the deal would close. When they met, Edgar steered clear of numbers and all went well. Three weeks later he went back with an offer letter in his briefcase.

The parties quickly settled at $7.1 billion, a hair above Edgar's original offer. At the eleventh hour, to save face and keep a hand in the entertainment business, Matsushita asked to hold back 20 percent of MCA and cut the final price to a prorated $5.7 billion. Their Hollywood foray was more or less a wash.

By March 31, when the *Wall Street Journal* broke the story, the deal was done but for the signing. When my friend Ronald Perelman and the German media company Bertelsmann (another CAA client) suddenly expressed interest in MCA, I told them Seagram was too far along. After reviewing the proposed contract with Edgar and his father, I felt so sure about the outcome that I left to join my family in the Bahamas.

On April 6, DuPont bought back nearly all of Seagram's shares for $8.8 billion, more than enough cash for MCA. I returned to L.A. for the closing at Shearman & Sterling, Seagram's attorneys. As I descended to the firm's lobby to greet Matsushita's delegation and escort them to the twenty-first floor, I wasn't sure what to expect. Would they begrudge their five-year escapade? But shaking hands with Morishita alleviated my concerns. He and his associates were warm and forthcoming—even gleeful. They wanted out of show business as fervently as Edgar wanted in.

As we gathered for the signing, Matsushita's group sat along one side of the big table and Seagram's principals and chief advisers sat along the other. Herb Allen stood in a neutral corner. I had to make a quick choice. Matsushita had vaulted me into the major leagues in M&A and I'd always be grateful. But Seagram was my future.

I sat down next to Edgar and watched him sign my last big deal for CAA.

CHAPTER SEVENTEEN

GONE

THROUGH ALL THE DEAL MAKING, I KEPT AGENTING. ONE day in 1995, I called Barbra Streisand with big news: I'd found a home for her romantic comedy *The Mirror Has Two Faces*. TriStar wanted Barbra to produce, direct, and star. The money was excellent for an actress who was fifty-two, an age when leading roles become exceedingly scarce. "They'll pay you eight million dollars against a percentage of the gross," I told her.

"That's it?"

"Barbra, it's a great deal," I said. "Plus, you get to make the movie you want to make."

In the Brooklyn accent she never lost, she said, "Why can't you get me what Redford gets?" Always strangely competitive with Bob, Barbra launched into a lecture about sexism in Hollywood and how women were overlooked and underpaid. She was right, of course. Despite inroads by players such as Sherry Lansing and Dawn Steel, it remained an uphill fight. But she was going on and on and on. Maybe it was the pressure of the corporate work, or too little sleep. Maybe I had taken one too many such calls in twenty-seven years of massaging celebrity egos. But I blurted out something an agent should never say to a superstar. "Barbra," I said, "you know my fifteen-year-old son? All he and his friends think about is girls, but you're no longer on their list."

Barbra laughed—but I wasn't sure what kind of laugh it was. Amused, or outraged? Horrified, I started laughing myself, pretending it was all a joke. Then I changed the topic to a minor deal point and wound the call up as fast as I could. As I laid the phone down, wincing, I saw my assistant staring at me. "You're gone, aren't you?" she said.

Yes, I was gone.

I gave Ron the blow by blow and told him how upset I was. "You've got to get out of the agency business," he said, empathetic as always.

Yet Ron couldn't admit that his job was eating him up, too. One Saturday he took a call from his most challenging client, Sylvester Stallone. No matter how methodically Ron explained why he should do a certain movie, Sly would lose interest and hit some erase-the-last-hour button and make him start over. Ron was extraordinary in these situations. He showed not one iota of impatience, not with Sly on the line or to me afterward. But this particular call was over the top even for Stallone, ten numbingly repetitive hours. I am not exaggerating. I think Sly broke Ron for good that day.

Like me, Ron yearned for the status and ease of the buy side. He'd recently caught a ride to New York on a company jet with Terry Semel, the co-CEO at Warner. With a stack of scripts to read in between business calls, Ron worked five hours straight. Terry, meanwhile, had a little something to eat. He picked up a screenplay, leafed through it for an hour, laid it down, and had a glass of wine. He read a few more pages. Then he took a nap.

"He's a buyer," Ron told me afterward, wistfully. "He does whatever he wants. Everyone calls him, and he doesn't have to call anybody back." That sounded pretty good.

I NEVER STOPPED LOVING ARTISTS AND THE CREATIVE PRO-cess. I never lost my fascination for the magic of making something from nothing. But agenting was a young person's game, and you could run just so long and so far. At forty-eight, having run since my first day at William Morris, I was tired.

I was tired of getting up at 6:00 a.m. and squeezing in a workout while on the phone with Europe.

I was tired of rolling through three hundred calls a day, talking till my throat was raw.

I was tired of having lunches and dinners scheduled three months out.

I was tired of flying six hundred hours a year, the equivalent of one workweek a month.

I was tired of owning six tuxedoes for the thirty obligatory events between November 1 and Christmas.

I was tired of returning calls till 7:00 p.m., going to dinner till 10:00, coming home to a mountain of pink message slips, calling Japan till midnight—and starting all over again six hours later.

I was tired of submerging myself—*drowning* myself—in the lives of my clients and their families and significant others. Our clients' worries about the size of their trailers and how big their billing would be had come to seem increasingly petty. The truth is I'd always disliked having to see to people's creature comforts, making sure our actors and directors had fresh guava and the perfect nanny. *You're an adult; run your own life!*

If anything, the M&A work had made me more restless. With a few multibillion-dollar deals under my belt, even a fifty-million-dollar film package began looking small. But I couldn't have one without the other. Our core business was the platform that sustained everything else.

Meanwhile, though, the skies were darkening over our core business. Reality television, which William Morris dominated, was crowding out our scripted programs. Fewer movies were produced each year, reducing demand for our clients. Prices had slumped for midtier actors and directors, a warning sign for our A-list. *It won't be long,* I thought, *before the studios begin to squeeze our gross percentages—or to reject our packages altogether.* In ten years, did I want to be like an overworked mechanic trying to keep an old car on the road? (While CAA remains a force in entertainment, almost everything that I feared has come to pass. Growth in television is confined to cable—where talent makes much less than it does at the networks—and in the movie business there are very few gross-percentage players left.)

It was time for a change.

—————

ON APRIL 11, 1995, TWO DAYS AFTER SEAGRAM AND MATSU-shita closed, the *New York Times* ran a story headlined NEW THRILLER: WILL OVITZ GO TO MCA? Five years earlier, when the rumor mill had me replacing Lew Wasserman, I wasn't ready to leave CAA. This time the buzz was real. Edgar's first pick was Barry Diller, who turned him down; I was his second choice. He made his mind up at the NBA All-Star weekend in Phoenix, where he and I and our eldest sons spent time together. The Bronfmans were all about family, and Edgar liked the way Chris and I got along. He told me, "That's when I knew you were the right person."

For a long time I had wondered what it might be like to lead a studio. Time Warner and MCA topped my list. Michael Eisner had repeatedly asked me to join him at Disney, but I kept saying no. I had held out for one of my dream jobs, and now I had been rewarded. I was confident I could handle it. I could read a screenplay as well as any executive out there and break down a balance sheet better than most. And I still had the growth plan I'd suggested to Matsushita five years earlier. I wanted to turn back the clock to the golden era of MGM—to, in effect, make MCA into CAA plus a massive production department.

Once Universal had a critical mass of CAA clients under contract, it could expand in every sector. We'd produce more movies and TV shows (especially sitcoms, which paid better in syndication than dramas), more books and music albums. The same talent would help give us a digital presence in mobile telephony and video games. Soon everyone would be carrying a cell phone, and those phones would be receptacles for data-rich content. With Ron replacing Sid Sheinberg and Bill Haber running Universal Television, I had no doubt we could flourish. Edgar was a hands-off chief executive. I was wary of Edgar senior and Charles Bronfman, but I thought I'd be able to get things done.

I was about to become a very wealthy man. When I was younger, cash was my ticket out. I'd made lots of it since. But I yearned to *accumulate* money—to build equity—which felt different from merely making it. Once an agent stopped working, there was no accrued equity to fall back on. I watched the runaway growth at Microsoft, where Bill Gates had built one of the world's largest companies. Fortunes were beginning to be made off the internet. Executives I considered as my peers—Michael Eisner, Barry Diller—were raking in hundreds of millions in stock options. My appetite for corporate buccaneering grew as I worked with Herb Allen and mingled with Fortune 50 CEOs in Sun Valley. It grew further whenever I lost an auction to an art collector with deeper resources. I wanted to play in that league, too.

And in truth I had always been faintly embarrassed to be an agent. As much as CAA had professionalized our field, it would never be a noble calling. I wanted to be one of the six people who could say yes to a movie without scrounging to assemble all the elements ahead of time. My master plan was to put in five years at a public company, then move on to a third act in public service and charity work. I dreamed of using my negotiating skills for the government—helping hammer out nuclear treaties, for instance—or of running the International Red Cross. I was tired of helping people who *could* help themselves, but who preferred to pay me to do things for them. I wanted to start helping people who couldn't help themselves, who actually needed the help. I wanted to give back on a large scale, but I felt I needed the credential of a public company job first. I was still looking for respect and validation.

USING RON AS MY AGENT, I ASKED EDGAR FOR 10 PERCENT of MCA and agreed to take 5 percent. I was attacked later for being greedy, but it struck me as a reasonable ask, given the circumstances. Many large companies set aside up to 10 percent of their stock for employee options, and the math that worked for me to run this large corporation was simple. I was walking away from CAA, worth at least $350 million at the time. Five percent of a $6.6 billion company came to $330 million in equity, enough to recoup the cost of leaving CAA, cover Ron and Bill and their equity in the agency, and pay for the other senior agents I wanted to bring along. I'd be taking a sharp pay cut, but it was all about the equity. I thought we could grow MCA to a dramatic multiple of that $6.6 billion.

By late May of 1995, Edgar and I had an understanding in principle. As he flew to Montreal to report to the Seagram board, I tried to tamp down the growing angst at CAA. On June 1, I gathered the staff to confirm I'd been approached but that nothing was decided.

I wasn't lying; I was teetering like mad. As Edgar's discussions with his father and uncle dragged on, I began to worry that he wasn't as in charge as he'd led me to believe, and that I'd have to answer to three bosses, not one. Worse, to three bosses who were related and who would naturally side with each other against me. I asked for more money—requesting that they pay my taxes, among other deal points—but it was basically a stall. I began to realize that I was having trouble sleeping because it wasn't so easy to just pick up and leave. CAA was not something outside me. It *was* me.

Ron pleaded with me to carry the negotiations through, for both of our sakes. "It's time to try something new," he said. "You need a bigger playpen and you've trained your whole life for this. Besides, how bad can we do compared with Lew and Sid?"

I met with Edgar in Los Angeles to close. Hours later, Edgar asked to see me again. "We're going to have to renegotiate," he said. "They won't accept the terms." *They*, of course, were his father and uncle.

I actually felt relieved. "That means you're not in control," I said.

"Michael," he said, "Seagram is a large public company. My father and his brother are major shareholders. This is how public companies work. I could push our thing through, but in the long run it wouldn't be healthy for either of us."

I needed at least three years to turn Universal around, and the job made no sense if all three Bronfmans weren't fully behind me—if I might not be afforded the time to break the company apart in order to remake it. I broke the news to Ron, who calmly said that he understood.

When I called Edgar to pull the plug, it was a short conversation. I hung up and felt another wave of relief.

I might have been sick of client service, but I still loved my company. I loved the people I worked with and the building we worked in. I was swamped by a tidal wave of love for CAA.

I convened the entire staff in our theater and announced that none of us were leaving. I could feel relief surge through the room, and the whole company rose into a standing ovation. As people hugged one another, I watched the Young Turks—Lovett, Huvane, and Lourd—who were standing together in the front row. They kept their arms folded, resentfully, and I suddenly felt real alarm. I recognized the mulish look on their faces; it was just the way the five of us had felt at William Morris twenty years earlier: restless, underappreciated, ready to make a move. The difference was that they had great clients—whom Ron and I had given them—considerable authority, and financial security.

Yet I believed I could patch things up with the Young Turks, if only to buy time for an orderly succession while I scouted our next play. I liked the possibility of Time Warner, where Gerald Levin looked shaky. Ron and I could work miracles there.

We could do anything as long as we hung together.

RON ASKED TO TAKE ONE MORE STAB FOR ME AT MCA. Halfheartedly, I told him to go ahead. I figured he could ascertain whether there remained any chance to make a deal where we could run the company without interference.

Early in July, Ron called from New York one afternoon. "Guess what?" he said. "I've met with Edgar and there's been a change in plans. He wants me to run MCA and I think I'm going to do it."

I felt completely numb; frozen with disbelief. The job on the table, chief operating officer, was what I'd negotiated for Ron in my last go-round with Edgar, with one big difference: I was out of the picture. (Edgar would bring in Frank Biondi as the CEO Ron reported to.) After a long silence, when I felt that I could speak without my voice breaking, I told Ron how much I needed him, what it meant to have him at my side. I'm great at pitching even when I'm not sincere, and I was a thousand percent sincere, so it was my greatest pitch ever. I was sure he'd be won over.

What came back, in a burst of rage, were all of Ron's pent-up grievances. How I had undernegotiated for him with Edgar and overnegotiated for Bill Haber because I'd valued them equally in my ask. How I had made a big mistake by walking away from MCA, and how it had always been all about me, never about him. How it was time to strike out on his own, to be recognized as something more than my consigliere.

I tried to sell him for two hours, as the knot in my stomach swelled into my throat. Finally, my voice faltered and I gave way. His mind was made up. I felt absolutely crushed. Ron was leaving, and taking the best, most human part of me with him. It felt like I was getting divorced.

AFTER I HUNG UP, I TRIED TO ADD UP THE MISTAKES I'D made with Ron over the years. One problem was money, our way of keeping score. Both Ron and Bill banked big slices of my corporate deals even though they'd had next to nothing to do with them. But knowing Ron's feelings, I should have done more. I could have bought Bill out and passed Ron his equity. Or kept Bill and split everything in thirds. It might not have been fair, but it would have been worth it. Money was important to me, but not as important as Ron's friendship.

My second error was even dumber, because it wouldn't have cost a dime to fix. From the start, CAA was antihierarchical. We dispensed with the usual title pyramid and rotated the heads of our departments; I introduced everyone as my partner. For years my business card had just my name, no title. But once I started meeting with Fortune 50 CEOs, I needed formal standing, so in 1990, I became CAA's chief executive officer. Ron was named president.

I should have made Ron the CEO and called myself the chairman. Because he'd never brought the matter up, it never occurred to me what that kind of recognition might have meant to him. When I looked at my partner, I still saw the brash young man with the *cojones* to flirt with Geneviève Bujold. I saw the guy who hung out with the biggest stars in the world like he'd grown up with them. I had forgotten that Ron was a high school dropout who craved approval just as much as I did—maybe even more.

The biggest problem was that our friendship never quite recovered after I put him in handcuffs for his poker debts. I had instinctively moved to protect our company, rather than to protect Ron from himself. I don't think I was wrong to do that. I *do* think I was wrong to behave, afterward, as if the crisis had never happened. It made it less scary for me. I should have taken Ron aside to talk to him about how he was doing, reestablished that unshakable bond, made it clear that I was with him through thick and thin. But men like me weren't too good about opening up, about acknowledging our fears. And so his resentment festered.

I didn't want to be who I'd become, and Ron didn't, either. But we were who we were. To this day Ron tells people, "I'm the best number two in the world." And I have to hand it to him—he's lasted as Universal's number two for more than twenty years, through four different owners. I couldn't have done that.

As I was about to learn in the most painful way possible, I suck at being number two.

––––––––––

BILL HABER WANTED TO TRY TO SUSTAIN THE OLD MAGIC, but I couldn't stay at CAA without Ron. (Bill would leave a few months later, as he'd long threatened, to work with the Save the Children Foundation.) I was upset because I'd had no idea Ron was so upset. I was upset by the prospect of working without him. And I was upset that I'd have to work with the Young Turks, who now evidently hated me, without him.

When I went to Herb Allen's conference in Sun Valley a few days after Ron told me he was leaving, I saw Ron and Edgar together, laughing, and I felt nauseated. At the first session, a friend named Peter Barton came up, noticed how out of sorts I was, and said, "Good move—you lost your partner." Before I could ask if he was being sarcastic or sympathetic, he walked away. I had no idea what he meant; all I knew is that I felt like a little boy lost in a department store. I left the conference two days early. It would have been wise to talk to a psychotherapist, but I wasn't eager to make myself that vulnerable. I had the idea that real men toughed it out.

I dragged myself back to work and went through the motions. One day Jay Moloney stormed into my office and shouted, "I want to see the books!" He actually pounded my desk. "I want to see the books right *now*!" No one but the owners of the agency saw our finances; it had long been part of the company culture that you didn't discuss your compensation with anyone but Ron, Bill, and me.

I stood. I knew the other Young Turks had put him up to it because none of them had the balls that Jay had. And I knew that Jay loved me, but that having seen my methods—and my workouts—he also feared me. The distance that fact created between us had always made me wistful, but now I used it. "You've got two seconds to leave through the door," I said. "Or you're leaving headfirst through the window."

Jay hesitated, then slunk out. Having looked up to me for so long, he evidently felt like a kid whose parents are divorcing. He blamed me for Ron leaving, and for the factionalism that had begun to splinter the agency. But he was also clearly not himself. The incident was my first hint of the drug problem that Jay had begun to fall prey to. And it was a clear signal that my time at CAA was up. I owned what these younger men wanted: the power.

MICHAEL EISNER HAD KEPT PURSUING ME. IN THE SPRING, when the Bronfmans and I were talking, he'd said, "Why go to Universal when you could come to Disney as my partner?" His wife, Jane, was insisting he slow down after his quadruple bypass, and she repeatedly begged me to make him take it easy, and to help him however I could. She believed it could literally save his life. Once Disney agreed to acquire Capital Cities/ABC for $19 billion, a deal that closed that August, Michael needed help more than ever—and that, for me, was the clinching factor. The merger would create the world's largest entertainment company, one way too big for one person to run, especially one who was ailing. Michael offered me the job of co-CEO.

Wounded by all that had just happened, I told myself that Disney would be a coat of armor, complete with a steely press office to ward off reporters. As Michael transitioned to a less intensive role as chairman, he could oversee the macro stuff and be the Voice of Walt on Disney's Sunday-night TV shows. I'd run the day-to-day and focus on Europe and Asia, all the unglamorous detail work he didn't want to do. By my midfifties, I'd have a sparkling credit to my name and a good chunk of cash to segue into government or philanthropy.

The move came with risks; I knew how Michael treated his deputies. John Angelo, one of Eisner's closest friends, had told me flatly, "Michael is incapable of sharing with anyone." Just the previous year, Michael had told me he was going to fire Jeffrey Katzenberg, who was by then his motion picture and animation chief, and who'd become indispensable after Frank Wells's death. As Michael ranted in his den about Jeffrey in the most vituperative language, Jane and I begged him to reconsider. He listened to us, and relented. (After Eisner refused to give him Wells's title, Jeffrey left Disney later that year to cofound DreamWorks SKG with Steven Spielberg and David Geffen.)

But I believed that I was immune to Michael's rages and suspicions. After Ron, he was my next-best friend. And I thought he could fill some of the void. "Okay," I told Michael. "I'm in."

CHAPTER EIGHTEEN

NUMBER TWO

IN AUGUST 1995, ON A FAMILY VACATION IN ASPEN, MICHAEL and I took a hike to hash out my role and title. For some time he'd been saying that only two people in L.A. could replace him: Barry Diller and me. After his operation, he sent a letter to that effect to his board. A number of directors told me I had their support. More than one added that they hoped I'd bring CAA's team-first culture to Disney, where backstabbing was a blood sport. But Sid Bass, the company's largest shareholder, would prove to be entirely in Eisner's pocket. Naive and easily manipulated, he was a rubber stamp for whatever changes Eisner wanted to make—which turned out to be none.

It worried me a little that Michael's plan for us was in constant flux. First we were going to be co-CEOs. Then he floated the idea of staying on as chairman and making me sole chief executive. More recently he'd talked about making Disney and ABC separate operational entities, one for each of us to run. Titles didn't really matter, we agreed. We'd be full partners, like Goizueta and Keough at Coca-Cola or Daly and Semel at Warner.

As my September start date neared, Michael decided to keep the CEO title for himself and make me president and COO, reporting directly to the board. He'd had the same arrangement with Frank Wells.

I asked how he planned to insert me over his incumbent execs. "They all work for me," he said, "so they're all going to work for you." Fair enough. I assumed I'd start as number two and move up from there.

Now, in Aspen, he informed me that he was tweaking our arrangement. Until I "earned" being COO, I'd report to him rather than the board. I needed time, he said, to transition from a small private company to a gigantic public one. I knew I faced a learning curve, but I had counted on my friend to support me in public and advise me in private. He assured me that time would resolve the issue, but I felt baited and switched.

That was the first yellow flag. The second came a day or two later when I was flying on a Disney jet to L.A. with Joe Roth, Michael's studio chief and a longtime client of mine. I'd made Joe's original deal with Disney at a time when the studio needed more producers on the lot. Now he told me he was worried that I'd outflank him by developing movies with CAA clients. I assured him I had no such thing in mind. (To avoid crowding Joe, I would stay out of film production at Disney.) What shook me was discovering that Joe had wanted my job for himself, so he'd be rooting for me to fail.

The third flag popped up that evening at Eisner's house in Bel Air, where I went to review the press release about my hiring. As Michael greeted me in his dining room, I was surprised to see Stephen Bollenbach, Disney's CFO, and Sandy Litvack, the company's general counsel and a man widely detested by Eisner's subordinates. We'd barely shaken hands when Bollenbach declared he wasn't reporting to me. Litvack then said the same thing. In the tense silence, my first thought was that Michael had orchestrated the showdown to clear the air—a move I might have made in his place. I waited for him to back me up and set Bollenbach and Litvack straight. But he averted his eyes and let me hang there.

I tried to engage my new colleagues and explain that I was going to be COO and that they'd report to me but it would be collegial—that I was just there to help. But they were adamant. I didn't know that Michael had recruited Bollenbach by implying he'd replace Frank

Wells. I didn't know that Litvack had his own designs on the job; Eisner had always dismissed him to me as "a functionary." One came out of real estate and the other out of litigation. Neither had any experience with talent, or with making and distributing films, television, or books.

When Michael and I took a break in his son's bedroom, he seemed as flustered as I was. He stroked people by reflex, promising everyone autonomy, but obviously we couldn't all have autonomy. A menschy CEO would never have let Bollenbach and Litvack into his house, let alone allowed them to ambush me without a word of reprimand. I pleaded for Michael's support. He assured me he'd work it all out. "Steve and Sandy don't have your creative background," he said. "You're the one for this job."

I stepped out to call Judy. "Michael just threw me under the bus," I told her. "No matter what I do, I'm going to fail in this job. I think I just made the biggest mistake of my career."

The next day I assembled my brain trust and posed the nuclear option: should I call the whole thing off? Bob Goldman was pessimistic but stopped short of telling me to bail; Sandy Climan was on the fence; and Ray Kurtzman thought I should make the best of it. I agreed, glumly. I was too far down the road to turn back, particularly after having gone so far down a similar road with Universal. But from that evening at Eisner's house on, I had a ball in the pit of my stomach that never left.

Eisner was working on a memoir with a writer named Tony Schwartz. Minutes after I called him, following my meeting with the brain trust, to say that I was in, he told Schwartz exactly what I'd told my wife the night before—that he'd just made the biggest mistake of his life. He wondered if he could take his offer back.

I wish he had.

IN A BIG COMPANY YOU'RE DEFINED BY WHOM YOU REport to and who reports to you. With Michael cutting me off from the board and boxing me in from the executives below, I felt pinioned from the start. Taking meaningless meetings would get me and Disney nowhere. But there was another way to build the company—through M&A. I'd come from a racing yacht called *CAA* that I could turn on a dime. Now I was on the *Titanic* and I needed to steer it before I'd made any friends in the bridge. Which alarmed the officers in the bridge, which panicked Eisner, which freaked me out and made me steam full speed ahead into the iceberg.

That's the short version.

My first week on the job, I reached an agreement with Brad Grey, a top-notch TV producer and talent manager who would later run Paramount. In return for exclusive rights to his productions and an open line to his artists (from the *Saturday Night Live* gang to the writers who'd create *The Sopranos*), Brad would get a production deal at our film studio. It would be a major statement to the creative community. But neither Joe Roth nor Bob Iger, who ran ABC, wanted Brad on the lot. Eisner backed his lieutenants without explaining why. No deal.

The next day I tackled Michael about the Tele-TV concept he'd ripped off from me. Though I'd never been happy with his duplicity, now we could start fresh. Why not combine Tele-TV and the copycat version he'd established with Americast and GTE and pull in the same direction? He dismissed the idea.

Over the next several months I put forward new ideas in publishing, music, digital technology, and international operations. I had tentative deals with Tom Clancy, Michael Crichton, and Stephen King—three of the four bestselling authors in the world—for exclusive rights to their books, movies, and miniseries. Disney would be a publishing powerhouse. Michael said no. Then I brought him a handshake agreement to buy G. P. Putnam's Sons, Clancy's publisher, for $350 million. He wasn't interested. (Later snapped up by Penguin and subsequently merged with Random House, Putnam is now worth well over ten times what we'd have paid for it.) I arranged for my longtime client Janet Jackson to jump from Virgin to Disney in a seven-album,

$75 million deal. It could have pumped new life into our Hollywood Records label and fixed Disney's cheapskate image. "We'll grow our own stars," Michael said. Hollywood Records would not grow a single star under Eisner.

I flew to Tokyo to see Masayoshi Son, the head of the tech-focused SoftBank, about his minority stake in Yahoo, then the chief Web portal. Based on preliminary discussions with Eisner and other board members, I was plying a strategy to get Disney online. I could see our cartoon characters leading millions of Yahoo home page viewers to news and weather sites while selling Disney merchandise and promoting Disney movies.

To my surprise, Son said he would sell his shares for a mere $250 million. Given what was about to happen to the internet, his stake would have been a bargain at quintuple the price. Fired up, I rushed from lunch to the airport, flew ten hours to LAX, and went straight to the office at 10:00 the next morning—I didn't even shower or shave. I entered Eisner's inner sanctum to find him with Stanley Gold, an influential Disney board member. "You're not going to believe this!" I told them. "We have a shot to buy Masa Son's piece of Yahoo."

"That's the stupidest idea I've ever heard," Michael said. Wheeling into mountaintop mode, he pronounced that people went online for information, not entertainment. It wasn't just that he was wildly wrong; it was that my supposed partner was deliberately embarrassing me in front of Stanley. Because my vulnerable spot, as Eisner knew, is my sense of dignity, his tactic was devastating. Humiliated, I left without another word.

With 80 percent of Disney's revenue deriving from North America, I tried to shift us toward a healthier domestic-foreign split. I met in Beijing with Jiang Zemin and Zhu Rongji, China's leaders, on a host of issues of mutual interest: a Disney theme park, joint film and TV production, piracy and intellectual property. On the strength of this budding relationship, I had high hopes for a Chinese Disneyland and a busy pipeline of coproductions. The timing was perfect. We'd be planting the Disney flag early enough to get in on China's economic explosion. But Michael showed no interest and the initiative died, an untold waste.

Michael contended that Disney was an "operations company," making acquisitions secondary. While I knew Michael liked to stay in-house, the ABC merger had given me hope. Before we agreed to work together, he had acknowledged that Disney needed to grow in every area I was now addressing. And Michael knew exactly what he was getting when he got me: a deal maker.

EARLY ON AT DISNEY, I GOT A CALL FROM UCLA HOSPITAL. They had been about to sew up a hole in Jay Moloney's heart, a congenital defect, when they'd discovered "heavy drugs" in his blood. They'd canceled the surgery, then called me because Jay had listed me as his emergency contact. I was touched that Jay still thought of me as a surrogate father, even as I suddenly made sense of his increasingly strange behavior over the past few years: the days he'd miss work and then show up, bruised and out of it, with a story about having been mugged.

A few months later, David O'Connor called me, nearly frantic: Jay was holed up in his house on Mulholland Drive, lost in drugs. David and I went up there together, kicked three hookers out of the house, and flushed a lot of cocaine down the toilet. Jay was remorseful, self-hating, a wreck. "I love you, Jay, you're like a son to me," I said. "But I'm not going to stand by and let you kill yourself."

"Okay," he said, wearily.

I had distanced myself from Jay when he began to fall apart. I felt he should have control over the drugs, rather than vice versa; that he was betraying himself, and was therefore no longer worthy of my affection and support. That was a bad mistake, and looking at him now, so defeated, I wanted to do anything I could to make him better. I found myself wishing fervently that I'd paid more attention to Jay's neediness, his wounded side, from the beginning. He was so talented and I was so laser focused on my own needs that I had just let him go, let him make money for all of us, let him chase the misbegotten dream of becoming just like me.

David and I drove him down the hill to Turner's, the liquor store on Sunset, where I had a UCLA internist I trusted waiting in a car in the parking lot. We marched him to the doctor's car, and Jay reluctantly got in—then tried to scramble back out. We held the door closed, remonstrating with him through the glass. Finally, he gave up, and let himself be driven to UCLA to get cleaned up before going into rehab.

He went through rehab five times over the years, but each time he came back a little further away, a little more lost. CAA finally asked him to leave. I would later offer him a job with me in my next gig, at AMG; I thought that if Jay rededicated himself to others it could help bring him back. But he declined; he was too far gone. In November of 1999, I got a call from David O'Connor: Jay was dead. He'd hung himself in the shower of his home. He was thirty-five. I was shocked and devastated, but not really surprised.

At his memorial service, I called him "a passing comet" who "lit up our lives." But it was Bill Murray, as usual, who nailed it. Looking out at the mourners, all of nineties' Hollywood, Bill said, "There are so many people sitting here today who I would so much rather be eulogizing."

———

AS THE DISPUTE OVER JEFFREY KATZENBERG'S UNPAID compensation headed for the courts, Michael let me try to settle it. I'd be dealing with both Jeffrey and his friend and adviser David Geffen, which would be tricky. David and I had fallen out back in 1980, when he was producing *Personal Best* and our dispute over writer-director Bob Towne's compensation delayed the start date. I respected David's considerable achievements, but hard as I tried to stay on his good side, he seemed to feel slighted that I didn't confide in him or, perhaps, defer to him. I would have been wiser to befriend him and take his counsel— given his intellect and influence, that was an error in judgment. But I preferred keeping my own counsel.

This once, however, our interests were aligned. We arrived at a figure of $90 million—a fabulous deal for Disney, given Jeffrey's contributions to blockbusters such as *The Lion King*. I brought the agreement to Eisner, who turned it down flat. It was left to me to break the bad news to Jeffrey, a further mortification. (The parties later settled out of court for a reported $250 million.)

The guy who closed everything was now closing nothing. I couldn't discuss the problem with anyone without looking even weaker, so I revved up, working harder than ever, sleeping only four hours a night, pushing for a breakthrough like a man possessed. Jane Eisner called me in a fury: "Your crazy work ethic is pressuring my husband. He's putting in too many hours. It's against doctor's orders!" I believed if I could get *one* thing to work, one new artist or acquisition, maybe everything would turn around. If insanity is doing the same thing over and over and expecting a different result, I had become stark raving mad.

I made plenty of mistakes. I came in like a whirlwind, far too frenetic for Michael's taste. (He used to complain to me about just that quality in Frank Wells.) In trying to keep the Brad Grey deal confidential, I failed to build consensus before bringing it to the boss. I was at sea in Disney's hierarchy and fiefdoms. It was hard to downshift from CAA, where I did as I pleased at my own headlong pace.

But my instincts were good. In a 2005 article headlined WHAT IF EISNER HAD LISTENED TO OVITZ?, *Fortune* looked at six of my proposals. The magazine judged one, a merger of Sony and Hollywood Records, a long-term negative (I'd argue that the advent of digital music would now make that deal a winner). My plan for an NFL team in L.A. was called a push. But the article rated four other ideas (Yahoo, Putnam, the Katzenberg settlement, and a joint venture with Sony PlayStation) as big positives for the Magic Kingdom had Eisner said yes.

I did get a few things done when I immersed myself in the nitty-gritty of operations. I came up with the idea for ABC's *One Saturday Morning*, a two-hour block of children's programming they launched after I left. I mediated for executives who were at odds with Michael or one another or both—a tidy subset at Disney headquarters, which was hardly a Magic Kingdom. When Tim Allen walked off *Home Improvement*, putting a syndication deal worth hundreds of millions into jeopardy, I met with him and worked things out.

But for the most part I ran in place. My directives were ignored; my suggestions vanished down the memory hole. More than one person at Disney later told me that Eisner went around me to everybody who mattered. He directed Larry Murphy, who led the planning group, to report on our meetings but to sit on anything I proposed. He did the same with Dean Valentine, head of TV animation, who fawned to my face while feeding the press anonymous negative quotes about me. *Just humor him*, Michael said, and they did.

Unable to quit without losing my severance, I was a lame duck awaiting the ax. In mid-September 1996, Sandy Litvack barged into my office. "Michael doesn't want you at the company anymore," he said, triumphantly.

"Go tell Michael to come tell me himself," I said. After a twenty-something-year relationship with my so-called friend, I thought I deserved to be fired face-to-face. Michael didn't appear.

He had volunteered to throw the party for my fiftieth birthday that December. *Hang in till then*, I told myself, *and perhaps not all will be lost*. He repeatedly suggested that we'd figure out a soft landing so I wouldn't be totally embarrassed in the community: I'd stay on Disney's board for a year after leaving management, or serve the company as a consultant. (He reneged on those promises, too.)

Three days before my birthday, Michael summoned me to his late mother's apartment in New York to sign off on my resignation "by mutual consent." He said he still wanted to stay friends and host my party—a bizarrely crazy idea that wouldn't happen, of course, but one that was quintessential Eisner. I shook his hand glassily and walked out. Twenty years later, I still have no interest in ever sitting down with him again. Even if he made the most spectacular apology in the world, he's incapable of true change.

By the time I returned to my apartment, three blocks away, my letter of resignation had already been hand delivered. It was signed by Sandy Litvack.

———

I SPENT A QUIET BIRTHDAY AT HOME IN BRENTWOOD WITH Judy and our three children. For once, I didn't answer the phone. Then I flew to Aspen for a week to be alone and think. I was livid with Eisner and furious at myself. I felt awful, worthless, an utter failure.

Intellectually, I knew it wasn't my fault. From the moment of the ambush in Bel Air, Michael had withheld the support he'd promised. It had been deliberate, and cruelly so. But I couldn't process what had happened intellectually; the emotions were too strong. Betrayal really sets me off. I had to walk out of the movie *Betrayal*—based on the Harold Pinter play about a man who carries on a long affair with his friend's wife—because it stirred up so many churning feelings. My dad once told me, "You give your all to your friends and clients, and you expect the same back. But you're not going to get it. They'll betray you. I was in sales—I know." I had argued with him then, but now I decided he was right.

A week of hard thinking about Michael Eisner wasn't nearly enough. It took me half a year to feel normal again, and longer than that to make sense of Michael's behavior. I think he was sincere when he wooed me, in his weakened postsurgical state. But then Michael recovered. And the better he felt, the worse I looked to him. I was four years younger and vastly more energetic. Ovitz the Savior became Ovitz the Rival.

In my first week on the job, Eisner told me to fire Bob Iger. He thought Bob was stupid, or so he said. I thought he was being rash and said so: "Bob Iger knows ABC cold." I later spent three hours over dinner with Iger—who'd heard of Eisner's dissatisfaction—persuading him not to leave. I told him Eisner had a short attention span, and would soon be on to someone else. That was true: he promptly told me to fire Dennis Hightower, our head of television. Dennis was our only high-ranking African American executive, and I told Michael, "That's a terrible idea for me or you." Hightower stayed.

In 2005, after Eisner resigned under pressure and Iger replaced him, I finally grasped the method behind Eisner's madness: he saw Iger as a future successor. Bob has led Disney to new heights as CEO. He built the business with high-wire acquisitions and a stronger foreign profile, more or less what I'd tried a decade earlier. He made big M&A bets on Pixar, Marvel, Lucasfilm, and Fox, and built the Shanghai Disney Resort. Bob was smart about it. First he changed the culture, dismantling the strategic planning group and erasing Eisner's imprint. And then he empowered the people around him, as any successful leader must.

I still think I could have run a big public company, given time to learn and adjust. But I never could have run *that* company as Eisner's number two. Disney's culture under Michael was too ingrained and ingrown. I lacked the power to change it or the temperament to blend in.

Bert Fields later told me that Eisner didn't want me at Disney so much as he wanted me out of CAA, in order to weaken the agency's power—all agencies' power. I'd been a thorn in Disney's side for too long, so he pulled it out. Humiliating me every day was just a bonus.

RIGHT AFTER I GOT FIRED, TEDDY FORSTMANN CALLED and said, "I want you to go on the board of Gulfstream," an aerospace company his equity firm owned. "It'll help you."

"Thanks," I said, touched by his loyalty. "But I can't. It won't be good for Gulfstream—I'll be getting a lot of bad publicity."

"You're on the board," he said, and hung up.

The bad publicity came, and it was pretty bad. Headlines everywhere, stories of my fall. Within days of my departure, a group of Disney shareholders brought suit against the company and me. They charged that I'd broken my contract and that my $130 million, no-fault payout was a fiduciary breach. In 2004, as the action headed toward trial in Delaware's Court of Chancery, I seized it as a chance for vindi-cation. I was raring to go, to tell the world what had really happened.

The judge, Chancellor William B. Chandler III, was sharp and attentive. And after he listened to thirty-seven days of testimony, his 175-page decision was strongly in my favor. Chandler found that I was "a poor fit with [my] fellow executives" at Disney, but he rejected the plaintiffs' claim that I'd been untruthful or derelict in my duties. In approving my contract with the company, he observed, Disney's direc-tors were well aware I needed "downside protection" before taking the job. I was walking away from up to $200 million in booked CAA com-missions. My severance would offset my losses if I were fired without cause—which I was.

While Chandler cleared the board of impropriety, he had harsh words for their conduct. Disney's directors "fell significantly short of the best practices of ideal corporate governance," he wrote. He called Eisner a "Machiavellian" CEO who stacked his board with cronies and "enthroned himself as the omnipotent and infallible monarch of his personal Magic Kingdom."

That's the tragedy that can befall the company man: we come to believe we are the company.

CHAPTER NINETEEN

THE THIRD VALLEY

CAA WAS RELENTLESS IN CHASING NEW BUSINESS, AND whenever we gained a client, someone else lost one. When I left the agency, after twenty years of dog-eat-dog, a lot of dogs out there had livid scars and long memories.

You might think that I'd still have a few friends at CAA itself. After all, Ron and Bill and I had sold the agency to the new leadership team on fire-sale terms, essentially floating them a zero-interest loan and having them pay us back out of earnings across four years, all so the agency would continue to thrive. But when I was at Disney, Richard Lovett routinely spewed about me in staff meetings, neutralizing me the way I used to neutralize anyone who crossed us. Even years afterward, when Lovett ran the memorial services for Marty Baum and Ray Kurtzman, he refused to let me speak. Given how close I'd been to Marty and Ray, I found that very painful. Bryan Lourd and Kevin Huvane felt the anxiety of influence, not wanting to be compared to me; Lourd would later insist that the agency leave the I. M. Pei building and move to Century City. And David O'Connor, who I'd thought of as a friend, was mad at me because I hadn't included him among my designated heirs. That wasn't a verdict on his qualities—it was simply that, as a lit agent, David didn't generate nearly as much income as the others. (The agency's new leaders included him in their ranks—then later pushed him out.) The group had plenty of reasons to dislike me, I suppose—no one ever really likes the boss, especially one as demanding as I was—but they also felt that I'd abandoned them. Companies are families, too.

I found it even more painful that Ron was still being less than complimentary about me to everyone. After I parted ways with Disney, I had lunch with him, trying to coax him to leave Universal and start a management or production company with me. I told him that ever since we'd suddenly stopped talking thirty times a day it had been tougher on me than him, because I wasn't pissed off. He could work his grievance out by venting, but I just felt deserted. He nodded, then said evenly that he had no interest in forming a company together.

Ron also told me that he'd bought a place in Point Dune, in Malibu, and that he had his eye on the adjacent property, owned by Berry Gordy. But he said that at $5.5 million, it was too expensive. I owned a place in Malibu, and I'd always wanted to buy Berry Gordy's place. Now, thinking that Ron was priced out, I did. A week later, Ron called, incensed, and said, "We have a problem. I went to buy Berry Gordy's house—and you have it in escrow. I was the one who told you about it, and I want to buy it." I told him I'd think about it. And that was our last conversation for years.

The truth is, I was mad. I was stewing about remarks he'd made that had gotten back to me—that I was like Secretariat, hopeless without the right jockey—and I was stung that he had so little interest in working with me again. So I wanted him to sweat a little before I gave it to him, which led me to behave like an asshole. Ron called everyone—Herb Allen, Barry Diller, David Geffen, random people out of the phone book—to complain about what I'd done, and the dispute wound up in the *New York Times*. A few weeks later I finally gave him the property, handling the transaction through our mutual business manager, and Ron lives there to this day.

IN 1999, TWO YEARS AFTER MY CRASH-AND-BURN AT DIS-
ney, I formed a new production and management company, Artists
Management Group. With my smart, accomplished partners, Rick
and Julie Yorn, I intended for us to become the leading provider of
mobile content, even as we kept a profitable foot in old media. The idea
was that in their downtime after writing a television show, say, our
creators would create three-minute comedy episodes for mobile
phones; compile seven of those and you'd have a twenty-one-minute
episode of a sitcom. We'd push sports scores and restaurant information to your phones (as is now common) and make short-form television you could view on any screen (an idea Jeffrey Katzenberg got
headlines for in 2017).

Structurally, AMG was designed to be free from CAA's constraints. It could produce content and represent artists simultaneously,
without any conflict. Scaling up quickly, we placed a stellar roster of
writers under contract to our TV production arm, and in our first six
months we sold thirteen TV pilots to the networks. And then, slowly
at first but with increasing speed, we did a face-plant.

One big problem was that the smartphone-adoption rate and
bandwidth needed for large numbers of people to receive programming on their phones weren't in place yet. We taped Robin Williams
reading the front page of the *New York Times* and riffing off it—a bit
we thought would be a repeatable, snackable way of advertising our
wares. But when we tried to upload it to Verizon's network, it simply
didn't transmit. We intended to be two years ahead of everyone else,
but we turned out to be five years ahead not only of everyone else, but
of the technology.

We also ran into a gale-force headwind from entrenched businesses
like the TV networks, which felt threatened; from skeptics who bad-
mouthed AMG all over town; and from CAA, which perceived our
model as a dagger aimed at its heart. I had no intention of stealing the
agency's clients, figuring there was plenty of work for everyone, but

when Mike Menchel left CAA to join us and brought along his long-time client Robin Williams, the agency declared war. They told their clients that if any of them hired AMG as their managers, they'd lose CAA as their agents. The day after Richard Lovett announced this edict, Ron Meyer dropped by the agency to tell the staff, "You're doing the right thing."

As AMG began to founder, CAA worked to poach Robin Williams back. I visited Robin in his dressing room at the Universal Amphitheater, where he was performing, and saw Bryan Lourd there. *Good God, who taught you that trick?* I thought. I wasn't shocked by Bryan's behavior; he was doing what I would have done. I was shocked that Robin's wife, Marsha, had allowed Bryan to infiltrate and undermine me. I remembered how grateful she'd seemed in the nineties when I'd gone to bat for her and Robin, reaming out *People* magazine for breaking its promise to the couple and trumpeting the fact that Marsha had been Robin's nanny when they met. So I took her betrayal personally. I saw Marsha not long ago in San Francisco, and I felt sick to my stomach.

Worse by far was that after Robin left, I heard that Barry Levinson was thinking of leaving, too. Barry was my oldest client and one of my closest friends; we'd talked every day for twenty-seven years. Each Christmas he sent me a pint of Chivas Regal with a handwritten note about our year together, and I was always deeply touched. I went to Barry and begged him to stay. I said I was devastated—*devastated*—that he'd even think of doing that to me. He said it was done; he'd made a business decision. Friends, trying to cheer me up afterward, told me exactly that: "It's just business."

I said, "No, it's not." What Barry and Robin and Marsha did to me, when I was at my lowest moment? I carry that within me still.

In April of 2000, I met Bryan Lourd to try to make peace with the agency. We took a walk around the outside of the CAA building and I told him that my father was very ill with leukemia (he would die in June), and that I didn't want to fight with anyone anymore. I just wanted to run my business and let them run theirs. The following day,

I received a two-page handwritten letter from Bryan laying out in precise, lawyerly detail all the reasons I was a horrible person.

I got out of AMG in 2002, selling its assets to The Firm and taking a loss of tens of millions. Days later, I made the spectacular miscalculation of meeting with a writer from *Vanity Fair*. By then my joust with David Geffen was well into its third decade, and I had it on good authority that David and his friends had sabotaged the last-ditch financing I had needed to keep AMG going. On a mutual friend's advice—which turned out to be terrible—I'd even gone to see David in his offices at Amblin Entertainment, and warned him that if he didn't stay out of my affairs, "I'll beat the living shit out of you." He didn't stay out. So I vented to *Vanity Fair*. It would have been fine if I'd confined my remarks to Geffen. But in my fury I characterized my various nemeses as "the Gay Mafia." The idea was more absurd than poisonous because a number of the men I'd named (Michael Eisner, Bernie Brillstein, Bernie Weinraub at the *New York Times*, Ron Meyer) weren't gay. But the sentiment was as stupid as it was offensive, and both it and the loss of control that led me to utter it were out of character. Every problem I tried to solve I now ended up making worse—the opposite of my traditional MO.

I'd always thought it was vital to mix business and friendship. I was learning, painfully, that it was better to keep those realms far apart. Business always gets personal.

―――――――――

THEY ONLY WIN IF THEY KILL YOU.

They didn't kill me. In the years that followed, I tried to bring a pro football team to Los Angeles (didn't happen, long story) and to become the head of the International Red Cross (didn't happen, end of story). I thought back on the career path I'd taken and realized that I would have been much happier as an artist or an architect—happier in an arena where you don't make five new enemies every time you create something.

Meanwhile, I turned my attention to Silicon Valley. Intrigued, early on, by software and the internet, I'd dreamed of remaking MGM or MCA as a digital-age studio. In the early nineties I flew to Redmond, Washington, and had a four-hour dinner with Bill Gates and Steve Ballmer of Microsoft to talk about what was coming. I met with Andy Grove, the CEO of Intel, to see how our companies might mesh, and before I left CAA, Intel built a media lab there to give us a jump on the internet age. I picked the brains of dozens of tech innovators at Allen & Company retreats and other industry conclaves. I especially admired Ron Conway, the Bay Area's leading "angel" investor in embryonic start-ups.

In 1999, Ron phoned to say, "I know a young man up here who's extraordinary. He's starting a company that's ahead of its time, and he'd like to meet you."

The company was LoudCloud, and the young man was Marc Andreessen, who as an undergrad had invented the Web browser. Three years later, at twenty-four, he monetized the browser as Netscape and landed on the cover of *Time*. Three years after that, partnering with Ben Horowitz, Marc imagined how start-ups might use business software on the network (what people now call the cloud) instead of sinking capital into costly servers. Way ahead of the herd, he saw that everyone would soon be connected to the digital network. *Wired* magazine fittingly named him its first "Wired Icon" under the headline: THE MAN WHO MAKES THE FUTURE.

When we met, at an L.A. restaurant, I expected a geek from central casting. What I got was someone six foot five, an athletic-looking guy with a winning smile. He did dress like a geek—he was wearing patterned shorts and white socks—but he was hyperarticulate, insatiably curious, and voraciously well read. He was Michael Crichton on steroids.

Marc invited me north to meet with Ben Horowitz. Ben is a brilliant manager and entrepreneur in his own right, and together he and Marc were a formidable team. They asked me to join the LoudCloud board, and so began a new chapter of my life.

Another board member was Bill Campbell, a legendary mentor to people like Steve Jobs at Apple and Sergei Brin and Larry Page at Google. I learned an enormous amount from Bill, who had nearly impeccable judgment (when the venture capital firm Kleiner Perkins sent him to Amazon to fire Jeff Bezos, Bill came back from their meeting and said, "You can't fire him"). But at one point he and I got into it in a board meeting. LoudCloud was in big trouble: its stock had sunk below a dollar a share and was about to be delisted. Bill thought we should just work our way through the rough patch, but I suggested that the board members demonstrate their faith in the company by buying stock. Bill, no fan of smoke and mirrors, screamed, "Ovitz, that's the dumbest fucking thing I've ever heard!" After a shocked moment, everyone cracked up. I bought half a million shares of Loud-Cloud stock, some of the other board members followed suit, and soon our shares were back up over a dollar. In 2007, Hewlett-Packard bought the company, now renamed Opsware, for $1.65 billion.

As Marc and Ben led me into their world, I felt like a privileged student in a graduate school of one. After they sold Opsware, I asked Marc about joining their angel investment group. "Funny you should mention that," he said. "Ben and I are thinking about doing something more formal." As their venture capital firm began to take shape, I coached them about how to make Andreessen Horowitz stand out. The idea that took was to offer a full menu of business services—a novel approach in venture, whose stars tend to be one-man bands who freelance out of a larger firm.

In other words, Marc and Ben set out to be the CAA of Silicon Valley. They borrowed our roots to give themselves gravitas the same way I had borrowed from Lew Wasserman and Sun Tzu. In essence, the firm linked all the partners' networks and added specialists to strengthen the whole organism. No individual "owns" an account at Andreessen Horowitz; investments are chosen by joint approval of the general partners, with the entire staff having a say. Then the team provides in-house experts to assist its start-ups with recruitment, budgeting, operations, sales, publicity, IPO rollouts—whatever an entrepreneur might need.

While other venture firms seek out executive talent for their clients, Andreessen Horowitz goes further. It develops ties with the Valley's best software engineers, designers, and product managers, helping them with introductions and career counseling. At times it connects these engineers and managers to one of its portfolio companies, but often there's no direct payoff. It does the same for top Valley executives, much as CAA negotiated employment contracts for studio executives. Andreessen Horowitz aims to forge long-term relationships that might eventually prove helpful at a future start-up, or as part of future deal flow. And Marc and Ben's thesis has worked brilliantly. They have rapidly established themselves as one of the nation's top five venture firms, with prescient investments in Facebook, Skype, Stripe, Airbnb, GitHub, Instacart, Lyft, and Pinterest, among many others. As Marc told the *New York Times*, "We'll wire up talent first with the goal of knowing and building relationships with all the best people. It's more like a Hollywood talent agency."

Meanwhile, the talent agencies themselves have become small parts of giant conglomerates. A few years ago, a young exec at TPG, the private equity firm that has bought 52 percent of CAA, casually told me, "I own CAA." That hit me hard. CAA is still a force in entertainment, but the real heirs to Ron and me are Ari Emanuel and Patrick Whitesell, who've turned William Morris Endeavor into a multihyphenate business, a new octopus. Ari is now an agent, a producer, an advertiser, and an investment banker. Naturally, he trained at CAA. And, naturally, Ari and Patrick met at InterTalent, which Ron Meyer worked so hard to put out of business. You can't kill the good ones. William Morris learned that after we left to start CAA, and CAA learned it when Ari and Patrick rose up to battle them.

———

IN 2009, I FOUND MYSELF AT WHAT I THOUGHT WAS A SO-cial dinner at a New York restaurant. Across the table were three dear friends: Marc Andreessen; his wife, Laura; and Herb Allen III, the son of the Herb Allen who'd brought me to Sun Valley all those years ago.

I'd known young Herb since he was ten, and he now ran the family business. I'd introduced him to Marc in 2000, believing that he should get the Allen firm out of old media and into tech and that Marc would be the best possible adviser in that transition, and I felt as close to him as I did to his father. Herb had maintained his father's old-school style—the wood-paneled office walls, the sweater vests—and he possessed his father's quiet humor, indifference to trends, and outsized loyalty.

This was my new inner circle. As I took my seat, I saw three solemn faces. Had someone died?

"This," Marc said gravely, "is an intervention." I tensed, knowing what was coming. Lately I'd been spending two days a week at Andreessen Horowitz. Now I was about to be triple-teamed into picking up stakes and making northern California my base of operations.

I spent my life solving other people's problems and steering the conversation away from myself. But that night I was trapped. First Marc pounded on me, with Laura chiming in. Then Herb took over. I squirmed for three hours as they discussed how I needed to change. My face flushed. My ears rang. It's tough to resist heartfelt counsel from three people you trust, especially when they're three awfully smart people.

As we rose from the table, Marc said, "Cortez, dude!" His reference to the Spanish conquistador who burned his ships to prevent his crew from returning to Europe made me laugh. That night was the kick in the pants I needed. I tore up my travel schedule and flew the next day to San Francisco, where I took an apartment. Andreessen Horowitz made me a special partner and assigned me to several portfolio companies.

I decided to study Silicon Valley the same way I'd studied the entertainment industry when I was twenty-three. I began networking, taking eight to ten meetings a day with founders and engineers. At first I wore a suit, then I left the tie at home, and pretty soon I was business casual, which proved both more comfortable and a psychic relief.

Many of the founders I met were dimly aware that I'd consulted

with Steve Jobs, both about the entertainment business and later, after
he bought Pixar, to help resolve tensions between him and Michael
Eisner at Disney. That gave me some credibility, as did my work launching CAA, Hollywood's ultimate start-up. So with the right introduction it was relatively easy to get a meeting with almost anybody. I met
with Peter Thiel and Max Levchin, who'd founded PayPal and become
leading investors in tech. I met with Kevin Systrom, who'd founded
Instagram. I met with Reid Hoffman, the LinkedIn founder. I took
separate meetings at Facebook with Mark Zuckerberg and Sheryl
Sandberg. I met with Eddy Cue at Apple. And so on—377 meetings
that first year alone.

Getting a second meeting with the superstars was harder; you had
to prove in the first meeting you had something to offer. But I gradually developed a strong network, growing close not only to a number
of founders, but also to venture capitalists such as Michael Abramson,
the youngest partner at Sequoia Capital; Josh Kushner of Thrive Capital; Steve Loughlin at Accel; Danny Rimer and Mike Volpi at Index
Ventures; and tech banker Quincy Smith. The players in the Valley
first made their marks in their twenties, as Ron and I did when we
started CAA, so I felt right at home with the ambient energy and ambition. Young people make their own rules.

I learned my most important lesson when two MIT engineers
came to me with unproven technology to improve mobile payments.
Acting as their agent, I called John Donahoe, the CEO of eBay, whom
I'd met with earlier, and asked him to take a look for PayPal, which
eBay had acquired. John brought two of his senior engineers to the
meeting, and they began picking the code and the technology apart,
asking nasty and insinuating questions. Accustomed to protecting my
directors when studio execs got rough, I finally stood and told my guys,
"They can't talk to you like this! We're going." The engineers stared at
me and said, "What are you talking about? It's totally fine."

I sat back down; eBay ended up buying the tech. And as we walked
out, John Donahoe put his arm around me and said, "You've just
learned something very important about the Valley. There are no

manners here, just brain challenges. It's about getting to the truth of the idea any way you can."

IF HOLLYWOOD IS LIKE HIGH SCHOOL WITH MONEY, AS people often say, the lesson from that eBay meeting is that Silicon Valley is a true meritocracy. The best idea with the best execution wins. In Hollywood I was always going to be judged against my own legacy at CAA, whereas in Silicon Valley I was judged simply on the ideas I brought to the whiteboard. My big mistake, in retrospect, had been starting AMG when I should have moved to Silicon Valley and become a principal in the tech revolution. The Valley ringingly echoes my shouted belief that hard work and good ideas are an unstoppable combination. The press is full of worries about the rise of China, but I remember the same worries about Japan a generation back, and what I see in the tech community makes me confident that American ingenuity will withstand this challenge, too.

It wasn't long before taking general meetings began to pay off. In 2009, Peter Thiel, who'd funded the data-analytics start-up Palantir with $200 million from his own funds, asked me to help his CEO, Alex Karp, expand the company from working solely with the federal government and law enforcement into the world of business. We narrowed the potential areas to attack to three: health (where insights on disease vulnerability or drug efficacy could be teased out of big data), advertising (which had grown increasingly focused on metrics), and finance. Alex and I, who became fast friends, chose finance because the sector had gotten crushed in 2008 and the banks were eager for new ideas. At the next Allen conference that summer, I introduced Alex to Jimmy Lee, a top investment banker at J.P. Morgan, which I knew had been unable to reliably price its underwater mortgages in the wake of the great recession.

Alex blew Jimmy away and we made a deal with Morgan to launch a three-month pilot program. Alex and I worked with Alex's cofounder, Stephen Cohen, and Stephen's engineers, Nima Ghamsari and Rosco Hill. They customized one of the company's algorithms so it would scrape thousands of hitherto uncorrelated data points about a given property and its location to determine a fair bid-ask spread. This allowed local branches to make speedy, accurate decisions. Settlements that used to take an average of twenty-seven days now got done in two. Jimmy Lee was overjoyed.

Our success with mortgage pricing rapidly led to a spate of other ventures in banking. When I started working with Palantir, it had fewer than a hundred engineers; today it has two thousand. I was given adviser shares in the company, and I purchased an additional stake, betting on its future. Valued at $600 million then, Palantir is now valued at more than $20 billion. In the Valley you only get paid for performance, and options vest slowly (usually over four years), but the upside can be much greater than in Hollywood.

Through Alex, I met his brilliant cofounder, Joe Lonsdale, who was just leaving Palantir to launch a venture fund, Formation 8. As the fund went on to invest in hugely successful companies such as Oculus and Illumio, I advised Joe and got even more great advice in return. He was my road map to the Valley; he always knew where tech was going and which young entrepreneurs were going to take it there.

I also became friends with Alex's engineers, Nima and Rosco. In 2012, when they launched Blend, which allows you to secure a mortgage with just ten clicks on your cell phone, I helped them raise seed money from Herb Allen, Peter Thiel, and Andreessen Horowitz, and I invested myself. Blend is currently valued at $500 million. When Rosco went on to found Perpetua Labs, which advises companies how to grow by doing data analytics, I invested and began advising that company, too.

Ben Horowitz introduced me to three robotic-engineering PhDs from Carnegie Mellon who were developing smart toys at a start-up called Anki. Ben called me the minute they left him, and the minute I hung up with Ben I drove to Anki's office, which was in the skid-rowiest part of San Francisco's Mission District. I walked up a darkened staircase and knocked on an unprepossessing door. It opened onto a huge room that was empty except for three guys sitting around a card table and playing with slot cars. I happen to be a slot-car freak, and I instantly fell in love with the fact that (a) you could control their cars with your phone and (b) their cars didn't need slots—they were smart cars that could drive all over the floor. I began working with Anki's CEO, Boris Sofman, and his two cofounders, Hanns Tappeiner and Mark Palatucci, and soon (much more thanks to them than me) the company had a great second product: a personalized, plucky, six-inch robot named Cozmo.

Through a Founders Fund venture capitalist named Brian Singerman, one of the best young investors I have met in the Valley, I invested in and began advising Stemcentrx, a bioscience company exploring novel ways to cure cancer. Stemcentrx eventually sold to AbbVie for $9 billion, and I got a 4x return as well as a terrific science education. One thing I really love about Silicon Valley is that each day brings you different fascinating problems, and you're always learning how the world—and sometimes the universe—works.

I also consulted for an amazing entrepreneur named Gurjeet Singh, a PhD in applied mathematics who was the founding CEO of a big-data-sifting business called Ayasdi. A remarkably composed man, Gurjeet taught me a lot about life. After his grandmother died, he remained steadfastly cheerful, and I said, "How are you able to be that way? My mother died two years ago, and I still grieve for her every day." He said, "Well, as a Sikh, I believe she's going to come back, so I'm happy for her." That gave me a comforting way to think about my parents' deaths, at a time when I'm beginning to contemplate my own.

I'm now working with at least twenty-five other companies, and new ones get in touch every week. I find that my "value add," as they say, is advising on how to monetize a technology, how to market it, and how to avoid some of the pitfalls I fell into at CAA. I don't always know the right move—who does?—but I can often help steer founders away from mistakes of inexperience: from making short-sighted hires, or needlessly alienating a rival who might become a collaborator, or not planning for the long term. Founders are much more interested in my mistakes (which can often be generalized to their situation) than in my successes (which were often particular to the agency business).

When I met Brian Chesky in 2013, I was astounded that this 2004 graduate of the Rhode Island School of Design, a former competitive bodybuilder with no coding experience, had cofounded and led one of the great start-ups of his era, the "sharing economy" juggernaut that is Airbnb. After providing occasional help to Airbnb over the years, I recently met with Brian to brainstorm about how Airbnb could keep growing. In one of our sessions, we discussed an "end to end" or "door to door" experience, and spent three hours whiteboarding how the company could curate your entire trip, from the time you left home. I told him, "Go larger, tackle the total vacation experience." The following year, Airbnb announced its "Trips" service, where hosts will introduce travelers who want to experience local living from everything to a dinner party to a Tai Chi class. It's currently available in fifty-one cities around the world.

Brian asked, "How did you learn to think so big at CAA?" I reminded him that Airbnb had consistently thought big: it hadn't been at all content with its original business of renting out air mattresses on floors. Then I added that one way to conceptualize how to think in business is a martial-arts precept: "If you aim at the target, you lose all your power. You have to hit *through* the target to really smash it." To get where you want to go, you have to set out to go even further.

IN 1998, ONCE OUR KIDS WERE ALL OUT OF THE HOUSE FOR good, I began building my dream home in Beverly Hills, high on the hillside. It's essentially three interlocking boxes made only of glass, oak, plaster, and steel. A house that doubles as an art gallery, it reminds visitors of a miniature MoMA with bedrooms. It contains my favorite paintings and sculptures from forty years of collecting: modern and contemporary paintings, Ming furniture, African antiquities, Rembrandt etchings, and turn-of-the-century Japanese bronze flower vases, as well as my library of more than three thousand art monographs. The design and build of the house took eleven years, and I drove my architect, Michael Maltzan, crazy. I had the contractor redo the plaster three times till it was perfectly smooth. I also had him fine-tune the "reveals," or tiny strips at the base of the walls, to get them just so, which required a team of six guys with sandpaper and toothbrushes. The worst day of all was the day I moved in, because then it was done.

At around the same time, my life took an unexpected turn. After being together since we were teenagers, Judy and I recognized that our lifestyles had diverged—she drawn to her horse ranch in Ojai; I migrating from L.A. to the Bay Area to New York, always on the move. We agreed to live our lives separately, though we'd remain married and the best of friends. We still talk almost every day.

In 2010, at Ted Forstmann's Aspen conference, I met a woman I'd encountered several times before. But this time was different. We had a drink, which became a dinner, which became a conversation that shows no signs of slowing down. Tamara Mellon and I love a lot of the same books and movies and art. We enjoy learning new things in each other's worlds. Best of all, we find ourselves laughing all the time. Tamara is gifted, witty, and kind enough to laugh at my jokes. She appreciates my eclectic interests and loves that I love what she does. She cofounded Jimmy Choo at twenty-seven, almost exactly my age when we founded CAA. She built the company by designing thousands of women's shoes and bags, many of them now iconic. After a bruising struggle with the company's shareholders, she is now creating a new business. I'm having a blast watching her and making suggestions to protect her interests.

An added treat is Tamara's fifteen-year-old daughter, Minty. She designed her own clothes at an early age, competes in national horseback-riding tournaments, and is socially graceful, with a wide circle of friends. It's daunting to have a teenage daughter in my life again, but it's also tremendous fun. She's always playing me new music and introducing me to fashion trends—because of her I knew about Snapchat the instant it came out. I was touched when, for her eleventh birthday, she asked me to get her a cake with a Lichtenstein painting on it. Minty has become totally enmeshed with my family.

Eric lives in L.A. and is married to a delightful woman named Kendall, who brings him to life and makes him happy. He's always been his own man. After becoming an early employee of the gaming company Zynga, he used the money he made there to put himself through Northwestern Law School, and now he hopes to work for the FBI. Somehow he came out Republican, despite my best efforts, so I know he'd make a great G-man. He and Kendall are now expecting their first child.

Kim, the artist in our family, started a fashion business in her twenties called Kimberly Ovitz. I was impressed and pleased that her first line, which featured lots of monochrome black and white, was heavily influenced by minimal artists like Ad Reinhardt, Ellsworth Kelly, and Robert Ryman. (Likewise, Eric haunts museums, and Chris is buying numerous prints for his house.) Kim also lives in L.A., and in addition to her work as a designer she consults with numerous fashion and digital companies on marketing and strategy.

Jordan Harris, who's still a vital part of our family fifteen years later—he was the best man at Chris's wedding—is now at NYU's Stern School of Business while working at Code Advisors. He has a real interest in tech.

I also tried for years to get Chris to go into tech and to move to San Francisco. I had him meet with Marc Andreessen and Peter Thiel, and they tried to talk him into moving to the city. But he stayed in Los Angeles to make his own way. And he finally did. At the Goldman Sachs Internet Conference a few years ago, I stood apart with the bank's Gary Cohn—later to become Donald Trump's first economic adviser—and watched Chris work the room. Gary grinned, recognizing my bursting pride. Chris may have learned the social skills from me, but he was much more candid and factual with the people he was talking to than I ever was. He wasn't trying to sell them. Chris is now working on his third start-up, Workpop, an H.R. technology company disrupting the service economy. I never make an angel investment without running it by Chris and his wife, Ara Katz. Ara is an entrepreneur who is the cofounder of Seed, which is focused on improving consumers' health through the microbiome, and she is a gentle, deeply grounded soul. To my surprise—I thought she was a touchy-feely hippie when I met her—she's became the core of our family, and someone whose perspective I rely on constantly.

Chris and Ara recently had a boy, Pax, and I FaceTime with him every day if we're not together. He is the light of my life. Ara is the best mother I've ever seen—she's totally anti-screen, except for FaceTime—and Pax reminds me of me as a little boy, the curious and emotional kid I was before Sarah got her hooks into me. As a grandfather, I plan to do everything right, to fix the numerous mistakes I made as a parent.

CHAPTER TWENTY

GENTLEMEN

OVER THE YEARS I KEPT HEARING THAT RON WAS STILL FU-
rious at me. Someone who was on Universal's plane with him recently
told me, "He ripped you for thirty minutes. It sounded like you and he
had just had a fight *yesterday*." I finally had had enough. A couple of
years ago, I called Ron and said, "Look, everywhere I go I keep hearing
from people that you're saying terrible things about me. I'm sure some
of your complaints are completely justified, but they can't all be, because we had twenty-five good years together. We're getting up there in
age, and I'd like not to leave the planet with this breach between us."

Somewhat to my surprise, he instantly said, "I'd like that, too." We
met for lunch at my Japanese place, Hamasaku. I opened it on a lark
sixteen years ago in a Korean strip mall in Westwood, and it's become
quite popular. It's so nonchic it's chic. After shaking hands and sizing
each other up, we made some small talk as we looked over the menus.
It felt both uncomfortable and, strangely, warmly familiar. Over sushi
we discussed how to work through our issues, or if we even could. We
left a second meeting up in the air. After pondering the problem, I
called Ron and said, "I think it'd be best if we had a mediator who can
listen to both of us, and help us interpret each other, and referee if
necessary. Why don't you come up with some possible people, and I'll

come up with some, and we'll find someone who works for both of us?"
I was trying to be sensitive to him, for a change.

"Why don't you do it?" he said. "I'm sure whoever you pick will be
great." Same old Ron.

I found a UCLA professor to mediate. Ron and I met at a coffee
shop in the basement of her office, and then went up to her office for a
two-hour session, our first of three. Ron started talking and didn't stop
for half an hour. He immediately acknowledged that he'd spent twenty
years denigrating me to anyone who would listen. He said, "I was the
guy taking care of the agency while you were running around all over
the world—you had the big profile, but I was doing all the hard work.
And you should have bought out Bill Haber and given me the stock. I
deserved it." I said that he wasn't generating the income I was. He responded that without him the business would have fallen apart.

I said, "Look, I was insensitive to you. I wasn't going to get rid of
Haber, because I was scared to rock the boat. But I *should have* done
something—anything!"

He said he was still furious and resentful about the house in Malibu, but when I started to explain, he talked over me. He wasn't going
to let me express my feelings; he was still the keeper of our collective
emotions. So the first session didn't end particularly well.

The second one went better, with the mediator's help. I got a chance
to apologize, and Ron accepted my apology and seemed mollified.
Then he owned up to all his rancor and sabotage, which was a form of
apology, or at least of candor. Yet even as we worked to get our feelings
out, I felt destroyed because Ron kept confirming my worst fears: every
time anyone in town had struck a match of accusation against me, Ron
had dumped on a truckload of gas. "No one was better equipped to put
you away than me," he said. I told him, "Ron, *you* were unhappy at
CAA, so you kind of shoved it to me. I apologize for missing the signs
that you were unhappy, but you could have just *told* me." He smiled a
little and said, "Yeah—but you didn't want to hear it."

After the sessions, we began meeting for lunch. We even brought
Tamara and Ron's wife, Kelly, into it. Just like old times, sort of. He'd

talk about his job; I'd talk about how I don't have a job. Ron followed up, he checked in, he was courteous and thoughtful, he made me feel like I was the only thing on his mind. It was seductive, particularly as more and more time passed without strife. But a voice in my head kept saying, "You were wrong about his feelings for the last ten years at CAA—he handled you beautifully, then. So what makes you certain you're right now?" Part of me wanted to believe in his sincerity and the promise of our old friendship, part of me was still angry, part of me felt sorry for him, part of me felt sorry for both of us. Still, we began talking two, three times a week, easing toward a renewal of our intimacy. I'd missed it so.

In September of 2016, Ron and I were publicly interviewed together one night by Jim Miller, who'd just published an oral history of CAA. I had to walk into the Directors Guild Theater using a cane, having just had surgery to fuse my entire spine. Under my suit, I was wearing a brace that made me look like a Teenage Mutant Ninja Turtle, and I was in considerable pain. The doctors told me that 90 percent of the reason my spine was so damaged was that I'd exercised every day of my life, never giving my body a rest, and absorbed all those punishing hits and falls in martial arts. I would have laughed, hearing that, only it hurt too much.

The two of us had agreed before the event not to go negative. My goal for the evening was to defuse the feud in public, and I think Ron's goal was to demonstrate that he was the Mr. Nice Guy of legend. But neither of us knew what might get said if we really got back into it. Just before going onstage, Ron and I went into the bathroom. As we each stood at a urinal, who should come in to piss alongside us but Jeffrey Katzenberg, who in Miller's book had said that I "consistently dealt in ways that were destructive, deceitful, and in bad faith." *Look who's talking*, I thought. We both said "Hello," but it was awkward. After pissing on each other for years, here we all were pissing side by side. Welcome back to Hollywood!

Ron and I walked onstage to a warm round of applause: all six hundred seats were filled. I saw old colleagues like Rick Nicita and

Sandy Climan and John Ptak and Fred Specktor and Paula Wagner, as well as a number of producers, including Larry Gordon and Joel Silver. All the industry trade papers and websites were there, too, eager to take the measure of what had become a legendary success story—and implosion.

Jim Miller started us talking about the years at William Morris, when we signed Rob Reiner and Sally Struthers together, and Ron got a big laugh when he called the agency's Sam Weisbord "an ugly little piece of shit guy." When we got into the founding of CAA, Ron said, "Mike was the natural leader—there was never a question." The conversation was affable and reflective. I recalled how he and I planned our moves together thirty times a day, and Ron won more laughs when he said, "It was a much more gentlemanly business before we started. Once Mike and I were let loose, no one was safe." He added, confirming my core belief, "There was no one else who understood what we were doing or how we were doing it except each other."

When Miller inquired about the roots of our breach, Ron soft-pedaled the issue, saying that my move into corporate deal making was organic: "Our clients weren't adversely affected by it, and more business was coming in." But, he noted poignantly, "It was much more *personal* to me" because my focus on bigger game made him feel less worthy, made him feel "disenfranchised from our relationship." I jumped in to say that I'd been blind to his feelings, and that in trying to build a wider network "I didn't realize I was sacrificing relationships that were more important to me."

Ron said, "I also have some responsibility. I did not tell Mike that I was unhappy. I felt that if I had confronted Mike, he wouldn't have handled it well, and I would have put the place on tilt." What we were both finally realizing, onstage, was that we'd each unwittingly sacrificed our relationship in order to save CAA—whereas if we'd just focused on making sure we were both happy, CAA would have done even better. The irony was right out of O. Henry.

We discussed the ugly breakup calmly, and at last we got to Berry Gordy's Malibu house. I decided, weighing the crowd, Ron, and my own feelings, to finally fess up. "I was pissed off," I said. "I made a mistake. I shouldn't have bought the property." I looked out at the crowd and waited a beat, using timing I'd picked up from David Letterman. "One of the reasons I made the mistake," I added, jerking my head at Ron, "was I didn't have him to advise me not to." Ron grinned, and the audience broke up.

Afterward, I basked in the kind words and notes of appreciation from old friends and colleagues. The lore had long been that I screwed Ron over and got my just deserts, but that evening seemed to shift the communal story line some and make people realize that it had been a *folie à deux*. Nearly everyone was astonished to see a vulnerable, ruminative Michael Ovitz, the me I'd always kept hidden. At CAA, I wouldn't have known how to show that side of myself—or wanted to.

That same reconciling impulse made me reach out to David Geffen. We met at Marea in New York, shook hands, and had a civil lunch. He told me, "My biggest problem with you was that I tried to be your friend, but you wouldn't be friends with me!" The old me would have argued, would have objected that that wasn't the whole story. But I just said, "You're right." I was there to make peace, and David said he wanted the same. We were two guys in our seventies, looking to fix what we'd broken. Ronnie later told me that David didn't have anything bad to say about me afterward. That made me smile a little: the win, nowadays, is breaking even. But I'll take it.

A FEW MONTHS BACK I VISITED THE OLD CAA BUILDING, which I still own. After Ron and Bill left the agency, I bought them out of the building; they were afraid that no one would want to occupy it if CAA left. Operating out of fear is bad business. Three months after the agency's departure, Sony leased the building from me for twenty years.

But now the building was empty again, needing a new tenant, so I took a tour. Sony had divided my not-huge office into two small offices; well, fair enough. The atrium was still airy and inspiring, yet it had no one to catalyze anymore, no one to inspire. The building felt drained, empty not just of the old bustle but of the magic, the power. It felt *small*. It felt like your childhood house does, when you go back as an adult. When we first inhabited the building, the whole mighty team of us, we were giants. We could walk outside and reach downtown, the Pacific, or Tokyo in a single bound. I was hit by the magnitude of what I'd done in that building, and it seemed kind of amazing: this kid from the Valley, with no stature, no tenure, no network to rely on, reshaping the entertainment business.

Bullied as a child, I spent my life bullying back. My clients sometimes viewed me as a superhero, and I did try to play that role—swooping in to help anyone who was down or ill or just in need of advice, fighting for the underdogs. I thought I was one of the good guys. Yet I was increasingly visited by the doubt that troubles every superhero: Had I become a vigilante? Plenty of people saw me as just that—a hired gun who took the law into his own hands. But that verdict misses all the loyalty and the love. Bob De Niro summed me up pretty well. Someone once asked him, "Why don't you leave Ovitz? He's such a tough asshole." De Niro said, "Yeah, but he's *my* tough asshole."

In my empty fortress, I realized that I wasn't out of the Valley yet. I'm free of it in my daily life, and in my bank account, but I'll never be free of it in my brain. You carry your origins with you. Still, those origins drove me here, and built this place, and attracted so many bright, funny, creative colleagues. In the silence, I discovered that the only thing I really miss about the agency business was the camaraderie: my comrades and friends and the passionate way we spent our lives together.

I miss the people.

INDEX